CONCISE GUIDE TO
Consultation-Liaison Psychiatry

Third Edition

D0645931

American Psychiatric Press
CONCISE GUIDES

Robert E. Hales, M.D., M.B.A.
Series Editor

CONCISE GUIDE TO
Consultation Psychiatry

Third Edition

James R. Rundell, M.D.
Program Director, National Capital Area Integrated, Military
Psychiatry Residency Program, Washington, D.C.
Associate Professor of Psychiatry, Uniformed Services
University of the Health Sciences, Bethesda, Maryland

Michael G. Wise, M.D.
Professor and Vice Chair, Department of Psychiatry, University
of California, Davis, Sacramento, California
Adjunct Professor of Psychiatry, Uniformed Services
University of the Health Sciences, Bethesda, Maryland

American
Psychiatric
Press, Inc.

Washington, DC
London, England

Copyright © 2000 American Psychiatric Press, Inc.
ALL RIGHTS RESERVED

Manufactured in the United States of America on acid-free paper
03   02   4   3   2
Third Edition

American Psychiatric Press, Inc.
1400 K Street, N.W., Washington, DC   20005
www.appi.org

Library of Congress Cataloging-in-Publication Data

Wise, Michael G., 1944–
    Concise guide to consultation psychiatry / Michael G. Wise, James R. Rundell. —
3rd ed.
        p.   cm. — (Concise guide series)
    Includes bibliographical references and index.
    ISBN 0-88048-946-
    1. Consultation-liaison psychiatry.   I. Rundell, James R., 1957–   II. Title   III. Concise
guides (American Psychiatric Press)
RC455.2.C65 W573 2000
616.89—dc21

                                                                                        99-052943

British Library Cataloguing in Publication Data
A CIP record is available from the British Library.

CONTENTS

Introduction to the American Psychiatric
Press Concise Guides xxi

1 EFFECTIVE PSYCHIATRIC CONSULTATION
  IN A CHANGING HEALTH CARE
  ENVIRONMENT 1
  History 1
  Psychiatric Illness in Medical-Surgical
    Outpatients and Inpatients 2
  Cost-Effectiveness of Psychiatric Consultation 3
  Approach to the Consultation 4
    Consultation Style 4
    Patient Confidentiality 4
    Patient Follow-Up 5
  Consultation or Liaison Psychiatry? 6
  Outpatient Consultation Psychiatry 7
  References 7
  Additional Readings 9

2 MENTAL STATUS EXAMINATION 11
  Noncognitive Components of the Mental
    Status Examination 12
    General Appearance and Behavior 12
    Mood and Affect 12
    Thought Processes and Content 13
    Perceptions 13
    Abstracting Abilities 14
    Judgment and Insight 14
  Cognitive Components of the Mental
    Status Examination 15
    Level of Consciousness 15
    Attention 15
    Speech and Language 15

Orientation 16
Memory. 16
Screening Mental Status Examinations . . . 16
Mini-Mental State Exam 17
Other Useful Tests of Cognitive Function . . . 17
The Neurological Examination 22
The Consultation Psychiatrist as
Neuropsychiatrist 23
References 26
Additional Readings 27

3 DELIRIUM 29

Epidemiology 30
Clinical Characteristics 30
Diagnostic Criteria 30
Prodrome 32
Temporal Course 32
Neuropsychiatric Impairment 32
Perceptual Disturbances 33
Psychomotor Disturbances 33
Sleep-Wake Cycle Disturbances 33
Differential Diagnosis 34
Treatment and Management 34
Reverse Remediable Etiologies 34
Medication Management 37
Environmental Interventions 40
References 41
Additional Readings 42

4 DEMENTIA 45

Epidemiology 45
Clinical Characteristics 46
Cortical and Subcortical Dementia Concept . . . 46
Degenerative Dementias 46
Differential Diagnosis and Evaluation 52
Mental Status Examination 52

History 53
Laboratory Data 53
Neuroimaging 53
Neuropsychological Testing 53
Treatment and Management 55
References 57
Additional Readings 59

5 DEPRESSION 61
Epidemiology 61
Clinical Characteristics 62
Diagnostic Criteria 62
Primary and Secondary Etiologies 63
Differential Diagnosis 64
Treatment and Management 65
Reverse Etiology 65
Pharmacological Management 65
Electroconvulsive Therapy 75
Medical Psychotherapy 76
References 77
Additional readings 79

6 MANIA 81
Clinical Characteristics 81
General Considerations 81
Diagnostic Criteria 81
Differential Diagnosis 82
Treatment and Management 83
General Considerations 83
Pharmacological Management 83
References 90
Additional Readings 92

7 ANXIETY AND INSOMNIA 93
Anxiety and Anxiety Disorders 93
Epidemiology 93

Biology of Anxiety 94
Clinical Characteristics 94
Differential Diagnosis 101
Treatment and Management 102
Insomnia 108
Treatment of Insomnia 109
References 112
Additional Readings 114

**8 SOMATOFORM AND RELATED
DISORDERS 117**
Somatization 119
Definitions and Theoretical Concepts 119
Evaluation 120
Epidemiology 120
Clinical Characteristics and Specific
Management Strategies 120
Somatization Disorder (Briquet's Syndrome) 122
Undifferentiated Somatoform Disorder 123
Hypochondriasis 125
Conversion Disorder 127
Body Dysmorphic Disorder (BDD) 129
Pain Disorder 130
Somatoform Disorder Not Otherwise Specified . . . 132
Psychological Factors Affecting
Medical Condition 132
Factitious Disorders 132
Malingering 135
Differential Diagnosis 136
Other Somatoform and Related Disorders 136
Medical Disorder 137
Secondary Psychiatric Disorders 137
Adjustment Disorder 137
Anxiety Disorders 138
Depressive Disorder 138
Substance-Related Disorders 138

Psychotic Disorder 138
Delusional Disorder, Somatic Type 139
Additional Treatment and Management
  Considerations 139
  Approach to the Patient 139
  Physical Reactivation and Physical Therapy 140
  Relaxation Therapies, Meditation, and
    Hypnotherapy 141
  Cognitive Therapy 141
  Group Psychotherapy 141
References 142
Additional Readings 146

9 SUBSTANCE-RELATED DISORDERS . . . 147

DSM-IV Substance-Related Disorders 147
Alcohol-Related Disorders 149
  Introduction 149
  Classification, Diagnosis, and Management 149
Sedative-, Hypnotic-, or Anxiolytic-Related
  Disorders 157
  Introduction 157
  Classification, Diagnosis, and Management 157
Opiate (Narcotic)-Related Disorders 159
  Introduction 159
  Classification, Diagnosis, and Management 160
Amphetamine-Related Disorders. 162
  Introduction 162
  Classification, Diagnosis, and Management 163
Cocaine-Related Disorders 165
  Introduction 165
  Classification, Diagnosis, and Management 165
References 168
Additional Readings 170

10 IMPORTANT PHARMACOLOGICAL ISSUES. 171

Adherence to Pharmacological Treatment 171
Drug Actions 171
    Drug Absorption 171
    Drug Distribution 173
    Drug Receptors 173
    Drug Metabolism 174
    Drug Elimination 174
Drug Interactions 175
    Drugs Being Taken by the Patient 175
    Monoamine Oxidase Inhibitors and Diet 179
    Other Drug Interactions 179
Cytochrome P450 system. 179
Neuroleptic Malignant Syndrome 180
    Clinical Characteristics 180
    Epidemiology 184
    Differential Diagnosis. 186
    Treatment and Management. 189
References 190
Additional Readings 192

11 VIOLENCE AND AGGRESSION 193

Emergency Consultation 193
    The Combative, Actively Violent Patient 193
    A Person Who Is Threatening Violence 195
    A Person Who Has Already Committed Violence. . . 196
Physiological Basis for Violence and Aggression 196
Differential Diagnosis of Violence and Aggression . . . 196
Treatment and Prevention of Chronic Aggression 197
    Pharmacological Treatment 197
    Nonpharmacological Treatment 197
References 199
Additional Readings 200

12 PAIN AND ANALGESICS 201

Pain Terminology 202
   Nociceptive (Peripheral) Versus Central Pain 202
   Acute, Continuous, and Chronic Pain 205
Pain Behavior, Suffering, and Psychiatric Diagnoses . . 207
   Depression 208
   Anxiety 209
   Somatoform Disorders 209
Aids to Diagnosis 210
   Minnesota Multiphasic Personality Inventory 210
   Projective Tests 210
   Pain Drawing 210
   Visual Analogue Scale 211
   Sadomasochistic Index (Pain-Prone) 211
Analgesics 211
Opiates (Narcotics) 212
   Dependence 212
   Addiction 212
   Adverse Effects 214
   Pharmacological Adjuvants 214
Treatment and Management of Chronic Pain 215
References 217
Additional Readings 218

13 PERSONALITY, RESPONSE TO ILLNESS, AND MEDICAL PSYCHOTHERAPY 219

Personality and Response to Illness 219
   Psychological Regression 219
   Levels of Ego Defenses 220
Personality and General Medical Conditions 220
Personality Disorder 222
   Definition 222
   Clinical Characteristics 223
   Differential Diagnosis 225
Treatment and Management 225

General Considerations 225
Pharmacotherapy 226
Group Psychotherapy 227
Clinic and Ward Management 227
Medical Psychotherapy 228
Definition 228
Selection Process 229
Setting 229
Associative Anamnesis 230
Formulation 231
References 231
Additional Readings 232

14 MEDICOLEGAL ISSUES IN CONSULTATION 233
Confidentiality 234
Competency Versus Capacity 235
Informed Consent and the Right to Refuse
    Medical Treatment 237
Signing Out Against Medical Advice 238
Do-Not-Resuscitate Orders 238
Advance Directives 239
Guardianship 239
Involuntary Hospitalization 240
Restraints 240
References 241
Additional Readings 242

15 SUICIDALITY 243
Epidemiology 243
Completed Suicides 243
Attempted Suicides 245
Clinical Features and Risk Factors 247
Psychiatric Disorders Associated With
    Increased Suicide Risk 247

Medical Disorders Associated With
    Increased Suicide Risk 248
Approach to the Patient 249
    Epidemiological Risk Assessment 249
    Individual Risk Assessment. 249
Treatment and Management 249
    Identifying the Risk Level. 249
    Protecting the Patient 250
    Treating or Removing Risk Factors 251
References 252
Additional Readings 254

16 GERIATRIC PSYCHIATRY 255
Epidemiology. 255
Psychiatric Disorders 255
    Delirium. 255
    Dementia 256
    Depression 256
    Anxiety 256
    Psychosis 257
    Substance-Related Disorders 258
Diagnostic Evaluation 258
    Clinical History 258
    Physical Examination 258
    Mental Status Examination 259
    Laboratory Findings. 259
Treatment and Management 259
    Treatment of Medical Problems 259
    Age-Related Pharmacological Issues 260
Electroconvulsive Therapy 264
Psychotherapy 264
Elder Abuse. 265
Conclusion 265
References 266
Additional Readings 268

**17 SPECIAL CONSULTATION-LIAISON
   SETTINGS AND SITUATIONS** **269**

Pregnancy and the Postpartum Period 269
   Psychopharmacology During Pregnancy and
      Lactation. 269
   Postpartum Psychiatric Disorders. 271
   References. 271
Pediatric Consultation-Liaison 272
   Developmental Perspective 272
   Family Focus 273
   Consultation Process 273
   Administrative and Legal Issues 274
   Psychopharmacology 274
   Reference 275
Burns 275
   Epidemiology 275
   Delirium. 275
   Mood Syndromes 276
   Psychoactive Substance Use Withdrawal
      Syndromes. 276
   Pain Management 276
   Psychosocial Issues in Burn Patients
      Likely to Die. 277
   Psychiatric Issues in Recovery 277
   References. 278
Cancer. 279
   Primary Psychiatric Disorders 279
   Secondary Psychiatric Disorders 279
   Anticipatory Nausea and Vomiting 281
   Pain Management 281
   Delivering Bad News 282
   References. 282
Death and Dying 283
   Depression 283
   Anxiety 283

Pain 284
References. 284
Neurology and Neurosurgery 285
Head Injury 285
CNS Infection 285
Primary and Metastatic CNS Tumors 286
Subcortical/Limbic System Disease 287
Normal Pressure Hydrocephalus 287
Poststroke Depression. 287
References. 288
HIV Disease and AIDS 288
AIDS 289
HIV Infection Without AIDS 290
Psychopharmacological Issues 290
Suicide Assessment 291
References. 291
Organ Transplantation 292
Transplant Donors. 292
Transplant Recipients 293
Rating Scales 293
Perioperative Issues 293
References. 295
Critically Ill Patients and the Intensive Care Unit. 296
Mental Status Examination 296
Changes in Medical-Surgical Management 297
Psychopharmacological Treatment 297
Respirators 298
Intra-Aortic Balloon Pump 298
References. 299
Male Erectile Disorder (Impotence) 299
History. 299
Evaluation 301
Treatment 301
Reference 301
Additional Readings for This Chapter 302

Index 303

List of Tables

1–1.   Recent Trends Affecting the Practice of
        Consultation-Liaison (C-L) Psychiatry 2

1–2.   Characteristics of Effective Psychiatric
        Consultation 5

2–1.   Components of the Mental Status
        Examination. 12

2–2.   Cortical Mapping of Brain Dysfunction 24

3–1.   DSM-IV Diagnostic Criteria for Delirium. 31

3–2.   Differential Diagnosis of Delirium: Emergent
        Diagnoses—WHHHHIMP 35

3–3.   Common Medications Associated
        With Delirium. 36

3–4.   Differential Diagnosis of Delirium
        Using Mnemonic I WATCH DEATH. 37

3–5.   Assessment of the Patient With Delirium 38

3–6.   Guidelines for Haloperidol Dosage 40

4–1.   Distinguishing Features of Cortical and
        Subcortical Dementias 47

4–2.   DSM-IV Diagnostic Criteria for Dementia of the
        Alzheimer's Type 48

4–3.   DSM-IV Diagnostic Criteria for Vascular
        Dementia 50

4–4.   Hachinski Ischemia Scale 51

4–5.   Laboratory Tests in the Assessment of
        Dementia 54

4–6.   Treatment and Management of Dementia 56

5–1.   Mnemonic for Diagnostic Criteria for Major
        Depressive Syndrome. 62

5–2.   Medical Conditions and Toxic Agents Associated
        With Secondary Depressive Disorders 66

5–3.	Differentiating Depression and Dementia	68
5–4.	Antidepressants	70
5–5.	Clinical Situations for Which Psychostimulants Are an Important Treatment Option	75
6–1.	Mnemonic for Diagnostic Criteria for Manic Episode: GIDDINESS	82
6–2.	Causes of Secondary Mood Disorder, Manic	84
6–3.	Antimanic Medications	87
7–1.	Medical and Toxic Causes of Anxiety and Panic	96
7–2.	Benzodiazepines: Oral Compounds, Dosages, Absorption Rates, and Pharmacokinetics	103
7–3.	Sedative-Hypnotic Medications	110
8–1.	Differential Diagnosis of Physical Complaints	118
8–2.	Psychiatric Evaluation of a Patient Referred for Somatization	121
8–3.	Management of Somatization Disorder	124
8–4.	Some Signs, Symptoms, and Diseases Simulated in or Caused by Factitious Behavior	134
8–5.	Steps to Take When Factitious Disorders Are Suspected	135
9–1.	DSM-IV Substance Abuse and Dependence	148
9–2.	CAGE Screen for Diagnosis of Alcoholism	150
9–3.	Substance Intoxication and Its Management	152
9–4.	Substance Withdrawal Syndromes and Their Management	154
9–5.	Clinical Cues That Warn of Possible Narcotic Abuse or Dependence in General Medical Patients	161
10–1.	Medication Treatment Principles in the Consultation-Liaison Setting	172
10–2.	Drug Interactions Important in Consultation-Liaison Psychiatry	176
10–3.	Cytochrome P450 Enzyme–Drug Interactions	181
10–4.	Clinical Characteristics of Neuroleptic Malignant Syndrome and Their Frequency (%)	185

10–5.	Risk Factors for Neuroleptic Malignant Syndrome (NMS)	186
10–6.	Clinical Characteristics of Serotonin Syndrome and Their Frequency	189
11–1.	Procedure for Physical Restraint	194
11–2.	Pharmacological Management of Chronic Aggression.	198
12–1.	Pain Terminology	204
12–2.	Characteristics of Central Pain	205
12–3.	Psychiatric Syndromes to Look for in Patients With Chronic Pain.	209
12–4.	Comparison of Opiate Potency and Dosage	213
12–5.	Management Principles for Patients With Chronic Pain.	215
12–6.	Behavioral Treatment Methods for Pain	216
13–1.	Defenses: Common Responses to Illness.	221
13–2.	Medical Causes of Personality Change.	223
13–3.	Clinical Characteristics of Frontal Lobe Syndromes.	224
13–4.	Elements of Medical Psychotherapy Formulation	230
14–1.	Common Statutory Exceptions to Confidentiality Between Psychiatrist and Patient	234
15–1.	Suicide Risk Factors in the General Population . .	244
15–2.	Factors Associated With Suicide in Medical-Surgical Patients	246
15–3.	SAD PERSONS Scale	248
15–4.	Lines of Questioning During Examination of a Potentially Suicidal Medical Patient	250
16–1.	Clinical Features of Geriatric Depression	257
16–2.	Pharmacokinetic Changes Associated With Aging	261
16–3.	Suggested Strategies for Psychiatric Consultation for Geriatric Patients	266

17–1.	Psychiatric Manifestations of Chemotherapeutic Agents 280
17–2.	Biopsychosocial Screening Criteria for Solid Organ Transplantation 294
17–3.	Medications That May Cause Male Erectile Disorder (Impotence) 300

List of Figures

2–1.	Mini-Mental State Exam, With Instructions for Its Administration. 18
12–1.	Pain Drawing 203
14–1.	Factors in Selection of Competency Tests 237

INTRODUCTION

to the American Psychiatric Press Concise Guides

The American Psychiatric Press Concise Guides Series provides, in an accessible format, practical information for psychiatrists, psychiatry residents, and medical students working in a variety of treatment settings, such as inpatient psychiatry units, outpatient clinics, consultation-liaison services, and private office settings. The Concise Guides are meant to complement the more detailed information to be found in lengthier psychiatry texts.

The Concise Guides address topics of special concern to psychiatrists in clinical practice. The books in this series contain a detailed table of contents, along with an index, tables, figures, and other charts for easy access. The books are designed to fit into a lab coat pocket or jacket pocket, which makes them a convenient source of information. References have been limited to those most relevant to the material presented.

Robert E. Hales, M.D., M.B.A.
Series Editor
American Psychiatric Press Concise Guides

EFFECTIVE PSYCHIATRIC CONSULTATION IN A CHANGING HEALTH CARE ENVIRONMENT

■ HISTORY

Consultation-liaison (C-L) psychiatry began in the 1920s to 1930s with the development of general hospital psychiatry units and the psychosomatic medicine movement (Lipowski 1996). Rockefeller Foundation grants in 1934 and 1935 aided this developmental process by establishing closer collaboration between psychiatrists and other physicians. The number of C-L psychiatry services grew, and by the 1960s to 1970s, a subspecialty scientific literature had developed. In 1974, the Psychiatry Education Branch of the National Institute of Mental Health (NIMH) decided to support the development and expansion of C-L services throughout the United States (Eaton et al. 1977). By 1980, NIMH supported 130 programs and materially contributed to the training of more than 300 C-L psychiatry fellows (Lipowski 1996). Federal budget cuts in the 1980s dramatically decreased the number of stipends. Nevertheless, C-L psychiatry continued to grow and develop during the 1980s (Lipowski 1996). More recently, as primary care expanded its scope of practice and influence, C-L psychiatrists have found themselves well suited to teach and consult with primary care physicians. Several significant historical trends affected C-L psychiatry during the 1990s (Table 1–1).

TABLE 1–1.	**Recent trends affecting the practice of consultation-liaison (C-L) psychiatry**

Managed health care's limitations and reallocation of health care resources

Reimbursement for psychiatric consultations and mental health care is limited.

"Carve outs" of psychiatric services separate physical from mental health.

Psychiatrists must justify psychiatric services by demonstrating cost offset.

Shift of medical care and psychiatric consultation from inpatient to outpatient settings

Psychiatric consultation is conducted directly in primary care settings.

Shorter hospital stays limit inpatient psychiatric consultation and follow-up and transfer treatment to the outpatient setting.

Multidisciplinary teams

C-L psychiatrists increasingly work on multidisciplinary teams (e.g., with neuropsychologists, medical social workers, behavioral health psychologists, developmental pediatricians, behavioral neurologists, and psychiatric nurse practitioners).

Subspecialty units now often include psychiatrists (e.g., transplantation, physical medicine and rehabilitation, pain clinics).

Combined residency training

The number of combined residency training programs in psychiatry–internal medicine or psychiatry–family practice has increased. The effect of this increase on C-L psychiatry training programs is not yet clear.

■ PSYCHIATRIC ILLNESS IN MEDICAL-SURGICAL OUTPATIENTS AND INPATIENTS

In outpatient community samples, fewer than 25% of patients with psychiatric disorders see mental health providers; most are seen by primary care providers (Simon and Walker 1999). In primary care settings, epidemiological surveys typically find that 10%–15% of patients have well-defined anxiety or depressive disorders (Eisenberg 1992). Not surprisingly, primary care physicians write the majority of prescriptions for antidepressant (Simon et al. 1993) and anti-anxiety medications (Mellinger et al. 1984).

Medical conditions, particularly chronic illnesses, significantly increase the likelihood that a person will develop a mood disorder, anxiety disorder, or substance-related disorder (Wells et al. 1988). As many as 30%–60% of general hospital inpatients have diagnosable psychiatric disorders (Strain 1982; VonAmmon et al. 1989). Depression, anxiety, and cognitive dysfunction each have been shown to predict longer hospital stays and greater hospitalization costs, even after accounting for demographics, degree of physical impairment, type of hospital unit, medical diagnosis, and circumstances of admission (Levenson et al. 1990; Saravay et al. 1991).

■ COST-EFFECTIVENESS OF PSYCHIATRIC CONSULTATION

Psychiatric consultation in general hospital patients and medical-surgical outpatients reduces mortality, morbidity, length of stay, and hospital costs (Hall et al. 1996). Maintaining the financial viability of C-L services is essential in sustaining these cost-effective operations. Because centralized billing departments often place a lower priority on psychiatric billing than on more lucrative surgical and procedure-based reimbursements, a psychiatric consultation service must have direct input into its billing process. For each consult, the consultant should list all appropriate medical and psychiatric diagnoses and provide specific diagnostic criteria for each major psychiatric diagnosis. In addition, he or she should rate the level of complexity of the case. The complexity of the case, number of diagnoses, amount of time spent, and amount of information included in the note all may significantly alter the level of billing submitted for an initial consult. Finally, the C-L chief should work closely with the hospital administration to define and document sources of cost savings produced by the C-L service.

■ APPROACH TO THE CONSULTATION

Consultation Style

The relative merits of an open-ended interview compared with a structured clinical examination are debated (Shakin-Kunkel and Thompson 1996). The two styles are not mutually exclusive, and both are necessary to obtain valuable longitudinal and cross-sectional information. Structured examination is necessary for some historical data and for parts of the mental status examination. However, most information needed to make a diagnosis and a biopsychosocial formulation is obtained by simply listening. Much data are gained from patients' responses to open-ended questions such as "What brings you into the clinic?" "How has this illness affected your life?" and "Why do you think your doctor asked the psychiatrist to see you?" Several personal and professional attributes are important to being an effective C-L psychiatrist. These are summarized in Table 1–2.

Patient Confidentiality

Most patients seen in psychiatric consultation have never seen a psychiatrist before, did not request the consultation, and have not been informed about the consultation. Maintaining absolute doctor-patient confidentiality is not possible for a psychiatric consultant (Simon and Walker 1999). The physician requesting the consult is the identified "customer" and expects an answer to the consultation, even if the patient benefits from the consultation. It is best to explain this dual relationship to the patient from the start. The primary care outpatient or inpatient record is a relatively public document. Notes regarding consultation visits are available not only to the referring primary care physician but also to other medical providers in the health care system.

TABLE 1–2.	**Characteristics of effective psychiatric consultation**

Respond promptly to consultation requests.

Establish the level of urgency—emergent, urgent, or routine.

Wear a white coat—on your shoulders and in your brain.

Determine the central question—time to address comprehensively all biopsychosocial issues a patient may have, especially in inpatient settings, is rare.

Be flexible—perform consultations in medical-surgical inpatient and outpatient settings.

Respect patients' rights to know that the identified "customer" is the consulting physician.

Review medical data and collect essential information.

Use the biopsychosocial model—consider predispositions, precipitants, and strengths.

Make a well-reasoned differential diagnosis—consider medical, neurological, and psychiatric syndromes.

Make specific recommendations that are brief, goal oriented, and free of psychiatric jargon.

Discuss findings and recommendations with consultees in person whenever possible.

Follow up a patient in the hospital and arrange outpatient care.

Recognize the value and role of medical psychotherapy for outpatient consultations.

Do not take over aspects of the patient's medical care unless asked to do so.

Read medical journals and remain part of the medical community.

Educate medical administrators about cost-offset advantages of psychiatric consultation.

Work with the business office and staff to optimize reimbursement.

Patient Follow-Up

Psychiatric consultants generally should follow up patients until they are discharged from the hospital or clinic or until the goals of the consultation are achieved. This is necessary for three reasons. First, urges to "sign off" on patients are frequently related more to negative reactions toward patients than to resolution of the presenting symptoms. Second, symptoms can recur, and a premature sign-off creates bad feelings and may lead to reconsultation. Finally, follow-up instills confidence that the C-L psychiatrist is available and willing to help.

Frequency and duration of psychiatric follow-up will vary widely depending on patient needs and financial circumstances (Simon and Walker 1999). Many patients receive maximum benefit from one or two consultation visits followed by management recommendations to the consulting physician. Some patients need a brief intervention, followed by referral back to the primary care physician. Other patients need immediate transfer to specialty mental health care clinics or units. In many situations, a period of shared follow-up with the outpatient primary care physician allows his or her continued involvement and learning.

■ CONSULTATION OR LIAISON PSYCHIATRY?

Liaison work is distinguished from consultation work in that the liaison psychiatrist casts an earlier and wider net, proactively seeking out psychiatric and medical comorbidity in a clinic or ward, and does not wait to see if the patient is identified and referred (Strain 1999). "Liaison psychiatry attempts to deal with the **denominator** of the prevalence of psychiatric morbidity in the medical setting, whereas consultation psychiatry, by the nature of the referral process, is involved only with the **numerator**" (Strain et al. 1988, p. 76). For example, Hammer et al. (J. S. Hammer, H. T. C. Lam, J. J. Strain, unpublished data, September 1993) screened all hospital admissions and showed that psychosocial assessment and treatment at the time of admission led to earlier discharges in patients with psychiatric comorbidity. For each dollar spent on this screening program, the hospital reported savings of $48. Unfortunately, health care payers are less willing to pay for psychiatrists to identify new patients than to assess and treat identified patients. More outcome-based research is needed to determine the most effective consultation models in different outpatient and inpatient settings.

■ OUTPATIENT CONSULTATION-LIAISON PSYCHIATRY

One of the most striking changes in health care over the last decade is the shift from inpatient to outpatient health care delivery. Cost pressures coupled with technological advances have led to dramatic decreases in hospitalization rates and length of stay (Simon and Walker 1999). These changes are shifting the focus of C-L psychiatry to the outpatient setting. C-L psychiatrists are ideally trained to consult on primary care patients and to coordinate integrated biopsychosocial treatment in outpatient medical clinics. Some psychiatric consultation services have established telephone lines and Internet-based consultation for primary care physicians and specialists.

Consultation psychiatrists are increasingly conducting outpatient consultation activities directly in primary care clinics. Fortunately, the transfer from working on inpatient medical-surgical units to an outpatient primary care setting is relatively easy and has several advantages (Simon and Walker 1999). First, patients who view their problems as "strictly medical" are less likely to resist a referral for psychiatric consultation when the visit occurs within the medical clinic. Second, the presence of a consulting psychiatrist in the clinic, even part-time, significantly increases opportunities for communication and follow-up. Third, regular contact in the primary care clinic allows discussions about ongoing management and "curbside consultations."

■ REFERENCES

Eaton JS Jr, Goldberg R, Rosinski E, et al: The educational challenge of consultation-liaison psychiatry. Am J Psychiatry 134 (March suppl):20–23, 1977

Eisenberg L: Treating depression and anxiety in primary care: closing the gap between knowledge and practice. N Engl J Med 326:1080–1084, 1992

Hall RCW, Rundell JR, Hirsch TW: Economic issues in consultation-liaison psychiatry, in The American Psychiatric Press Textbook of Consultation-Liaison Psychiatry. Edited by Rundell JR, Wise MG. Washington, DC, American Psychiatric Press, 1996, pp 24–37

Levenson JL, Hamer RM, Rossiter LD: Relation of psychopathology in general medical inpatients to use and cost of services. Am J Psychiatry 47:1498–1503, 1990

Lipowski ZJ: History of consultation-liaison psychiatry, in The American Psychiatric Press Textbook of Consultation-Liaison Psychiatry. Edited by Rundell JR, Wise MG. Washington, DC, American Psychiatric Press, 1996, pp 2–11

Mellinger G, Balter M, Uhlenhuth E: Prevalence and correlates of the long-term regular use of anxiolytics. JAMA 251:375–379, 1984

Saravay SM, Steinberg MD, Weinschel B, et al: Psychological comorbidity and length of stay in the general hospital. Am J Psychiatry 148:324–329, 1991

Shakin-Kunkel EJ, Thompson TL: The process of consultation and organization of a consultation-liaison psychiatry service, in The American Psychiatric Press Textbook of Consultation-Liaison Psychiatry. Edited by Rundell JR, Wise MG. Washington, DC, American Psychiatric Press, 1996, pp 12–23

Simon GE, Walker EA: The consultation-liaison psychiatrist in the primary care clinic, in The Essentials of Consultation-Liaison Psychiatry. Edited by Rundell JR, Wise MG. Washington, DC, American Psychiatric Press, 1999, pp 255–262

Simon G, VonKorff M, Wagner EH, et al: Patterns of antidepressant use in community practice. Gen Hosp Psychiatry 15: 399–408, 1993

Strain JJ: Needs for psychiatry in the general hospital. Hosp Community Psychiatry 33:996–1002, 1982

Strain JJ: Liaison psychiatry, in Modern Perspectives in Clinical Psychiatry. Edited by Howells JG. New York, Brunner/Mazel, 1988, pp 76–101

Strain JJ: Liaison psychiatry, in The Essentials of Consultation-Liaison Psychiatry. Edited by Rundell JR, Wise MG. Washington, DC, American Psychiatric Press, 1999, pp 3–11

vonAmmon CS, Wettstein RM: Emotional and cognitive dysfunction associated with medical disorders. J Psychosom Res 33: 505–514, 1989

Wells KB, Golding JM, Burnam MA: Psychiatric disorders in a sample of the general population with and without chronic medical conditions. Am J Psychiatry 145:976–981, 1988

■ ADDITIONAL READINGS

Ford CV, Fawzy FI, Frankel BL, et al: Fellowship training in consultation-liaison psychiatry; education goals and standards. Psychosomatics 35:118–124, 1994

Goldman L, Lee T, Rudd P: Ten commandments for effective consultation. Arch Intern Med 143:1753–1755, 1983

Holtz JL: Making a consultation service work: an organizational commentary. Psychosomatics 33:324–328, 1992

2

MENTAL STATUS EXAMINATION

The patient's mental status examination (MSE) reflects mental and psychological function at a particular point in time and is fully appreciated only when placed in the context of the patient's history. Mental status testing in a general hospital environment is difficult. Hospital rooms are noisy, and many distractions, such as intravenous alarms, a roommate who is groaning or loudly conversing with visitors, or a harried nurse or phlebotomist who must have immediate access to the patient, are present. In addition, the patient is sick, often frightened, and sleep deprived. Before testing, the clinician should always ensure that the patient has his or her usual sensory aids (e.g., hearing aid or glasses). The MSE is separated into two categories: noncognitive and cognitive (Table 2–1).

Anthony and colleagues (1982) examined all patients admitted to a general medical ward and found that 23 of 97 patients (24%) had dementia or delirium. Jacobs et al. (1977) administered a brief examination to consecutive medical admissions and found significant cognitive dysfunction in 37%. Unfortunately, physicians, nurses, and medical students often do not recognize that a patient is cognitively impaired. In one study (Knights and Folstein 1977), 37% of ward physicians, 55% of nurses, and 46% of medical students did not identify cognitively impaired general medical patients. In a study of elderly patients referred to an ambulatory geriatric evaluation service, the referring physician did not recognize that 73% of the patients had substantial cognitive dysfunction or that cognitive dysfunction was related to medications 75% of the time (Kallman and May 1989).

TABLE 2–1.   **Components of the mental status examination**

Noncognitive	Cognitive
General appearance and behavior	Level of consciousness
Mood and affect	Attention
Thought processes and content	Speech and language
Perceptions	Orientation
Abstracting abilities	Memory
Judgment and insight	

Source.   Adapted from Strub RL, Wise MG: "Differential Diagnosis in Neuropsychiatry," in *The American Psychiatric Press Textbook of Neuropsychiatry,* 2nd Edition. Edited by Yudofsky SC, Hales RE. Washington, DC, American Psychiatric Press, 1992, p. 231. Copyright 1992, American Psychiatric Press. Used with permission.

■ NONCOGNITIVE COMPONENTS OF THE MENTAL STATUS EXAMINATION

General Appearance and Behavior

The MSE begins the instant the clinician sees the patient. The patient's physical appearance, attitude, and behavior (such as increased or decreased body movements, posturing, pacing, tremor, and choreiform or dyskinetic movements) should be described without using jargon.

Mood and Affect

Mood is the patient's pervasive and sustained emotional state. Terms used to describe mood are *depressed, angry, elevated, euthymic, expansive,* and *irritable.* The parameters of *affect* are *range, intensity, lability,* and *appropriateness.* Affective range may be full (the patient shows a wide range of emotional states during the interview) or restricted to a particular state, such as depressed. Affective intensity among patients can also vary greatly (e.g., from the extreme rage seen in a borderline patient to the flat or affectless expression typically observed in a patient with Parkinson's disease). Affective lability indicates that the patient rapidly fluctuates from one affective state to another; this often implies a toxic or medical etiology. Affect is also described as either appropriate or inappropriate to the topic under discussion.

Thought Processes and Content

Thought processes and *thought content* are judged by the patient's quality and quantity of speech and his or her behavior (Wise and Strub 1999). When the clinician asks the patient a question, how does he or she respond? Is his or her answer responsive to the question asked (goal directed), or does he or she ramble purposelessly (tangential)? The pattern of thoughts is also an important measure of thought processes. The patient's thoughts may move extremely rapidly from one idea to another (flight of ideas), may not relate in an understandable way (loose associations), or may stop suddenly (thought blocking). The patient's thought content or major themes reflect the concerns of the patient. These can include obsessional preoccupation, suicidal or homicidal ideation, and irrational beliefs.

The patient's behavior also reflects thought content. A patient who is reluctant to talk and acts very suspiciously is usually paranoid, even if he or she denies it. The patient who denies misperceptions but is seen responding to hallucinations is another good example of the importance of observed behavior in the assessment of thought content.

Perceptions

Disorders of *perception* include illusions (misinterpretation of a real sensory experience), hallucinations (a sensory perception in the absence of an external stimulus), delusions (a fixed false belief), and ideas of reference (an incorrect interpretation that events have direct reference to oneself). Hallucinatory perception can be visual, auditory, tactile, olfactory (smell), gustatory (taste), or kinesthetic (body movement). Although cultural variations are important, hallucinations that occur in an awake individual are almost always symptomatic of a pathological process. Auditory hallucinations are more typical of primary psychiatric disorders. Visual hallucinations are typically associated with brain disease, although they also occur in nonpsychiatric patients with severe recent visual loss and in some patients with schizophrenia (Bracha et al. 1989). Tactile hallucinations occur commonly in patients who have had a limb amputation or substance-induced withdrawal delirium. "Phantom limb" sensation, the feeling that the limb is still present, occurs in a majority of amputees. Given time, the amputee's tactile hallucinations diminish and usually disappear. Olfactory, gustatory, or kinesthetic hallucinations are rare and are most commonly experienced by patients with partial seizures (Lishman 1987).

Abstracting Abilities

Educational level is a strong determinant in one's ability to *abstract*. The clinician usually conducts bedside testing by asking the patient to interpret simple proverbs. Concrete interpretations are commonly found in three groups: individuals with less than a high school education, individuals with schizophrenia, and individuals with dementia.

Judgment and Insight

Judgment is the individual's ability to correctly anticipate the consequences of one's behavior and to behave in a culturally acceptable way. Recent behavior is the best way to determine a patient's judgment. In general, *insight* is present if the patient realizes that a problem exists, that his or her thinking and behavior may contribute to that problem, and that he or she may need assistance.

■ COGNITIVE COMPONENTS OF THE MENTAL STATUS EXAMINATION

Level of Consciousness

Psychiatric consultation is often requested for patients who have a rapid or recent change in mental status. In most instances, the patient is either lethargic or agitated and disruptive after surgery or a medical intervention. In addition to changes in arousal, such patients often have altered thought content.

Attention

The capacity to direct and maintain one's *attention* while screening out extraneous and irrelevant stimuli is a fundamental yet highly complex cognitive function. Inattention (the breakdown of selective attention) and distractibility are common and clinically significant neuropsychiatric symptoms. Inattention can also complicate the entire evaluation process (Mesulam 1985). For example, an inattentive patient will frequently fail tests of memory or calculation on the basis of inattention alone. Digit span is a standard psychological test for attention.

Speech and Language

Brain disease, particularly dominant hemisphere insults, frequently disrupt a patient's *speech* and *language*. Speech defects include the slurred speech of the intoxicated patient, the soft trailing speech of the patient with Parkinson's disease, and the dysphonia and dysarthria of the patient with amyotrophic lateral sclerosis. Language disturbances, specifically aphasias, refer to defects in word choice, comprehension, and syntax. The patient's spontaneous speech should be observed and its rate, rhythm, and fluency described. Is speech fluent, and does the patient make sense? Next, comprehension must be tested. This is particularly important when the patient is on a respirator and normal speech is not possible. The clinician should ask yes-and-no type questions, for example, "Do you put on your socks before your shoes?" "Is there a tree in the room?" and "Can an elephant ride a tricycle?"

Orientation

The psychiatrist should record orientation in the spheres of self, place, situational awareness, and time. Serial measurement of orientation provides valuable longitudinal historical and treatment outcome data.

Memory

The clinician should ask the patient to remember four unrelated objects, such as tulip, eyedropper, ball, and brown. The patient should immediately repeat the words to ensure that he or she has properly heard and understood them. After the clinician engages the patient in conversation about other things for about 3 minutes, he or she asks the patient to repeat the words. If the patient cannot recall the words, the clinician should check to see if the words were not encoded into memory or were encoded but cannot be retrieved. These can be differentiated by giving the patient clues. Patients who did not learn the words are not aided by prompting, whereas patients who learned the words but cannot access them quickly will recall with prompting.

■ SCREENING MENTAL STATUS EXAMINATIONS

A number of bedside examinations are used to screen patients for cognitive dysfunction. Screening examinations have advantages and disadvantages. Sometimes a scored MSE will persuade a physician who doubts a psychiatrist's opinion but may believe "hard data." In addition, serial screening MSEs are useful when following the clinical course of a delirious or demented patient. Screening MSEs are very useful for physicians who do not normally perform an MSE as part of their examination. For the consultation psychiatrist, who is an expert in cognition and its measurement, screening MSEs are only one piece of a more extensive cognitive examination. **Caution:** In general, screening MSEs are insensitive and may miss mild to moderate cognitive impairment.

Mini-Mental State Exam

Folstein's Mini-Mental State Exam (MMSE; Folstein et al. 1975) is probably the most widely used and best-known screening MSE. The MMSE (Figure 2–1) takes about 5 minutes to administer, can be administered serially to follow up a patient's clinical course, and is a reliable and valid test in medical patients (Nelson et al. 1986).

Various MMSE cutoff scores are proposed to indicate delirium or a dementia. A score of 20 or less may indicate impairment (Folstein et al. 1975); however, Mungas (1991) proposed that a score of 0–10 corresponds to severe cognitive impairment, 11–20 to moderate impairment, 20–25 to mild impairment, and 25–30 to questionable impairment or intact function.

Other Useful Tests of Cognitive Function

The *Reitan-Indiana Aphasia Screening Test* is a pocket-sized, easily administered, brief aphasia screen. This test gives a reasonable survey of aphasic symptoms, including ability to copy, name, spell, write, read, calculate, and demonstrate use of an object (ideomotor praxis).

The *Set Test* is a test of verbal fluency designed to screen elderly patients for dementia (Isaacs and Kennie 1973). The patient is asked to name 10 items from each of 4 categories. A useful mnemonic to recall the categories is F-A-C-T (fruits-animals-colors-towns). The patient is asked to name 10 fruits, then to name 10 animals, and so on. The score is the total number of items named, with a maximum score of 40. In patients age 65 or older, scores below 15 are clearly abnormal and indicate impairment. (Note: this is not a timed test. It is an excellent test for frontal lobe dysfunction and is a great distraction after presenting 4 words to remember.)

FIGURE 2–1. **Mini-Mental State Exam, with instructions for its administration.**

Patient _____
Examiner _____
Date _____

Maximum score	Score	
		Orientation
5	( )	What is the (year) (season) (date) (day) (month)?
5	( )	Where are we: (state) (county) (town) (hospital) (floor)?
		Registration
3	( )	Name 3 objects; 1 second to say each. Then ask the patient all 3 after you have said them. Give 1 point for each correct answer. Then repeat them until he learns all 3. Count trials and record. Trials _____
		Attention and Calculation
5	( )	Alternatively spell "world" backwards.
		Recall
3	( )	Ask for the 3 objects repeated above. Give 1 point for each correct.

9   ( )

Language

Name a pencil, and watch (2 points)

Repeat the following: "No ifs ands or buts." (1 point)

Follow a 3-stage command:

"Take a paper in your right hand, fold it in half, and put it on the floor" (3 points)

Read and obey the following:

Close YOUR eyes (1 point)

Write a sentence (1 point)

Copy design (1 point)

Total score

ASSESS level of consciousness along a continuum

Alert   Drowsy   Stupor   Coma

(continued)

FIGURE 2–1.   **Mini-Mental State Exam, with instructions for its administration.** *(continued)*

Instructions for administration of Mini-Mental State Examination

Orientation

(1) Ask for the date. Then ask specifically for parts omitted, e.g., "Can you also tell me what season it is?" One point for each correct.

(2) Ask in turn "Can you tell me the name of this hospital?" (town, county, etc.). One point for each correct.

Registration

Ask the patient if you may test his memory. Then say the names of 3 unrelated objects, clearly and slowly, about one second for each. After you have said all 3, ask him to repeat them. This first repetition determines his score (0–3) but keep saying them until he can repeat all 3, up to 6 trials. If he does not eventually learn all 3, recall cannot be meaningfully tested.

Attention and Calculation

Ask the patient to begin with 100 and count backwards by 7. Stop after 5 subtractions (93, 86, 79, 72, 65). Score the total number of correct answers.

If the patient cannot or will not perform this task, ask him to spell the word "world" backwards. The score is the number of letters in correct order. E.g., dlrow = 5, dlorw = 3.

Recall

Ask the patient if he can recall the 3 words you previously asked him to remember. Score 0–3.

Language

Naming: Show the patient a wrist watch and ask him what it is. Repeat for pencil. Score 0–2.

Repetition: Ask the patient to repeat the sentence after you. Allow only one trial. Score 0 or 1.

3-Stage command: Give the patient a piece of plain blank paper and repeat the command. Score 1 point for each part correctly executed.

Reading: On a blank piece of paper print the sentence "Close your eyes," in letters large enough for the patient to see clearly. Ask him to read it and do what it says. Score 1 point only if he actually closes his eyes.

Writing: Give the patient a blank piece of paper and ask him to write a sentence for you. Do not dictate a sentence; it is to be written spontaneously. It must contain a subject and verb and be sensible. Correct grammar and punctuation are not necessary.

Copying: On a clean piece of paper, draw intersecting pentagons, each side about 1 in., and ask him to copy it exactly as it is. All 10 angles must be present and 2 must intersect to score 1 point. Tremor and rotation are ignored.

Estimate the patient's level of sensorium along a continuum, from alert on the left to coma on the right.

Source. Reprinted from Folstein MF, Folstein SE, McHugh PR: "Mini-Mental State, a Practical Method for Grading the Cognitive State of Patients for the Clinician." *Journal of Psychiatric Research* 12:189–198, 1975. Copyright 1975, Pergamon Press. Used with permission.

Draw a clock face is another useful bedside test. This task is easy to do and very instructive, particularly for documenting constructional apraxia (see Chapter 3 for a further explanation of this test).

The *Frank Jones Story* tests the patient's ability to conceptualize a situation and to solve a problem. The clinician asks the patient to explain the following story: "I have a friend by the name of Frank Jones whose feet are so big that he has to put on his pants by pulling them over his head." After the psychiatrist observes the patient's response, he or she asks the patient, "Can Mr. Jones do that?" A patient with normal cognitive function will typically laugh and then explain in an understandable way why it is impossible. When a patient with dementia hears the story, he or she usually will not laugh because he or she does not understand the problem. The patient also is unable to rationally explain his or her response. A patient with delirium usually will laugh because he or she finds the situation humorous. However, such a patient often will answer "No" and then give a bizarre explanation for that answer, for example, "He can't. Well, maybe he can if he unzips his fly"; "He just can't"; or "I guess so if he takes off his shoes."

■ THE NEUROLOGICAL EXAMINATION

A neurological examination is essential in any patient with cognitive dysfunction, suspected somatoform or conversion disorder with neurological complaints, or malingering. The examination does not need to be time-consuming. Often, the patient's history will suggest deficits.

A basic bedside neurological examination consists of the following:

1. Check deep tendon reflexes for symmetry. Check for the presence of a Babinski reflex. Some clinicians also check for primitive reflexes (snout, grasp, glabellar, and palmomental).
2. Check muscle strength for asymmetry, weakness, tone, or embellishment.
3. Observe the gait and associated arm movements.

4. Examine cranial nerve function.
5. Check the distribution of any sensory findings.
6. Check for signs of meningeal irritation, such as neck stiffness, headache, or Kernig's and Brudzinski's signs.

■ THE CONSULTATION PSYCHIATRIST AS NEUROPSYCHIATRIST

The ability to correlate neuropsychiatric or behavioral dysfunction with cortical anatomy is difficult. It requires effort and practice and is not an exact science. Approximate cortical localization of various cognitive and behavioral functions is summarized in Table 2–2.

Knowledge of brain-behavior relationships is important for psychiatrists to function well as consultants in the hospital setting. The consultation psychiatrist must understand neurological terminology. The following list contains a few of the commonly used neurological terms. The prefix *a-* means complete loss of ability (e.g., aphasia is the loss of ability to comprehend or express speech), and the prefix *dys-* means an impaired ability (e.g., dysphasia means an impairment in the ability to comprehend or express speech).

- *Dysarthria*—disturbance of articulation of speech caused by muscle dysfunction
- *Dysbulia*—decrease in willpower
- *Dyscalculia*—impaired ability to do mathematical calculations
- *Dysgnosia*—impaired ability to recognize the importance of sensory impressions
- *Dysgraphia*—impaired ability to express thought in writing
- *Dyslexia*—impaired ability to read
- *Dysphasia*—impaired ability to comprehend, elaborate, or express speech
- *Dyspraxia*—impaired ability to use objects correctly
- *Dysprosody*—speech that is not of the normal pitch, rhythm, and variation
- *Dystaxia*—impaired motor coordination

TABLE 2–2. **Cortical mapping of brain dysfunction**

Abnormality	Frontal	Dominant temporo-parietal	Dominant parietal
Motor	Motor impersistence	Dysgraphia	Ideokinetic (ideomotor) dyspraxia
	Inertia		Kinesthetic dyspraxia
	Impaired rapid sequential movements		
	Stimulus-bound behavior (e.g., echopraxia)		
Language	Broca's aphasia	Wernicke's aphasia	Dyslexia
	Transcortical aphasia	Driveling, word approximations, neologisms	Dysnomia
	Motor aprosodia[a]	Pure word deafness	
	Verbigeration	Dysgraphia	
		Dyslexia	
		Dysnomia	
		Letter and number agnosia	
		Sensory aprosodia	
Memory	Impaired short-term memory store	Impairment of rehearsed consolidated memory	
Other	Impaired concentration		Finger agnosia
	Global disorientation		Dyscalculia
	Impaired judgment		Right-left and east-west disorientation
	Impaired problem solving		Dysstereognosis
	Impaired abstraction		Dysgraphesthesis
	Right spatial neglect		Impaired symbolic categorization

[a]Nondominant frontal lobe.
Source. Adapted from Taylor et al. 1987.

Nondominant parietal	Nondominant temporoparietal	Occipital	Corpus callosum
Constructional dyspraxia			Inability to tie shoes with eyes closed
Dressing dyspraxia			Ideokinetic dyspraxia in hand ipsilateral to dominant hemisphere
Kinesthetic dyspraxia			Constructional dyspraxia in hand contralateral to dominant hemisphere
			Alexia without agraphia
	Impaired musical memory	Impaired visual memory	
Dysstereognosis			Dysstereognosis of hand ipsilateral to dominant hemisphere
Dysgraphesthesis			Dysgraphesthesis of hand ipsilateral to dominant hemisphere
Anosognosia			
Prosopagnosia			
Reduplicative paramnesia			
Left spatial neglect			

■ REFERENCES

Anthony JC, LeResche L, Niaz U, et al: Limits of the Mini-Mental State as a screening test for dementia and delirium among hospital patients. Psychol Med 12:397–408, 1982

Bracha HS, Wolkowitz OM, Lohr JB, et al: High prevalence of visual hallucination in research subjects with chronic schizophrenia. Am J Psychiatry 146:526–528, 1989

Folstein MF, Folstein SE, McHugh PR: 'Mini-Mental State': a practical method for grading the cognitive state of patients for the clinician. J Psychiatry Res 12:189–198, 1975

Isaacs B, Kennie AT: The set test as an aid to the detection of dementia in old people. Br J Psychiatry 123:467–470, 1973

Jacobs JW, Bernhard MR, Delgado A, et al: Screening for organic mental syndromes in the medically ill. Ann Intern Med 86:40–46, 1977

Kallman H, May HJ: Mental status assessment in the elderly. Prim Care 16(2):329–347, 1989

Knights EB, Folstein MF: Unsuspected emotional and cognitive disturbance in medical patients. Ann Intern Med 87:723–724, 1977

Lishman WA: Organic Psychiatry. Oxford, England, Blackwell Scientific, 1987

Mesulam M-M: Attention, confusional states, and neglect, in Principles of Behavioral Neurology. Edited by Mesulam M-M. Philadelphia, PA, FA Davis, 1985, pp 125–140

Mungas D: In-office mental status testing: a practical guide. Geriatrics 46(7):54–66, 1991

Nelson A, Fogel BS, Faust D: Bedside cognitive screening instruments: a critical assessment. J Nerv Ment Dis 174:73–83, 1986

Taylor MA, Surles FS, Abrams R: The neuropsychiatric evaluation, in The American Psychiatric Press Textbook of Neuropsychiatry. Edited by Hales RE, Yudofsky SC. Washington, DC, American Psychiatric Press, 1987, pp 3–16

Wise MG, Strub RI: Mental status examination, in Essentials of Consultation-Liaison Psychiatry. Edited by Rundell JR, Wise MG. Washington, DC, American Psychiatric Press, 1999, pp 13–25

■ ADDITIONAL READINGS

Blessed G, Tomlinson BE, Roth M: The association between quantitative measures of dementia and of senile change in the cerebral grey matter of elderly subjects. Br J Psychiatry 114:797–811, 1968

Feher EP, Doody R, Pirozzolo FJ, et al: Mental status assessment of insight and judgment. Clin Geriatr Med 5:477–498, 1989

Fogel BS, Eslinger PL: Diagnosis and management of patients with frontal lobe syndromes, in Medical Psychiatric Practice, Vol 1. Edited by Stoudemire A, Fogel BS. Washington, DC, American Psychiatric Press, 1991, pp 349–391

Kiernan RJ, Mueller J, Langston JW, et al: The Neurobehavioral Cognitive Status Examination: a brief but differentiated approach to cognitive assessment. Ann Intern Med 107:481–485, 1987

Reitan RM: Validity of the Trail Making Test as an indicator of organic brain damage. Percept Mot Skills 8:271–276, 1958

Schwamm LH, Van Dyke C, Kiernan RJ, et al: The Neurobehavioral Cognitive Status Examination: comparison with the Cognitive Capacity Screening Examination and the Mini-Mental State Examination in a neurosurgical population. Ann Intern Med 107:486–491, 1987

Strub RL, Black FW: The Mental Status Examination in Neurology. Philadelphia, PA, FA Davis, 1977

3

DELIRIUM

Delirium is a transient, reversible, global dysfunction in cerebral metabolism that has an acute onset (more rarely, a subacute onset). Delirium occurs in about 15%–18% of patients on medical and surgical wards (Wise and Trzepacz 1999). Its prevalence is even higher in certain populations—30% in post–coronary artery bypass graft (CABG) surgery and 50% in post–hip surgery patients. The frequency increases with advanced age and in individuals with existing brain disease (e.g., dementia of the Alzheimer's type) (Kolbeinsson and Jonsson 1993). The mortality associated with this psychiatric disorder is high and is an indicator in 25% of impending deaths (Folstein et al. 1991). In addition to an increased risk of mortality, patients with delirium stay in the hospital longer than nondelirious patients (Marcantonio et al. 1994).

Delirium has many different labels: acute brain failure, acute brain syndrome, encephalopathy, confusional state, reversible dementia, and intensive care unit (ICU) psychosis. The term *ICU psychosis* should be abandoned. It infers a cause-and-effect relationship between the ICU setting and delirium. There is no more evidence for ICU psychosis than there is for ICU arrhythmia or ICU seizure. Delirium is receiving more attention from psychiatrists and other physicians. The American Psychiatric Association recently published delirium practice guidelines (American Psychiatric Association 1999).

■ EPIDEMIOLOGY

Patients who are at increased risk for delirium include the elderly (who often also have dementia and medical morbidity), patients with central nervous system (CNS) disorders (e.g., stroke, Parkinson's disease, HIV infection), postsurgical patients (e.g., postcardiotomy, posttransplant, post–hip surgery), burn patients, and drug-dependent patients who are experiencing withdrawal. Advancing age increases the risk, with age 60 or older usually cited as the highest risk group (Lipowski 1990). If children are excluded, the incidence of delirium increases with the age of the patient population studied. Studies by Inouye et al. (1989) and Francis et al. (1988) that used DSM-III-R (American Psychiatric Association 1987) criteria reported that 23% and 25%, respectively, of patients older than 70 had delirium during hospitalization. Increasing age is also associated with increasing prevalence of dementia, which is itself an independent risk factor for delirium.

Preexisting brain damage, whether preoperative CNS neurological abnormalities (Koponen and Riekkinen 1993; Marcantonio et al. 1994) or dementia (Kolbeinsson and Jonsson 1993), lowers the patient's threshold for developing delirium. The aging brain has less "cerebral reserve" and flexibility in the face of physiological perturbations, including changes in vasculature, decreased cholinergic activity, and increased monoamine oxidase activity; all of these may increase an individual's vulnerability to delirium. Even with a relatively minor insult, such as a urinary tract infection, elderly patients are more likely than younger adults to develop delirium.

■ CLINICAL CHARACTERISTICS

Diagnostic Criteria

DSM-IV (American Psychiatric Association 1994) diagnostic criteria for delirium are listed in Table 3–1. The core characteristics are impairment of consciousness and reduced ability to focus, sustain, or shift attention. Other DSM-IV criteria are an acute change in cogni-

---

TABLE 3–1. **DSM-IV diagnostic criteria for delirium**

A. Disturbance of consciousness (i.e., reduced clarity of awareness of the environment) with reduced ability to focus, sustain, or shift attention.

B. Change in cognition (such as memory deficit, disorientation, language disturbance, perceptual disturbance) that is not better accounted for by a preexisting, established, or evolving dementia.

C. The disturbance develops over a short period of time (usually hours to days) and tends to fluctuate during the course of the day.

D. There is evidence from the history, physical examination, or laboratory findings of [*] judged to be etiologically related to the disturbance.

[*] A general medical condition, diagnose delirium due to a general medical condition.

Substance intoxication or withdrawal, diagnose substance-induced delirium.

More than one etiology (e.g., more than one etiologic general medical condition, a general medical condition plus Substance Intoxication or medication side effect), diagnose delirium due to multiple etiologies.

Note. When a medical condition or substance use is the suspected cause but specific evidence is lacking, the diagnosis is delirium not otherwise specified (NOS).
Source. Reprinted from American Psychiatric Association: *Diagnostic and Statistical Manual of Mental Disorders,* 4th Edition. Washington DC, American Psychiatric Association, 1994. Copyright 1994, American Psychiatric Association. Used with permission.

tion (onset usually over hours to days) that is not better accounted for by dementia and mental status fluctuations during the day. When delirium is present, a specific diagnosis is made based on etiology. If an etiology is determined, the diagnosis is delirium due to a general medical condition (e.g., delirium due to hepatic encephalopathy or delirium due to hypoglycemia), substance-induced delirium (including medication side effects), or delirium due to multiple etiologies. If the clinician is unable to determine a specific etiology, a diagnosis of delirium not otherwise specified (NOS) is made.

Prodrome

Some patients manifest symptoms, such as restlessness, anxiety, irritability, distractibility, or sleep disruption, immediately prior to the onset of an overt delirium. Review of the patient's hospital medical chart, particularly the nursing notes, often reveals prodromal features.

Temporal Course

Two features of the temporal course of delirium are characteristic and assist in differential diagnosis: abrupt/acute onset of symptoms and fluctuation of symptom severity during an episode. Waxing and waning of symptoms typically occur, with relatively lucid intervals fluctuating with more severe symptoms; careful examination usually reveals continued, although more subtle, cognitive impairment even during lucid periods.

Neuropsychiatric Impairment

The patient with delirium has difficulty sustaining attention and is usually either distractible or unable to focus. Short-term memory is impaired. In the presence of impaired registration, memory difficulties may be secondary to attention deficits. After recovering from delirium, some patients are amnestic for the entire episode; others have islands of memory for certain experiences. Disorientation to time and place is typical in delirium. Patients often have visuo-constructional impairment, being unable to copy simple geometric designs or to draw more complex figures such as a clock face. Clock face drawing requires input from the nondominant parietal cortex for overall spatial proportions and relations, from the dominant parietal cortex for details like numbers or hands, and from the prefrontal cortex for understanding the concept of time. Many higher level executive functions are subserved by the prefrontal cortices, especially the dorsolateral region. These functions, including switching mental sets, abstraction, sequential thinking, verbal fluency, temporal memory, and judgment, are affected in delirium (Trzepacz 1994).

Patients with delirium often have disorganized thought patterns. The severity of the thought disturbance can range from tangentiality and circumstantiality to loose associations. At the most severe level of thought disorganization, speech may resemble a fluent aphasia (Wise and Trzepacz 1999). Language impairments range from mild dysarthria or mumbling to dysphasia or muteness. Word-finding difficulty, dysnomia with paraphasias, and reduced comprehension are common.

Perceptual Disturbances

The patient with delirium often experiences misperceptions, usually illusions or hallucinations. Illusions and hallucinations can be auditory or visual, but the latter are more common and always raise the suspicion of CNS disorder whenever they occur. Tactile, gustatory, and olfactory hallucinations are less common.

Psychomotor Disturbances

Some patients with delirium are hypoactive, others are hyperactive, and a significant number alternate between these two states. A hyperactive delirium, such as delirium tremens (DTs), is rarely undetected. This is not the case for hypoactive delirium. The patient with hypoactive delirium often goes unnoticed or is mislabeled as depressed, unmotivated, having a character disorder, or uncooperative. On neurological examination, motor findings may include tremor, myoclonus, asterixis, and reflex or muscle tone changes. The tremor associated with delirium, particularly toxic-metabolic, is generally absent at rest but apparent during movement (action or intention tremors).

Sleep-Wake Cycle Disturbances

During delirium, the patient's normal diurnal rhythm is often reversed, with lethargy during the day and arousal during the night. Normalization of sleep is an important treatment goal. Reduction of external cues during the night may increase disorientation or paranoia and result in agitation and "sundowning."

■ DIFFERENTIAL DIAGNOSIS

The differential diagnosis of delirium is extensive, and confusional states often have multiple causes. Francis et al. (1990) found that 56% of elderly patients with delirium had a single definite or probable etiology, and the remaining 44% had an average of 2.8 etiologies per patient. Because the differential diagnosis of delirium is so broad, a two-tiered diagnostic system is clinically useful. The first tier contains the emergent items, and the second tier contains other diagnostic considerations.

Emergent items are listed using the mnemonic WHHHHIMP (Table 3–2). These diagnoses are considered emergent because failure to recognize and treat the etiology immediately may result in injury or death to the patient. Medications are an extremely common cause of delirium (Table 3–3). A thorough review and correlation of the medication records (either administration or discontinuation) with behavioral change is important. The second, somewhat less emergent, tier considers other potentially contributory diagnoses. Table 3–4 summarizes these diagnoses with the mnemonic I WATCH DEATH. This mnemonic reminds the clinician that the morbidity and mortality associated with untreated delirium is significant.

Several important aspects of the physical examination, mental status examination, and laboratory examination of a patient with delirium assist with differential diagnosis. They are summarized in Table 3–5.

■ TREATMENT AND MANAGEMENT

Reverse Remediable Etiologies

The treatment of delirium has two separate and important aspects. The first is critical and bears directly on the survival of the pa-

TABLE 3-2.   **Differential diagnosis of delirium: emergent diagnoses—WHHHHIMP**

Wernicke's encephalopathy or **W**ithdrawal	Check for Wernicke's triad: confusion, ataxia, and ophthalmoplegia (lateral gaze paralysis most common).
Hypoxemia, **H**ypertensive encephalopathy, **H**ypoglycemia, or **H**ypoperfusion	Check for insulin-dependent diabetes. Check arterial blood gases, oxygen saturation, and current and past vital signs. Hypoperfusion or hypoxemia of the brain can result from several causes: decreased cardiac output, arrhythmias, pulmonary failure, carbon monoxide poisoning, hypotension, cerebral vascular insufficiency, and severe anemia.
Intracranial bleeding or **I**nfection	Examine for subarachnoid or intraparenchymal hemorrhage or subdural hematoma. Look for infectious processes (e.g., elevated white blood cell count, fever).
Meningitis or encephalitis	Check vital signs for fever and general or localizing neurological signs (e.g., meningismus with stiff neck). Also consider oncological and viral causes.
Poisons or medications	The most common causes of delirium are exogenous substances—prescribed and over-the-counter medications or illicit substances and toxins. Order a toxicology screen. Take a thorough medication history, particularly looking for drug-drug interactions.

Source.   Adapted from Wise MG, Brandt G: "Delirium," in *The American Psychiatric Press Textbook of Neuropsychiatry,* 2nd Edition. Edited by Hales RE, Yudofsky SC. Washington, DC, American Psychiatric Press, 1992, pp. 300–301. Copyright 1992, American Psychiatric Press. Used with permission.

tient—identification and reversal, when possible, of the reason(s) for the delirium. The second aspect of treatment is to reduce psychiatric symptoms of delirium with medications and environmental interventions regardless of whether psychosis or agitation is present (American Psychiatric Association 1999).

The patient with delirium should be placed near the nursing station, and vital signs should be checked frequently. A sitter should be employed if necessary. The medical staff must ensure good oxygenation and monitor fluid input and output. All nonessential medications should be stopped. If an etiology for the confusional state

---

TABLE 3–3. **Common medications associated with delirium**

Analgesics: meperidine, opiates, nonsteroidal anti-inflammatory drugs

Antibiotics: acyclovir, ganciclovir, amphotericin B, interferon, cephalosporins, rifampin, isoniazid, tetracycline, gentamicin, ticarcillin

Anticholinergics: antihistamines, antispasmodics, atropine, benztropine, phenothiazines, scopolamine, promethazine, tricyclic antidepressants, trihexyphenidyl, belladonna alkaloids

Anticonvulsants: phenobarbital, phenytoin, valproic acid

Anti-inflammatories: Adrenocorticotropic hormone, corticosteroids, nonsteroidal anti-inflammatory drugs

Antineoplastic drugs: methotrexate, tamoxifen, vinblastine, vincristine, asparaginase, aminoglutethimide

Antiparkinsonian drugs: amantadine, bromocriptine, L-dopa, carbidopa

Cardiac drugs: β-blockers, captopril, clonidine, digitalis, lidocaine, mexiletine, methyldopa, quinidine, tocainide, procainamide

Sedative-hypnotics: barbiturates, benzodiazepines, glutethimide

Sympathomimetics: amphetamine, cocaine, ephedrine, epinephrine, phenylephrine, theophylline

Others: cimetidine, disulfiram, lithium, metrizamide, ranitidine, quinacrine

---

Source. Adapted from Wise MG, Brandt G: "Delirium," in *The American Psychiatric Press Textbook of Neuropsychiatry,* 2nd Edition. Edited by Hales RE, Yudofsky SC. Washington, DC, American Psychiatric Press, 1992, pp. 300–301. Copyright 1992, American Psychiatric Press. Used with permission.

TABLE 3–4. **Differential diagnosis of delirium using mnemonic I WATCH DEATH**

Infection	Encephalitis, meningitis, syphilis, HIV disease, sepsis
Withdrawal	Alcohol, barbiturates, sedative-hypnotics
Acute metabolic	Acidosis, alkalosis, electrolyte disturbance, hepatic failure, renal failure
Trauma	Closed-head injury, heatstroke, postoperative states, severe burns
CNS pathology	Abscess, hemorrhage, hydrocephalus, subdural hematoma, infection, seizures, stroke, tumors, metastases, vasculitis
Hypoxia	Anemia, carbon monoxide poisoning, hypotension, pulmonary failure, cardiac failure
Deficiencies	Vitamin B_{12}, folate, niacin, thiamine
Endocrinopathies	Hyper/hypoadrenocorticism, hyper/hypoglycemia, myxedema, hyperparathyroidism
Acute vascular	Hypertensive encephalopathy, stroke, arrhythmia, shock
Toxins or drugs	Medications, illicit drugs, pesticides, solvents (see Table 3–3)
Heavy metals	Lead, manganese, mercury

Note. CNS = central nervous system; HIV = human immunodeficiency virus.
Source. Reprinted from Wise MG, Trzepacz PT: "Delirium (Confusional States)," in *The American Psychiatric Press Textbook of Consultation-Liaison Psychiatry.* Edited by Rundell JR, Wise MG. Washington, DC, American Psychiatric Press, 1996, p. 268. Copyright 1996, American Psychiatric Press. Used with permission.

is not identified immediately, further laboratory, radiological, and physical examinations are recommended.

Medication Management

There is no consensus on the symptomatic treatment of delirium. However, clinical experience indicates that neuroleptic medica-

TABLE 3–5. **Assessment of the patient with delirium**

Physical status

  History

  Physical and neurological examination

  Review of vital signs and anesthesia record if postoperative

  Review of medical records

  Careful review of medications and correlation with behavioral changes

Mental status

  Interview

  Cognitive tests (e.g., clock face, Trail Part A and B)

Basic laboratory—*consider in every patient with delirium*

  Blood chemistries (electrolytes, glucose, calcium, albumin, blood urea nitrogen, creatinine, electrolytes, serum glutamic-oxaloacetic transaminase [SGOT], bilirubin, alkaline phosphatase, magnesium, PO_4_, Venereal Disease Research Laboratory [VDRL])

  Complete blood count

  Serum drug levels (e.g., digoxin, theophylline, phenobarbital, cyclosporine)

  Arterial blood gases or oxygen saturation

  Urinalysis and collection for culture and sensitivity (C&S)

  Urine drug screen

  Electrocardiogram

  Chest X ray

Laboratory—*order as indicated by clinical condition*

  Electroencephalogram

  Lumbar puncture

  Brain computed tomography (CT) or magnetic resonance imaging (MRI)

  Blood chemistries (e.g., heavy metal screen, B12 and folate levels, lupus erythematosus (LE) prep, antinuclear antibody (ANA), urinary porphyrins, human immunodeficiency virus [HIV])

Source. Reprinted from Wise MG, Trzepacz PT: "Delirium (Confusional States)," in *The American Psychiatric Press Textbook of Consultation-Liaison Psychiatry.* Edited by Rundell JR, Wise MG. Washington, DC, American Psychiatric Press, 1996, p. 267. Copyright 1996, American Psychiatric Press. Used with permission.

tion is helpful and that haloperidol, a potent antipsychotic with virtually no anticholinergic or hypotensive properties, that does not suppress respirations, that has minimal cardiotoxicity, and that can be given intravenously, is probably the drug of first choice. Other useful antipsychotic medications include droperidol and risperidone. Although droperidol is used by physicians for control of nausea and vomiting, and by anesthesiologists as a preanesthetic agent, it is a potent antipsychotic. Droperidol is approved for intravenous use but has a higher potential than haloperidol for causing orthostatic hypotension. Risperidone has less potential than haloperidol to cause unwanted extrapyramidal symptoms but must be taken orally. Less potent antipsychotic indications, such as chlorpromazine and thioridazine, are more likely to cause hypotension and anticholinergic side effects and are not recommended.

Regardless of the route of administration, the usual initial dosage of haloperidol in younger patients is 0.5–1 mg for mild, 2–5 mg for moderate, and 5–10 mg for severe confusion or agitation. The initial dosage for frail or elderly patients is 0.5 mg for mild, 1 mg for moderate, and 2 mg for severe confusion or agitation. The dose is repeated at regular intervals, but not before 30 minutes, until the patient is calmer. Often doses given only two or three times a day are needed in patients whose level of agitation does not mandate more emergent care. After the confusion has cleared, haloperidol is continued and tapered over 1–5 days, depending on the severity of the episode. Guidelines for haloperidol dosage are summarized in Table 3–6.

Benzodiazepines are the drugs of choice in the treatment of DTs, certain other drug withdrawal states, and complex partial seizure status. Intravenous midazolam and lorazepam are frequently used emergently to treat severe agitation. Benzodiazepines are used successfully as adjuncts to high-potency neuroleptics such as haloperidol. Small doses of intravenous lorazepam, particularly in patients whose symptoms have not responded to haloperidol alone, help to decrease agitation.

TABLE 3–6. **Guidelines for haloperidol dosage**

Level of agitation	Starting dose (mg)
Mild	0.5–2.0
Moderate	2.0–5.0
Severe	5.0–10.0

1. If haloperidol is used intravenously, clear the intravenous (IV) line with normal saline prior to bolus infusion. Heparin can precipitate IV haloperidol.

2. For elderly patients, use a starting dose of 0.5–2.0 mg.

3. Allow 30 minutes between doses; *check Q-T interval on the electrocardiogram before repeating* dose.

4. For continued agitation, double the previous dose.

5. If no improvement after three doses, give 0.5–1.0 mg lorazepam intravenously concurrently, or alternate lorazepam with haloperidol every 30 minutes.

6. Once the patient is calm, add the total milligrams of haloperidol and administer the same number of milligrams over the next 24 hours.

7. Assuming the patient remains calm, reduce the dose by 50% every 24 hours.

8. To convert to an oral dosage, double the iv dose required for 24 hours (divide oral dose bid or tid).

Source.   Adapted from Wise MG, Terrell CD: "Neuropsychiatric Disorders: Delirium, Psychotic Disorders, and Anxiety," in *Principles of Critical Care,* 2nd Edition. Edited by Hall JB, Schmidt GA, Wood LDH. New York, McGraw-Hill Inc, 1998, p. 973. Used with permission.

Environmental Interventions

Environmental interventions are sometimes helpful but are not a primary treatment. Both nurses and family members can frequently reorient the patient to date and surroundings. It may help to place a clock, calendar, and familiar objects in the room. Adequate light in the room during the night may decrease frightening illusions or hasten reorientation during awakenings. Rooms with windows may help the patient retain orientation. A private room for the patient with delirium is not recommended unless adequate supervision is provided. If the patient normally wears eyeglasses or a hearing aid, returning these devices may improve the quality of sensory input and help the patient better understand his or her surroundings.

■ REFERENCES

American Psychiatric Association: Diagnostic and Statistical Manual of Mental Disorders, 3rd Edition, Revised. Washington, DC, American Psychiatric Association, 1987

American Psychiatric Association: Diagnostic and Statistical Manual of Mental Disorders, 4th Edition. Washington, DC, American Psychiatric Association, 1994

American Psychiatric Association: Practice Guideline for the Treatment of Patients With Delirium. Am J Psychiatry 156:5 (suppl): 1–20, 1999

Folstein MF, Bassett SS, Romanoski AJ, et al: The epidemiology of delirium in the community: the Eastern Baltimore Mental Health Survey, in International Psychogeriatrics. Edited by Miller NE, Lipowski ZJ, Lebowitz BD. New York, Springer, 1991, pp 169–176

Francis J, Strong S, Martin D, et al: Delirium in elderly general medical patients: common but often unrecognized (abstract). Clinical Research 36(3):711A, 1988

Francis J, Martin D, Kapoor W: A prospective study of delirium in hospitalized elderly. JAMA 263:1097–1101, 1990

Inouye S, Horwitz R, Tinetti M, et al: Acute confusional states in the hospitalized elderly: incidence, factors, and complications (abstract). Clinical Research 37(2):524A, 1989

Kolbeinsson H, Jonsson A: Delirium and dementia in acute medical admissions of elderly patients in Iceland. Acta Psychiatr Scand 87:123–127, 1993

Koponen HJ, Riekkinen PJ: A prospective study of delirium in elderly patients admitted to a psychiatric hospital. Psychol Med 3:103–109, 1993

Lipowski ZJ: Delirium: Acute Confusional States. New York, Oxford University Press, 1990

Marcantonio ER, Goldman L, Mangione CM, et al: A clinical prediction rule for delirium after elective noncardiac surgery. JAMA 271:134–139, 1994

Trzepacz PT: Neuropathogenesis of delirium: a need to focus our research. Psychosomatics 35:375–391, 1994

Wise MG, Terrell CD: Neuropsychiatric disorders: delirium, psychotic disorders, and anxiety, in Principles of Critical Care, 2nd Edition. Edited by Hall JB, Schmidt GA, Wood LDH. New York, McGraw-Hill Inc, 1998, p. 973

Wise MG, Trzepacz PT: Delirium (confusional states), in Essentials of Consultation-Liaison Psychiatry. Edited by Rundell JR, Wise MG. Washington, DC, American Psychiatric Press, 1999, pp 81–93

■ ADDITIONAL READINGS

Berrios GE: Delirium and confusion in the 19th century: a conceptual history. Br J Psychiatry 139:439–449, 1981

Cole MG, Primeau FJ: Prognosis of delirium in elderly hospital patients. Can Med Assoc J 149:41–46, 1993

Fernandez F, Holmes V, Adams F, et al: Treatment of severe, refractory agitation with a haloperidol drip. J Clin Psychiatry 49:239–241, 1988

Frye MA, Coudreaut MF, Hakeman SM, et al: Continuous droperidol drip infusion for management of agitated delirium in an ICU. Psychosomatics 36:301–305, 1995

Liptzin B, Levkoff SE: An empirical study of delirium subtypes. Br J Psychiatry 161:843–845, 1992

Metzger E, Friedman R: Prolongation of the corrected QT and torsades de pointes cardiac arrhythmia associated with intravenous haloperidol in the medically ill. J Clin Psychopharmacol 13:128–132, 1993

Platt MM, Breitbart W, Smith M, et al: Efficacy of neuroleptics for hypoactive delirium (letter). J Neuropsychiatry Clin Neurosci 6:66–67, 1994

Riker RR, Fraser GL, Cox PM: Continuous infusion of haloperidol controls agitation in critically ill patients. Crit Care Med 22: 433–440, 1994

Tune L, Carr S, Cooper T, et al: Association of anticholinergic activity of prescribed medications with postoperative delirium. J Neuropsychiatry Clin Neurosci 5:208–210, 1993

4

DEMENTIA

Dementia is a syndrome of acquired persistent impairment of intellectual function. Multiple spheres of mental activity such as memory, language, visuospatial skills, emotion or personality, and cognition are compromised (Cummings et al. 1980). Early reviews reported that as many as one-third of dementia patients who initially present for evaluation have at least partially reversible dementia (Rabins 1983); however, more recent reviews suggest that reversible dementias occur in as few as 1% of outpatients who are evaluated (Wise et al. 1999). The principal causes of dementia are degenerative, vascular, demyelinating, traumatic, neoplastic, inflammatory, infectious, toxic-metabolic, and dementia syndromes associated with psychiatric disorders (Gray and Cummings 1996).

■ EPIDEMIOLOGY

The most commonly occurring dementia is dementia of the Alzheimer's type (DAT), accounting for approximately 50% of patients evaluated for progressive cognitive decline. Perhaps another 15%–20% show a combination of Alzheimer's disease and vascular pathology at autopsy (Wise et al. 1999). Vascular dementia is the second most common cause of dementia. It occurs in 17%–29% of patients with dementia, with an additional 10%–23% of patients exhibiting vascular dementia mixed with DAT. Together, DAT and vascular dementia account for 70%–90% of dementia patients (Gray and Cummings 1996). The largest group of potentially reversible dementias is psychiatric disorders. Other causes of potentially reversible dementias include alcohol, metabolic disturbances, hydrocephalus, and neoplasms.

■ CLINICAL CHARACTERISTICS

Cortical and Subcortical Dementia Concept

A popular and clinically useful mechanism for conceptualizing dementia, particularly degenerative dementia, is to divide it into cortical, subcortical, and mixed dementias. *Cortical dementias* are disorders producing dysfunction predominantly of the cerebral cortex, as characterized by the *A*s: amnesia, aphasia, apraxia, and agnosia (Gray and Cummings 1996). DAT is the classic example of a cortical dementia. *Subcortical dementias* are disorders primarily involving the deep gray and deep white matter structures, including the basal ganglia, thalamus, and frontal lobe projections of these subcortical structures. Examples of predominantly subcortical dementias include the dementias associated with Parkinson's disease, Huntington's disease, and striatonigral degeneration. *Mixed dementias* produce clinical syndromes with cortical and subcortical features. Vascular dementia is the most common type of mixed dementia. Table 4–1 presents clinical features that help to distinguish cortical and subcortical dementias.

Degenerative Dementias

Cortical Dementia: DAT

The diagnosis of DAT requires the gradual, progressive development of multiple cognitive deficits, including memory and nonmemory cognitive disturbances (American Psychiatric Association 1994). The diagnostic criteria for DAT are listed in Table 4–2.

The typical language disturbance is a fluent aphasia with anomia. Naming and comprehension are progressively impaired, whereas the ability to repeat is relatively preserved (Cummings and Benson 1986). Disturbances in executive cognitive functions include impaired abstracting, sequencing, planning, and organizing. Apathy, distractibility, overreliance on environmental cues, agitation, and a tendency to perseverate also may result from disturbed executive cognitive systems (Gray and Cummings 1996; Royall et al. 1992).

TABLE 4–1.	Distinguishing features of cortical and subcortical dementias	
Characteristic	**Subcortical**	**Cortical**
Language	No aphasia	Aphasia early
Memory	Recall impaired; recognition is better preserved than recall	Amnesia: recall and recognition impaired
Visuospatial skills	Impaired	Impaired
Calculation	Preserved until late	Involved early
Frontal systems	Disproportionately affected	Impaired to the same degree as other abilities
Cognitive processing speed	Slowed early	Response time normal until late in disease course
Personality	Apathetic, inert	Unconcerned or disinhibited
Mood	Depressed	Euthymic
Speech	Dysarthric	Normal articulation[a]
Posture	Bowed or extended	Normal, upright[a]
Coordination	Impaired	Normal[a]
Gait	Abnormal	Normal[a]
Motor speed	Slowed	Normal[a]
Movement disorders	Common (chorea, tremor, tics, rigidity)	Absent[a]

[a]Motor system involvement occurs late in the course of the cortical dementias.
Source. Adapted from Cummings JL (ed): *Subcortical Dementia.* New York, Oxford University Press, 1990, pp. 1–16. Copyright 1990, Jeffrey L. Cummings. Used with permission.

Subcortical Dementia

Parkinson's disease. Assessment of dementia in Parkinson's disease is complex because the effects of aging, depression (in perhaps half of all Parkinson's disease patients), and chronic disability must be considered in addition to the profound motor deficits (Gray and Cummings 1996). Parkinson's disease patients may

TABLE 4–2.	**DSM-IV diagnostic criteria for dementia of the Alzheimer's type**

A.   The development of multiple cognitive deficits manifested by both

    (1) memory impairment (impaired ability to learn new information or to recall previously learned information)

    (2) one (or more) of the following cognitive disturbances:

        (a) aphasia (language disturbance)

        (b) apraxia (impaired ability to carry out motor activities despite intact motor function)

        (c) agnosia (failure to recognize or identify objects despite intact sensory function)

        (d) disturbance in executive functioning (i.e., planning, organizing, sequencing, abstracting)

B.   The cognitive deficits in Criteria A1 and A2 each cause significant impairment in social or occupational functioning and represent a significant decline from a previous level of functioning.

C.   The course is characterized by gradual onset and continuing cognitive decline.

D.   The cognitive deficits in Criteria A1 and A2 are not due to any of the following:

    (1) other central nervous system conditions that cause progressive deficits in memory and cognition (e.g., cerebrovascular disease, Parkinson's disease, Huntington's disease, subdural hematoma, normal pressure hydrocephalus, brain tumor)

    (2) systemic conditions that are known to cause dementia (e.g., hypothyroidism, vitamin B12 or folic acid deficiency, niacin deficiency, hypercalcemia, neurosyphilis, HIV infection)

E.   The deficits do not occur exclusively during the course of a delirium.

F.   The disturbance is not better accounted for by another Axis I disorder (e.g., major depressive disorder, schizophrenia).

Source.   Reprinted from American Psychiatric Association: *Diagnostic and Statistical Manual of Mental Disorders,* 4th Edition. Washington DC, American Psychiatric Association, 1994. Copyright 1994, American Psychiatric Association. Used with permission.

show either mild spontaneous extrapyramidal features or exaggerated sensitivity to standard doses of neuroleptic medications. The illness progresses, often rapidly, with associated neuropsychological deficits in 60% and dementia in 25% of patients (Wise et al. 1999).

Huntington's disease. The clinical triad of dementia, chorea, and a positive family history define Huntington's disease. Huntington's disease patients have diminished cognitive speed, a memory retrieval deficit (characterized by poor spontaneous recall but preserved recognition memory), poor executive functions, and motor symptoms (Gray and Cummings 1996). The absence of aphasia and other cortical features distinguishes Huntington's disease from DAT (Folstein et al. 1990). Personality changes such as irritability or apathy are common and may antedate the onset of chorea. Depression is common in Huntington's disease.

Mixed Dementia

Vascular dementia. Chronic ischemic vascular disease, hemorrhage, and anoxia are the most common causes of vascular dementia. The accumulation of cerebral infarctions produces the progressive cognitive impairment termed *multi-infarct dementia*. In contrast to cortical dementias, vascular dementia is characterized by an abrupt onset, a stepwise progression, a fluctuating course, depression, pseudobulbar palsy, a history of hypertension, a history of strokes, evidence of associated atherosclerosis, and focal neurological symptoms and signs on examination. Table 4–3 lists the DSM-IV diagnostic criteria for vascular dementia (American Psychiatric Association 1994). Table 4–4 summarizes these features, which constitute the Hachinski Ischemia Scale, a valuable tool in differentiating vascular dementia from DAT. The ischemia score does not differentiate vascular dementia from vascular dementia *plus* DAT (Erkinjuntti et al. 1988).

Alcohol dementia. Alcohol dementia is found in approximately 3% of alcoholic patients, and subtle deficits occur in 50% (Cummings 1985); 45% of alcoholic patients who are older than

65 have dementia (Cummings and Benson 1992). Physicians tend to misdiagnose the alcoholic patient's dementia as Korsakoff's psychosis (Cutting 1982). In contrast to a patient with Korsakoff's psychosis, a patient with alcoholic dementia is probably female, has a failing intellect, has a drinking history of longer than 10 years of regular consumption (vs. binge drinking), has abnormal electroencephalogram (EEG) and computed tomography (CT) scan results, and has a more favorable outcome with abstinence or reduced consumption. In 10 studies of alcoholic patients, 66% had

---

TABLE 4–3. **DSM-IV diagnostic criteria for vascular dementia**

A. The development of multiple cognitive deficits manifested by both

  (1) memory impairment (impaired ability to learn new information or to recall previously learned information)

  (2) one (or more) of the following cognitive disturbances:
    (a) aphasia (language disturbance)
    (b) apraxia (impaired ability to carry out motor activities despite intact motor function)
    (c) agnosia (failure to recognize or identify objects despite intact sensory function)
    (d) disturbance in executive functioning (i.e., planning, organizing, sequencing, abstracting)

B. The cognitive deficits in Criteria A1 and A2 each cause significant impairment in social or occupational functioning and represent a significant decline from a previous level of functioning.

C. Focal neurological signs and symptoms (e.g., exaggeration of deep tendon reflexes, extensor plantar response, pseudobulbar palsy, gait abnormalities, weakness of an extremity) or laboratory evidence indicative of cerebrovascular disease (e.g., multiple infarctions involving cortex and underlying white matter) that are judged to be etiologically related to the disturbance.

D. The deficits do not occur exclusively during the course of a delirium.

Source.   Reprinted from American Psychiatric Association: *Diagnostic and Statistical Manual of Mental Disorders,* 4th Edition. Washington DC, American Psychiatric Association, 1994. Copyright 1994, American Psychiatric Association. Used with permission.

TABLE 4–4. **Hachinski Ischemia Scale**

Feature	Points
Abrupt onset	2
Stepwise progression	1
Fluctuating course	2
Nocturnal confusion	1
Relative preservation of personality	1
Depression	1
Somatic complaints	1
Emotional incontinence	1
History of hypertension	1
History of strokes	2
Evidence of associated atherosclerosis	1
Focal neurological symptoms	2
Focal neurological signs	2
Total scale score ≥ 7 signifies a vascular dementia	
Total scale score ≤ 4 signifies nonvascular dementia	

Source.   Adapted from Hachinski VC, Iliff LD, Zilhka E, et al.: "Cerebral Blood Flow in Dementia." *Archives of Neurology* 32:632–637, 1975. Copyright 1975, American Medical Association. Used with permission.

moderate to severe CT scan abnormalities (Cutting 1982). The CT scan results will normalize in some alcoholic patients with abstinence (Cummings 1985). Neuropsychological abnormalities associated with alcoholic dementia are partially reversible with abstinence.

Dementia Associated With Psychiatric Disorder: Pseudodementia

Pseudodementia implies a deceptive or false dementia, which may not be accurate (Cummings and Benson 1992). The term *dementia syndrome of depression* is more accurate in a subset of patients with depression and cognitive dysfunction.

Pseudodementia is associated with several psychiatric disorders; of these, depression is by far the most common psychiatric disorder that produces intellectual impairment. Cognitive abnormalities frequently occur in the elderly depressed patient and less commonly occur in the young depressed patient. Depressive pseudodementia usually has the following characteristics:

- Personal and/or family history of affective illness
- Sudden onset of symptoms
- Complaints about cognitive deficits and halfhearted efforts or "I don't know" responses to questions that test cognitive function by the patient
- Equal impairment of recent and remote memory
- Inconsistent results on tests of cognitive function

In contrast, the dementia patient usually does not have a psychiatric history, attempts to conceal disabilities, tries hard to perform cognitive tasks but fails, has memory loss for recent events greater than that for remote events, and consistently performs poorly on neuropsychiatric tests. Psychiatric disorders that are associated less commonly with dementia-like symptoms include somatization disorder, conversion disorder, malingering, factitious disorder, Ganser's syndrome, mania, and obsessive-compulsive disorder.

■ DIFFERENTIAL DIAGNOSIS AND EVALUATION

Mental Status Examination

An accurate diagnosis cannot be established without a careful mental status examination (MSE). The MSE serves as a probe of brain function but must be conceptualized as a structure built on a solid foundation of intact attentional systems (Gray and Cummings 1996). The consultant must first confirm that attention is undiminished, then the other major cognitive domains are assessed in a logical sequence. Chapter 2 describes the MSE.

History

The clinical history should be obtained and corroborated through reliable caregivers. The clinician should inquire into the type of onset (gradual vs. sudden) and pattern of progression (relentless vs. "stepwise"). The consultant must understand the typical features of an illness such as DAT in order to address potentially reversible etiologies.

Laboratory Data

Laboratory assessment is an important part of the psychiatric consultation of a potential dementia patient. Table 4–5 suggests a battery of laboratory tests to assess cognitive dysfunction. If specific clinical evidence for the cause of the dementia (e.g., evidence of hypothyroidism) is found, then appropriate tests are ordered. With no compelling evidence for a specific cause of dementia, the screening battery summarized in Table 4–5 should be used.

Neuroimaging

Atrophy is present on CT and magnetic resonance imaging (MRI) in most patients with DAT. Patients with DAT also usually have significantly larger ventricles than do age-matched control subjects. In general, correlations between ventricular enlargement and cognitive function are stronger than those between cortical atrophy and cognition (Giacometti et al. 1994). Areas of decreased lucency in the white matter are seen on head CT in most patients with vascular dementia. MRI is the most sensitive structural imaging technique for diagnosing vascular dementia (Gray and Cummings 1996).

Neuropsychological Testing

Neuropsychological testing is much more sensitive and specific than screening MSE tools such as the Mini-Mental State Exam (Chapter 2) and can 1) distinguish between mild dementia and normal aging in elderly individuals, 2) differentiate mild dementia

TABLE 4–5.   **Laboratory tests in the assessment of dementia**

Screening battery

Complete blood count

Erythrocyte sedimentation rate

Blood glucose

Blood urea nitrogen (BUN)

Electrolytes

Serum calcium and phosphorus

Thyroid-stimulating hormone

Vitamin B12 and folate levels

Fluorescent treponemal antibody absorption (FTA-ABS)

If unexplained fever or urinary symptoms present

Urinalysis

Urine culture and sensitivity

If unexplained fever or pulmonary symptoms present

Chest X ray

If cardiovascular symptoms present or evidence of vascular dementia

Electrocardiogram (ECG)

If risk factors for HIV present

Serum HIV test

If drug intoxication suspected

Serum drug level or toxic screen

Tests selected on the basis of specific symptoms or history

Blood gases

Heavy metals

Disease-specific tests (e.g., serum copper and ceruloplasmin for Wilson's disease)

Note.   HIV = human immunodeficiency virus.
Source.   Reprinted from Gray KF, Cummings JL: "Dementia," in *The American Psychiatric Press Textbook of Consultation-Liaison Psychiatry.* Washington, DC, American Psychiatric Press, 1996, pp. 276–309. Copyright 1996, American Psychiatric Press. Used with permission.

from the effects of low education or limited natural cognitive capacities, 3) provide detailed quantitative information that may help distinguish among different dementias, and 4) establish a baseline description of cognitive function that may be followed over time to determine whether the patient is undergoing progressive decline (Gray and Cummings 1996).

■ TREATMENT AND MANAGEMENT

The treatment and management of dementia has several objectives (Table 4–6):

1. *Treat reversible diagnoses.* These include medical and psychiatric disorders that can present with an apparent dementia (e.g., hypothyroidism, depressive pseudodementia). In addition, depression often accompanies and amplifies the cognitive dysfunction of dementias. If vascular dementia is suspected, daily aspirin therapy (325 mg/day) can be used to inhibit platelet aggregation (Meyer et al. 1989). Ticlopidine may ameliorate progressive ischemic injury in patients who fail to tolerate or respond to aspirin (Flores-Runk and Raasch 1993).
2. *Treat coexisting medical conditions,* which are frequently overlooked in patients with dementia.
3. *Consider treatments that restore cognitive function,* such as cholinesterase inhibitors in Alzheimer's dementia (e.g., donepezil, metrifonate, tacrine), or medication that may delay progression of the disease, such as daily aspirin therapy (325 mg/day) in vascular dementia. Several treatments may delay or slow the progression of DAT: vitamin E, selegiline, estrogen in postmenopausal women, and nonsteroidal anti-inflammatory drugs.
4. *Manage and treat behavioral problems.* Nonpharmacological interventions should be used whenever possible. The clinician should use simple vocabulary and repeat communications frequently. When medications are required, the physician must choose target symptoms, start medications at a low dose, in-

---

TABLE 4–6.   **Treatment and management of dementia**

Treat reversible diagnoses (e.g., hypothyroidism, depressive pseudodementia)

Treat coexisting medical conditions

Consider treatments that restore cognitive function or delay decline

    Vascular dementia—give daily aspirin therapy (325 mg/day)

    Alzheimer's dementia

        Augment cholinergic function (e.g., donepezil, metrifonate, tacrine)

        Delay progression (e.g., vitamin E, selegiline, estrogen in postmenopausal women, nonsteroidal anti-inflammatory drugs)

Manage and treat behavioral problems

    Use nonpharmacological interventions whenever possible

    When medications are required:

        Choose target symptoms

        Start at a low dose and increase slowly

        Monitor target symptoms and side effects closely

Provide a consistent environment and legal arrangements (e.g., powers of attorney, wills)

Support caregivers

---

crease the dosage slowly, and monitor target symptoms and side effects closely. If a major tranquilizer is necessary, a high-potency neuroleptic should be used and started at a very low dose (e.g., haloperidol 0.25 mg orally twice a day). Low-potency neuroleptics such as thioridazine and chlorpromazine should be avoided because of their potent anticholinergic and hypotensive side effects. Buspirone appears to help control agitation and aggressive behavior in some elderly patients. Propranolol may help control aggressive behavior in some patients but rarely may exacerbate depression. Clonazepam (0.5 mg) can be used to maintain sleep in patients with frequent awakening or nocturnal wandering; trazodone (25–100 mg) is useful for agitation and for patients with difficulty falling asleep (Pinner and Rich 1988).

5. *Provide a consistent environment.* The patient with dementia needs a safe, consistent, familiar, predictable environment. Early in the course of a dementing illness, the patient is usually most comfortable at home. If the patient has to leave home for unfamiliar surroundings, it may precipitate anxiety and/or deterioration in the patient's condition. The patient and the family should always be encouraged to make legal arrangements (e.g., powers of attorney, wills) before the patient becomes incompetent. Adequate nutrition, hydration, and vigilance for infections and other medical illnesses are important as well.

6. *Support caregivers.* The family and other caregivers of the patient with dementia require support, especially a caregiving spouse. The emotional strain and time demands placed on the caregivers of a person with dementia are often overwhelming. Caregivers need respites from these demands. A nationwide organization called Alzheimer Family Support Group offers such assistance. Two books that are "required" reading for caregivers are *The 36-Hour Day* (Mace and Rabins 1981) and *Understanding Alzheimer's Disease* (Aronson 1988).

■ REFERENCES

American Psychiatric Association: Diagnostic and Statistical Manual of Mental Disorders, 4th Edition. Washington, DC, American Psychiatric Association, 1994

Aronson MK: Understanding Alzheimer's Disease. New York, Scribners, 1988

Cummings JL: Clinical Neuropsychiatry. Boston, MA, Allyn & Bacon, 1985, pp 17–35

Cummings JL, Benson DF: Dementia of the Alzheimer's type: an inventory of diagnostic clinical features. J Am Geriatr Soc 34:12–19, 1986

Cummings JL, Benson DF: Dementia: A Clinical Approach. Boston, MA, Butterworth-Heinemann, 1992, pp 95–152, 217–265, 345–364

Cummings JL, Benson DF, LoVerme S Jr: Reversible dementia. JAMA 243:2434–2439, 1980

Cutting J: Alcoholic dementia, in Psychiatric Aspects of Neurologic Disease, Vol 2. Edited by Benson DF, Blumer D. New York, Grune & Stratton, 1982, pp 149–165

Erkinjuntti T, Ketonen L, Sulkava R, et al: Do white matter changes on MRI and CT differentiate vascular dementia from Alzheimer's disease? J Neurol Neurosurg Psychiatry 50:37–42, 1988

Flores-Runk P, Raasch RH: Ticlopidine and antiplatelet therapy. Ann Pharmacother 27:1090–1098, 1993

Folstein SE, Brandt J, Folstein MF: Huntington's disease, in Subcortical Dementia. Edited by Cummings JL. New York, Oxford University Press, 1990, pp 87–107

Giacometti AR, Davis PC, Alazraki NP, et al: Anatomic and physiologic imaging of Alzheimer's disease. Clin Geriatr Med 10:277–298, 1994

Gray KF, Cummings JL: Dementia, in The American Psychiatric Press Textbook of Consultation-Liaison Psychiatry. Washington, DC, American Psychiatric Press, 1996, pp 276–309

Mace NL, Rabins PV: The 36-Hour Day. Baltimore, MD, Johns Hopkins University Press, 1981

Meyer JS, Rogers RL, McClintic K, et al: Randomized clinical trial of daily aspirin therapy in multi-infarct dementia: a pilot study. J Am Geriatr Soc 37:549–555, 1989

Pinner E, Rich CL: Effects of trazodone on aggressive behavior in seven patients with organic mental disorders. Am J Psychiatry 145:1295–1296, 1988

Rabins PV: Reversible dementia and the misdiagnosis of dementia: a review. Hosp Community Psychiatry 34:830–835, 1983

Royall DR, Mahurin RK, Gray KF: Bedside assessment of executive cognitive impairment: the executive interview. J Am Geriatr Soc 40:1221–1226, 1992

Wise MG, Gray KF, Seltzer B: Delirium, dementia, and amnestic disorder, in The American Psychiatric Press Textbook of Psychiatry, 3rd Edition. Edited by Hales RE, Yudofsky SC, Talbott JA. Washington DC, American Psychiatric Press, 1999, pp 317–362

■ ADDITIONAL READINGS

Aharon-Peretz J, Cummings JL, Hill MA: Vascular dementia and dementia of the Alzheimer type. Arch Neurol 45:719–721, 1988

American Academy of Neurology AIDS Task Force: Nomenclature and research case definitions for neurologic manifestations of human immunodeficiency virus-type 1 (HIV-1) infection. Neurology 41:778–785, 1991

Bliwise DL: What is sundowning? J Am Geriatr Soc 42:1009–1011, 1994

Carlyle W, Ancill RJ, Sheldon L: Aggression in the demented patient: a double-blind study of loxapine versus haloperidol. Int Clin Psychopharmacol 8:103–108, 1993

Gupta SR, Naheedy MH, Young JC, et al: Periventricular white matter changes and dementia: clinical, neuropsychological, radiological and pathological correlation. Arch Neurol 45:637–641, 1988

Jones BN, Reifler BV: Depression coexisting with dementia: evaluation and treatment. Med Clin North Am 78:823–840, 1994

Petersen RC, Smith GE, Ivnik RJ, et al: Memory function in very early Alzheimer's disease. Neurology 44:867–872, 1994

Victor M: Alcoholic dementia. Can J Neurol Sci 21:88–99, 1994

Whitehouse PJ, Geldmacher DS: Pharmacotherapy for Alzheimer's disease. Clin Geriatr Med 10:339–350, 1994

5

DEPRESSION

■ EPIDEMIOLOGY

The lifetime prevalence rate for a major depressive episode is 12.7% for men and 21% for women. The 12-month prevalence rate is 7.7% for men and 12.9% for women (Kessler et al. 1994). The point prevalence for depression in the medically ill is 10%–36% for general medical inpatients and 9%–16% for general medical outpatients (Rouchell et al. 1999). Unfortunately, 59% of the individuals in the community who are depressed receive no treatment, fewer than 28% of *severely* depressed patients seen by primary care physicians are prescribed antidepressant medication, and, to make matters worse, 39% of the doses prescribed are subtherapeutic (Wells 1994). Mood disorders are present in 26% of the patients seen in outpatient primary care settings and account for more impairment than common medical disorders (Spitzer 1995).

The presence of major or minor depression in a medically ill patient has a significant effect on the patient's morbidity and mortality. For example, major depressive disorder is the best predictor of myocardial infarction, angioplasty, and death during the 12 months following cardiac catheterization (Carney et al. 1988). Patients with either major or minor depression following a stroke are 3.4 times more likely to die during a 10-year period than patients without depression (Morris et al. 1993).

■ CLINICAL CHARACTERISTICS

Diagnostic Criteria

The mnemonic SIG:E CAPS (Prescribe Energy Capsules) is a useful way to remember the diagnostic criteria for major depressive syndrome (Table 5–1). To diagnose *major depressive episode,* DSM-IV (American Psychiatric Association 1994) requires at least five of nine depressive symptoms, and one of the symptoms must be either 1) depressed mood or 2) loss of interest or pleasure, during the same 2-week period. DSM-IV also states that symptoms are excluded from the diagnosis if they are "due to direct effects of a general medical condition" or "due to the direct effects of a substance" (American Psychiatric Association 1994). This presents a problem, because major depressive disorder, many constitutional features of medical illnesses, and side effects of treatments for the medical disorder can produce the same symptoms. Thus, the decision to exclude certain symptoms when diagnosing depression in a patient who is medically ill is challenging.

Many consultation-liaison (C-L) psychiatrists, therefore, do not use DSM-IV's *exclusive* approach to diagnose major depressive

TABLE 5–1.	Mnemonic for diagnostic criteria for major depressive syndrome
SIG:E CAPS (Prescribe Energy Capsules)	
Sleep	Insomnia or hypersomnia
Interests	Loss of interest or pleasure in activities
Guilt	Excessive guilt, worthlessness, hopelessness
Energy	Loss of energy or fatigue
Concentration	Diminished concentration ability, indecisive
Appetite	Decreased appetite, >5% weight loss or gain
Psychomotor	Psychomotor retardation or agitation
Suicidality	Suicidal thought, ideation, plan, or attempt

disorder in medical-surgical patients. Cohen-Cole and Stoudemire (1987) recommended an *inclusive* approach to diagnosis; that is, count all symptoms toward the diagnosis of depression regardless of whether they are secondary to a physical or psychiatric process. This approach may lead to some false-positive diagnoses, but it is preferable to denying treatment to medically ill patients who are depressed and would benefit from treatment.

Some experienced clinicians favor the *substitutive* approach (i.e., substitute alternative diagnostic criteria for the diagnosis of depression) to the diagnosis of depression in patients who are medically ill. For example, Endicott (1984) substituted change in appetite or weight with tearfulness or depressed appearance, sleep disturbance with social withdrawal, indecisiveness with lack of reactivity to events, and loss of energy/fatigue with brooding pessimism. In other words, she used psychological symptoms to diagnosis depression when neurovegetative symptoms were confounded by medical illness.

The diagnosis of *dysthymic disorder* (three SIG:E CAPS symptoms present) in the medically ill is restricted in DSM-IV by the same exclusion criteria that complicate the diagnosis of major depressive disorder; the symptoms cannot be due to the direct effects of a substance or a medical condition. C-L psychiatrists commonly have two views of dysthymic disorder in the medical setting: 1) dysthymia is a chronic characterological mood syndrome, and 2) dysthymia is equivalent to *minor depression* (i.e., depression that falls just short of diagnostic criteria for major depressive disorder).

Illness and hospitalization are stressful events that can precipitate depression. This depressive reaction can meet the criteria for the diagnosis of *adjustment disorder with depressed mood,* one of the most common diagnoses made by C-L psychiatrists in the general hospital or clinic setting (Rouchell et al. 1999). Patients with adjustment disorder are candidates for psychotherapy.

Primary and Secondary Etiologies

The psychiatric consultant in the general hospital frequently finds that a major depressive syndrome is due to a specific medical or toxic etiology. The consultant should try to avoid the functional versus organic dichotomy that is often applied to psychiatric signs and symptoms in medical settings. A functional label implies that no biological component exists. The functional-organic split fosters the belief that psychiatric disorders are not medical, or even real. We recommend that clinicians use the terms *secondary* and *primary* instead. The term secondary refers to a psychiatric syndrome that occurs after a medical event or ingestion of a neuroactive substance; primary implies an autonomous psychiatric disorder that is unrelated to medical events. Secondary and primary are neutral terms already widely used in medicine.

■ DIFFERENTIAL DIAGNOSIS

The clinician must try to determine whether a medically ill patient has a mood disorder and, if a mood disorder is present, whether it is primary or secondary. Three areas of inquiry are helpful. First, to help establish the presence of major depression in a patient with severe medical illness, the clinician should look for psychological symptoms, such as guilt, worthlessness, helplessness, hopelessness, and suicidal ideation, rather than neurovegetative symptoms, such as fatigue, weight loss, and poor sleep. Second, the clinician should look for personal and family history of depression. Patients with primary unipolar depression typically have a history of multiple depressive episodes, with an average of five or six episodes over 20 years (Winokur 1986). First-degree relatives of unipolar depressed patients experience major depression seven times more frequently than control subjects. Third, the clinician should search for potentially reversible medical and toxic causes of the depressive syndrome. Dozens of medical conditions and neuroactive agents are associated with the onset of depressive syndromes. Most of these associations are anecdotal and are based on a temporal relationship between the event and the subsequent depressive episode; a temporal association does not mean that a cause-and-effect relationship exists. However, studies link some toxic or metabolic factors to the onset of major depressive syndromes. Table 5–2 is a list of conditions and toxic agents associated with secondary depressive disorders.

Other neuropsychiatric disorders, such as delirium, dementia, psychoactive substance use disorders, anxiety disorders, schizophrenia, somatoform disorders, and personality disorders, can resemble or accompany depression. The distinction between dementia and depression is often difficult; clinically helpful considerations are summarized in Table 5–3. Chapter 4 discusses the diagnosis of dementia in more detail.

■ TREATMENT AND MANAGEMENT

Reverse Etiology

The C-L psychiatrist's first job is to identify etiologies for the depressive syndrome that may be reversed or ameliorated (see Table 5–2). If no remediable etiology is found or if the depression does not resolve, the patient may need antidepressant treatment.

Pharmacological Management

Table 5–4 lists antidepressants, dosage ranges, and receptor affinities, which also determine side effects. For example, sedative potency and appetite stimulation are related to central nervous system (CNS) histamine-1 (H_1) receptor affinity, anticholinergic potency is related to peripheral muscarinic receptor affinity, and orthostatic hypotension is related to peripheral α_1 receptor affinity.

Tricyclic Antidepressants

Tricyclic antidepressants are used for a number of indications throughout the hospital and clinic. Besides depression, they are used for chronic pain, headache, insomnia, anxiety, panic, and bedwetting. Lower doses of tricyclic antidepressants are sometimes required in patients with liver disease, elderly and malnourished patients, and patients taking medications that slow antidepressant metabolism (e.g., fluoxetine). Higher antidepressant doses may be

TABLE 5–2. **Medical conditions and toxic agents associated with secondary depressive disorders**

Endocrine disorders

Addison's disease

Cushing's disease

Diabetes mellitus

Hyperparathyroidism

Hypopituitarism

Hypothyroidism

Infections

Encephalitis

Epstein-Barr virus

Hepatitis

Human immunodeficiency virus (HIV)

Pneumonia

Postinfluenza

Tertiary syphilis

Tuberculosis

Medications

Amphetamine withdrawal

Antihypertensives: methyldopa, clonidine, guanethidine, reserpine, diuretics

Barbiturates

Benzodiazepines

β-Blockers

Cholinesterase inhibitors

Cimetidine

Cocaine withdrawal

Corticosteroids

Disulfiram

Levodopa

Metoclopramide

(continued)

TABLE 5–2. **Medical conditions and toxic agents associated with secondary depressive disorders** *(continued)*

Medications *(continued)*

Chemotherapy agents: vinblastine, vincristine, procarbazine, L-asparaginase, amphotericin B, interferon

Nonsteroidal anti-inflammatories

Opiates

Oral contraceptives

Tumors

Central nervous system

Lung

Pancreas

Neurological disorders

Cerebrovascular disease

Dementia (particularly subcortical)

Epilepsy (particularly with a temporal lobe focus)

Huntington's disease

Multiple sclerosis

Parkinson's disease

Postconcussion

Progressive supranuclear palsy

Sleep apnea

Stroke

Subarachnoid hemorrhage

Others

Alcoholism

Anemia

Electrolyte abnormalities

Heavy metal poisoning

Hypertension

Systemic lupus erythematosus

TABLE 5–3. **Differentiating depression and dementia**[a]

	Depression	Dementia
Insidious onset	No	Yes
Psychological distress present	Yes	No
Frequently answers "I don't know"	Yes	No
Higher cortical function deficits (dysphasia, dyspraxia)	No	Yes
Remote memory less impaired than recent memory	No	Yes
Inconsistent mental status examination findings on repeated examinations	Yes	No
Past or family history of mood disorder	Yes	No
Aware of cognitive deficits	Yes	No
Neuroimaging study results usually abnormal	No	Yes

[a]Can occur together, especially in subcortical dementias. When a patient with dementia also has comorbid major depression, his or her cognitive deficits are greatly magnified.

needed in patients taking medications that induce hepatic enzymes (e.g., carbamazepine, phenytoin, and barbiturates).

Adverse effects.   A premedication orthostatic blood pressure check that reveals a decline in systolic blood pressure greater than 15 mm Hg is associated with a higher risk for significant orthostatic hypotension after starting treatment. Tricyclic antidepressants may lower seizure threshold. Maprotiline is the worst offender in this regard. In patients with cardiac illness, knowledge of the cardiac effects of tricyclic antidepressants is important. When tricyclic antidepressants are within normal therapeutic serum level ranges, they have little if any effect on left ventricular performance, even in patients with low ejection fractions. For patients with a history of angina, it is important to be aware that anticholinergic effects may increase the heart rate and slightly increase cardiac workload. Tricyclic antidepressants may, like type IA antiarrhythmic drugs such as quinidine, prolong ventricular depolarization by delaying conduction in the His-Purkinje cardiac conduction system. Ventricular dysrhythmias may actually improve. However, a patient who has preexisting bundle branch disease is at risk for second- or third-degree heart block (Glassman and Bigger 1981). Conduction delay will appear on the electrocardiogram as increased duration of the Q-Tc, QRS, and P-R intervals. Risk of sudden death increases if Q-Tc is greater than 440 msec (Schwartz and Wolf 1978).

Monoamine Oxidase Inhibitors

Depressive syndromes with prominent anxiety, phobias, panic, or obsessions have shown a better response to monoamine oxidase inhibitors (MAOIs) than to other antidepressants in some studies. MAOIs are also used when the symptoms have a poor response to another type of agent or the patient has a history of good response to an MAOI. The two MAOIs used in the United States, phenelzine (45–90 mg/day) and tranylcypromine (30–50 mg/day), irreversibly inhibit both MAO-A and MAO-B. Common initial daily doses are 30 mg and 20 mg, respectively.

Adverse effects.   MAOIs have the advantage in medically ill patients of having virtually no cardiac effects, relatively low sedative potential (except phenelzine), and no anticholinergic activity. Unfortunately, the potential for causing orthostatic hypotension is very high, sometimes occurring up to several weeks after the drug has been started. MAOIs can also produce hypertensive crises in the presence of tyramine-containing foods; MAOI use requires dietary counseling. Other potential adverse effects of MAOIs are anorgasmia, sedation (more common with phenelzine), activation (more common with tranylcypromine), dry mouth, urinary hesitancy, constipation, weight gain, edema, and myoclonic twitches. Another source of difficulty is concomitant use of MAOIs with sympathomimetics, other psychotropic agents, and meperidine. The use of these agents with MAOIs can result in a hypertensive crisis or severe serotonergic syndrome (Nierenberg and Semprebon 1993). Caution should be exercised when switching from an MAOI

TABLE 5–4. **Antidepressants**

Generic name	Trade name	Class	Initial dose (mg)[a]	Usual therapeutic dose range (mg)[a]
Amitriptyline	Elavil, others	Tertiary tricyclic	25–75	150–300
Clomipramine	Anafranil	Tertiary tricyclic	25	100–250
Doxepin	Sinequan, others	Tertiary tricyclic	25–75	150–300
Imipramine	Tofranil, others	Tertiary tricyclic	25–75	150–300
Trimipramine	Surmontil	Tertiary tricyclic	25–75	75–300
Desipramine	Norpramin, others	Secondary tricyclic	25–75	75–200
Nortriptyline	Pamelor, others	Secondary tricyclic	20–40	50–200
Protriptyline	Vivactil	Secondary tricyclic	10–20	20–60
Maprotiline	Generic only	Tetracyclic	25–75	75–300
Bupropion	Wellbutrin	Monocyclic phenylbutylamine	25–75 tid	300
Trazodone	Desyrel	Triazolopyridine	150	100–600
Amoxapine	Asendin	Dibenzoxazepine	50–150	100–600
Fluoxetine	Prozac	Straight-chain phenylpropylamine	20	20–60
Paroxetine	Paxil	Phenylpiperidine	20	20–50
Sertraline	Zoloft	Naphthylamine derivative	50	50–200
Venlafaxine	Effexor	Bicyclic cyclohexanol	25 tid	225–375
Nefazodone	Serzone	Phenylpiperazine	100 bid	300–600

Norepine-phrine reuptake blockade	Serotonin reuptake blockade	Dopamine reuptake blockade	Acetylcholine blockade	Histamine blockade	Orthostatic blood pressure
1	2	1	4	3	3
2	4	1	2	0	2
2	1	0	3	4	3
2	2	0	3	2	3
1	2	0	3	4	3
4	0	0	2	1	2
3	1	0	2	2	1
3	1	0	3	2	2
4	0	1	2	3	2
1	0	2	1	1	1
1	2	0	0	1	3
3	1	1	1	2	2
1	3	1	1	0	1
1	4	1	2	0	1
0	3	1	1	0	1
1	3	0	0	0	1
2	2	1	0	0	2

(continued)

TABLE 5–4.   **Antidepressants** *(continued)*

Generic name	Trade name	Class	Initial dose (mg)[a]	Usual therapeutic dose range (mg)[a]
Mirtazapine	Remeron	Tetracyclic	15	15–45
Riboxetine	Edronax	Methane sulphonate	4–6	4–10

Note.   0 = least effect, 4 = most effect.
[a]Doses for elderly and medically ill patients are often lower.
Source.   Adapted from Jachna JS, Lane RD, Gelenberg AJ: "Psychopharmacology," Edited by Rundell JR, Wise MG. Washington, DC, American Psychiatric Press, 1996,

to another antidepressant. A 2-week drug-free period is recommended to allow time for MAO to regenerate.

Selective Serotonin Reuptake Inhibitors

The selective serotonin reuptake inhibitors (SSRIs) are generally well tolerated by the depressed medically ill patient. SSRIs vary in the presence of active metabolites and elimination half-life. For example, fluoxetine, which has an elimination half-life of 1–3 days, is converted to norfluoxetine, which has a half-life of 7–9 days. Therefore, steady-state plasma levels are not reached for 5–6 weeks; a similar amount of time is required to clear norfluoxetine after discontinuation. In contrast, sertraline and paroxetine have short elimination half-lives (Nemeroff 1993). Venlafaxine blocks reuptake of norepinephrine and serotonin and appears to benefit some patients whose condition has not responded to SSRIs or other antidepressants.

Patients frequently ask how long they should continue taking SSRI (and other) antidepressant medication once depression is in remission. Recent data suggest (Reimherr et al. 1998) that relapse rates of patients in remission who stop taking SSRI medication are about twice as high 3 months later (49% vs. 26%) and 2.5 times higher (23% vs. 9%) 6 months after discontinuation.

Norepine- phrine reuptake blockade	Serotonin reuptake blockade	Dopamine reuptake blockade	Acetylcholine blockade	Histamine blockade	Orthostatic blood pressure
2	2	0	2	4	1
3	0	0	1	1	1

in *The American Psychiatric Press Textbook of Consultation-Liaison Psychiatry*. p. 968. Copyright 1996, American Psychiatric Press. Used with permission.

Adverse effects. The most common side effects are gastrointestinal distress, nervousness, sexual dysfunction, and insomnia. Almost all SSRIs inhibit enzymes in the cytochrome P450 system and can cause accumulation of medications metabolized by this system (see Chapter 10 for more details). Paroxetine is the most potent inhibitor of the important IID6 enzyme, followed by fluoxetine and sertraline. P450 IID6 metabolizes many antiarrhythmics, antidepressants, neuroleptics, codeine, oxycodone, and hydroxycodone (Ottson et al. 1993). In addition, about 7% of Caucasians are deficient in this enzyme and are considered slow metabolizers (Ottson et al. 1993).

Other Antidepressants

Several newer, nontricyclic, non-SSRI antidepressants, including bupropion, trazodone, venlafaxine, nefazodone, and mirtazapine, are available to the C-L psychiatrist (Table 5–4).

Adverse effects. Bupropion can be stimulating and causes fewer anticholinergic effects than do tricyclic antidepressants, little orthostatic hypertension, and few adverse sexual side effects (Jachna et al. 1996). However, bupropion may produce anxiety, agitation, insomnia, increased motor activity, gastrointestinal side effects, and headache. Trazodone's sedating properties and lack of anticholinergic side effects make it a widely used medication in C-L psychiatric patients. However, its association with priapism and orthostatic hypotension limits its use as a single agent. Trazodone is sometimes combined with an SSRI to address different sets of target symptoms. Trazodone has fewer cardiac effects than do other cyclic antidepressants and apparently does not slow conduction. However, it may exacerbate ventricular irritability, so it should be used with caution in patients with heart disease. Nefazodone appears to not be associated with a risk of priapism. Venlafaxine is an activating antidepressant that has a dose-related risk of hypertension; it also causes sexual dysfunction in men and women. Mirtazapine is moderately anticholinergic and very antihistaminic; therefore it is associated with increased appetite, weight gain, and significant sedation. Mirtazapine is well suited for certain patients (e.g., a patient with advanced cancer who is depressed, has no appetite, and cannot sleep).

Psychostimulants

Psychostimulant medications, such as methylphenidate (plasma half-life 1–2 hours) and dextroamphetamine, are useful in the treatment armamentarium. Table 5–5 lists situations in which psychostimulants are an important treatment option. Psychostimulants are fast-acting, well tolerated, and safe among the elderly and the medically ill (Massand et al. 1991). Usual dosage ranges are 5–20 mg/day for both methylphenidate and dextroamphetamine. Half-life is short, so two doses per day are usually given, one in the morning and one at noon or early afternoon. Doses later than 3:00 P.M. should be avoided so that sleep is not disturbed. When effective, the onset of action is usually within 2–3 days.

Adverse effects.   Few side effects occur; potential adverse effects include sinus tachycardia and other arrhythmias, blood pressure elevation, psychosis, insomnia, anorexia, and exacerbation of spasticity in patients with upper motor neuron disease. These side effects usually occur at doses much higher than those recommended. There is a bias against psychostimulant medications because of their potential for abuse. At the doses recommended in the treatment of depression in the medical setting, the risk is negligible.

Electroconvulsive Therapy

Electroconvulsive therapy (ECT) is a first-line treatment in depressed patients who are severely malnourished or dehydrated, who have catatonia, who have a previously documented good response to ECT, and who have delusional depression (Welch 1987). ECT's main adverse effect is anterograde and retrograde memory loss. This memory loss is usually mild and transient and disappears within a few weeks. Unilateral nondominant electrode placement decreases memory loss.

There are no absolute contraindications to ECT; however, some medical conditions increase the morbidity associated with ECT and require thoughtful review of the risks versus benefits. These include 1) conditions that cause increased intracranial pressure,

---

TABLE 5–5. **Clinical situations for which psychostimulants are an important treatment option**

When neurovegetative features of depression threaten health or life and a rapid response is needed

When cardiac and other adverse effects of other antidepressants should be avoided

When diagnostic uncertainty exists—a good response to a trial of a stimulant often helps confirm a diagnosis of depression

Terminally ill patients with profound psychomotor retardation

Treatment-resistant depression

Adult attention-deficit disorder

Late-stage human immunodeficiency virus disease (acquired immunodeficiency syndrome)–associated secondary mood disorders

Poststroke depression

Depression associated with subcortical dementias (e.g., dementia associated with Parkinson's disease)

---

2) conditions that increase the risk of serious hemorrhage, and 3) pathophysiological states that cause hemodynamic compromise, such as an acute myocardial infarction or malignant arrhythmias (Rouchell et al. 1999). The addition of β-blockers and antiarrhythmics before ECT reduces some of these risks. Mortality associated with ECT is less than 0.05% and is essentially the same as the risk of brief general anesthesia.

Medical Psychotherapy (see also Chapter 13)

The psychiatric examination is not complete without an attempt by the psychiatric consultant to understand the meaning of the illness to the patient. When past experiences or current level of psychological function are issues, talk therapy is often helpful. Because most hospital stays are short, brief therapies are used. For patients seen in outpatient consultation, cognitive therapy, psychodynamic psychotherapy, and supportive psychotherapy are available treatment options.

Cognitive therapy is particularly useful for patients with false beliefs about their illness. Examples of scenarios responsive to cognitive therapy include beliefs that illness represents punishment or weakness, unrealistic or distorted fears and expectations, and exaggerated or inappropriate responses to loss (Fava et al. 1988). Recent data suggest that cognitive-behavioral treatment of residual depressive symptoms may decrease the number of recurrences of full major depressive episodes (Fava et al. 1998a, 1998b). Evidence indicates that cognitive therapy may fare as well as medication for mild, moderate, and even severe depression (DeRubeis et al. 1999). Cognitive therapy is a sound treatment both in addition to antidepressant medication and instead of antidepressant medication in patients who cannot or will not take medication.

Some brief psychodynamic psychotherapies can be completed in 6–10 sessions. Supportive psychotherapy is indicated for a large portion of patients seen by C-L psychiatrists. The value to the patient of abreacting or "just talking" is often underestimated. Group psychotherapy promotes support, improves interpersonal relationships, models adaptive coping mechanisms, decreases loneliness, and helps the patient develop a sense of meaning in life. Spiegel (1990) used psychoeducational group therapy to treat depression in patients with metastatic breast cancer. He found that the patients in group therapy lived twice as long as the patients who received only routine oncological care.

■ REFERENCES

American Psychiatric Association: Diagnostic and Statistical Manual of Mental Disorders, 4th Edition. Washington, DC, American Psychiatric Association, 1994

Carney RM, Rich MW, Freedland KE, et al: Major depressive disorder predicts cardiac events in patients with coronary artery disease. Psychosom Med 50:627–633, 1988

Cohen-Cole SA, Stoudemire A: Major depression and physical illness: special considerations in diagnosis and biologic treatment. Psychiatr Clin North Am 10:1–17, 1987

Craig TJ: Epidemiology of psychiatric illness, in The Medical Basis of Psychiatry. Edited by Winokur G, Clayton PJ. Philadelphia, PA, WB Saunders, 1986, pp 541–561

DeRubeis RJ, Gelfand LA, Zang TZ, et al: Medications versus cognitive behavior therapy for severely depressed outpatients: mega-analysis of four randomized comparisons. Am J Psychiatry 156:1007–1013, 1999

Endicott J: Measurement of depression in patients with cancer. Cancer 53:2243–2248, 1984

Fava GA, Sonino N, Wise TN: Management of depression in medical patients. Psychother Psychosom 49:81–102, 1988

Fava GA, Rafanelli C, Grandi S, et al: Prevention of recurrent depression with cognitive behavioral therapy. Arch Gen Psychiatry 55:816–820, 1998a

Fava GA, Rafanelli C, Grandi S, et al: Six-year outcome for cognitive behavioral treatment of residual symptoms in major depression. Am J Psychiatry 155:1443–1445, 1998b

Glassman AH, Bigger T: Cardiovascular effects of therapeutic doses of tricyclic antidepressants: a review. Arch Gen Psychiatry 38:815–820, 1981

Jachna JS, Lane RD, Gelenberg AJ: Psychopharmacology, in The American Psychiatric Press Textbook of Consultation-Liaison Psychiatry. Edited by Rundell JR, Wise MG. Washington, DC, American Psychiatric Press, 1996, pp 958–1005

Kessler RC, McGonagle KA, Zhao S, et al: Lifetime and 12-month prevalence of DSM-III-R psychiatric disorders in the United States. Arch Gen Psychiatry 51:8–19, 1994

Massand P, Pickett P, Murray GB: Psychostimulants for secondary depression in medical illness. Psychosomatics 32:203–208, 1991

Morris PL, Robinson RG, Andrzejewski P, et al: Association of depression with 10 year post-stroke mortality. Am J Psychiatry 150:124–129, 1993

Nemeroff CB: Paroxetine: an overview of the efficacy and safety of a new selective serotonin reuptake inhibitor in the treatment of depression. J Clin Psychopharmacol 13 (suppl 2):18–22, 1993

Nierenberg DW, Semprebon M: The central nervous system serotonin syndrome. Clin Pharmacol Ther 53:84–88, 1993

Ottson SV, Wu D, Joffe RT, et al: Inhibition by fluoxetine of cytochrome P4502D6 activity. Clin Pharmacol Ther 53: 401–409, 1993

Reimherr FW, Amsterdam JD, Quitkin FM, et al: Optimal length of continuation therapy in depression: a prospective assessment during long-term fluoxetine treatment. Am J Psychiatry 155: 1247–1253, 1998

Rouchell AM, Pounds R, Tierney JG: Depression, in Essentials of Consultation-Liaison Psychiatry. Edited by Rundell JR, Wise MG. Washington, DC, American Psychiatric Press, 1999, pp 121–147

Schwartz PJ, Wolf S: QT interval prolongation as predictor of sudden death in patients with myocardial infarction. Circulation 57:1074–1077, 1978

Spiegel D: Can psychotherapy prolong cancer survival? Psychosomatics 31:361–366, 1990

Spitzer RL, Kroenke K, Linzer M, et al: Health-related quality of life in primary care patients with mental disorders: results from the PRIME-MD 1000 Study. JAMA 274:1511–1517, 1995

Welch CA: Electroconvulsive therapy in the general hospital, in Massachusetts General Hospital Handbook of General Hospital Psychiatry, 3rd Edition. Edited by Cassem NH. St. Louis, MO, Mosby-Year Book, 1991, pp 269–280

Wells KB, Katon W, Rogers B, et al: Use of minor tranquilizers and antidepressant medications by depressed outpatients: results from the medical outcomes study. Am J Psychiatry 151: 694–700, 1994

Winokur G: Unipolar depression, in The Medical Basis of Psychiatry. Edited by Winokur G, Clayton PJ. Philadelphia, PA, WB Saunders, 1986, pp 60–79

■ ADDITIONAL READINGS

Cathebras PJ, Robbins JM, Kirmayer LJ, et al: Fatigue in primary care: prevalence, psychiatric comorbidity, illness behavior and outcome. J Gen Intern Med 7:276–286, 1992

Forrester AW, Lipsey JR, Teitelbaum ML, et al: Depression following myocardial infarction. Int J Psychiatry Med 22:33–46, 1992

Frasure-Smith N, Lesperance F, Talajic M: Depression following myocardial infarction: impact on 6-month survival. JAMA 270: 1819–1825, 1993

Freedland KE, Lustman PJ, Carney RM, et al: Underdiagnosis of depression in patients with coronary artery disease: the role of nonspecific symptoms. Int J Psychiatry Med 22:221–229, 1991

Freedland KE, Carney RM, Lustman PJ, et al: Major depression in coronary artery disease patients with vs without a prior history of depression. Psychosom Med 54:416–421, 1992

Liberzon I, Goldman RS, Hendrickson WJ: Very brief psychotherapy in the psychiatric consultation setting. Int J Psychiatry Med 22:65–75, 1992

Mueller TI, Leon AC, Keller MB, et al: Recurrence after recovery from major depressive disorder during 15 years of observational follow-up. Am J Psychiatry 156:1000–1006, 1999

6

MANIA

■ CLINICAL CHARACTERISTICS

General Considerations

Lifetime prevalence rates for a bipolar manic episode are 0.4% (Kessler et al. 1997). Because bipolar disorder rarely presents after age 50, first-time manic episodes in older patients are almost always secondary. Numerous studies of patients with brain damage have found that patients who develop secondary mania have a significantly greater frequency of lesions in the right hemisphere than patients with brain injury who become depressed or develop no mood disturbance at all (McDaniel et al. 1999). The right-hemisphere lesions associated with mania are in specific structures that are connected to the limbic system. The right basotemporal cortex is particularly important because direct lesions of this cortical region are associated with secondary mania (Starkstein and Robinson 1992).

Diagnostic Criteria

The diagnosis of a manic episode requires elevated or irritable mood, at least three symptoms from a list of cardinal manic episode features (four if the mood is irritable), and impaired social or occupational functioning (American Psychiatric Association 1994). A hypomanic episode differs only in that social and occupational functioning are not impaired and may even be enhanced. Table 6–1 summarizes criteria for the diagnosis of a manic episode using the mnemonic GIDDINESS.

Secondary mania is due to specific identifiable medical or toxic factors. In DSM-IV (American Psychiatric Association 1994), sec-

TABLE 6–1.	Mnemonic for diagnostic criteria for manic episode: GIDDINESS

Grandiosity

Increased activity

Decreased judgment (risky activities)

Distractibility

Irritability

Need for sleep decreased

Elevated mood

Speedy thoughts

Speedy talk

ondary mania is called "mood disorder due to a general medical condition, with manic features" or "substance-induced mood disorder, with manic features." As in primary mania, the essential feature of this syndrome is a prominent and persistent elevated or expansive mood. According to DSM-IV, secondary mania is not diagnosed if the mood disturbance occurs in the context of delirium or dementia.

Differential Diagnosis

As with depression, the same three principles of diagnostic inquiry apply to mania. First, the diagnosis should be established—look for psychological and behavioral features of mania, such as grandiosity, spending sprees, and foolish investments. Second, review past and family history of mania, hypomania, and depression. The initial onset of primary bipolar manic episodes rarely occurs after age 50. The median lifetime number of affective (depressive plus manic) episodes in a bipolar patient is nine (Clayton 1986). Of patients with bipolar disorder, 63% have at least one family member with a mood disorder. Third, carefully review the chart, laboratory values, radiographs, physical examination findings, and medication history to identify potentially reversible etiologies. Table 6–2 lists medical conditions and neuroactive substances associated with secondary mania.

■ TREATMENT AND MANAGEMENT

General Considerations

The treatments for secondary and primary mania are similar, with two exceptions. First, in secondary mania the etiological agent is identified and removed, whenever possible. Second, lithium is not a first-line treatment for secondary mania because of increased side effects in patients who are medically ill and/or elderly. Table 6–3 is a summary of dosing information for the antimanic drugs: lithium, carbamazepine, valproate, gabapentin, lamotrigine, and topiramate.

Pharmacological Management

Lithium

Lithium is titrated within a rather narrow therapeutic range. Toxic effects occur at doses only moderately higher than those for therapeutic effects. Therefore, the clinician must monitor serum lithium levels carefully; the levels are typically drawn 12 hours after the last dose. The generally accepted therapeutic range of serum lithium concentrations is 0.6–1.2 mEq/L. Patients in an acute manic phase are best treated with lithium doses that achieve serum concentrations at the upper end of this therapeutic range. However, in severely ill medical patients, in elderly patients, or in those with renal disease, lower doses are typically used. Assuming normal renal function and no drug interactions (e.g., cyclosporine inhibits the kidney's secretion of lithium), lithium's half-life is 18–36 hours. Steady-state serum levels take 5–8 days to achieve, and clinical effects usually begin around 10–14 days. For this reason, concomitant neuroleptic or benzodiazepine use (e.g., clonazepam) is often necessary for acute control of agitation and psychosis.

TABLE 6–2.   **Causes of secondary mood disorder, manic**

Neurological conditions

Focal neurological lesions

   Tumors (gliomas, meningiomas, thalamic metastases)

   Cerebrovascular lesions (temporal, right hemispheric), including stroke and head trauma

   Temporal lobe seizure

   Thalamotomy

   Right hemispherectomy

   Huntington's disease

   Wilson's disease

   Postencephalopathic parkinsonism

   Idiopathic calcification of basal ganglia

Nonfocal neurological lesions

   Posttraumatic encephalopathy

   General paresis

   Neurosyphilis

   Multiple sclerosis

   Viral meningoencephalitis

   Cryptococcal meningoencephalitis

   Pick's disease

   Klinefelter's syndrome

   Kleine-Levin syndrome

   HIV encephalopathy

   Post–St. Louis type A encephalitis

Medications

   Alcohol

   Alprazolam[a]

   Amantadine

   Amphetamines

   Antiretroviral agents

   Baclofen

(continued)

TABLE 6–2.	**Causes of secondary mood disorder, manic** *(continued)*

Medications *(continued)*

Bromide

Buspirone

Captopril

Carbamazepine

Cimetidine

Clonidine withdrawal

Cocaine

Corticosteroids/corticosteroid withdrawal

Cyclobenzaprine

Cyproheptadine

Hallucinogens

Iproniazid

Isoniazid

Levodopa

Lorazepam

Methylphenidate

Metoclopramide[a]

Metrizamide

Phencyclidine

Procainamide

Procarbazine

Procyclidine

Propafenone

Sympathomimetic amines

Thyroid preparations

Tolmetin

Triazolam[a]

Yohimbine[a]

Zidovudine

(continued)

TABLE 6–2. **Causes of secondary mood disorder, manic**
(continued)

Systemic conditions

Hyperthyroidism

Hyperthyroidism with starvation diet

Uremia

Hemodialysis

Cushing's syndrome

Puerperal psychosis

Infectious mononucleosis

Niacin deficiency

Vitamin B12 deficiency

Carcinoid

Use of hyperbaric chamber

Postoperative excitement

Premenstrual psychosis

Other

Aspartame

L-Glutamine

Source.   Adapted from Cassem NH: "Depression," in *Massachusetts General Hospital Handbook of General Hospital Psychiatry,* 3rd Edition. Edited by Cassem NH. St. Louis, MO, Mosby Year Book, 1991, pp. 237–268; Goodwin FK, Jamison KR: *Manic-Depressive Illness.* New York, Oxford University Press, 1990, p. 505; Larson EW, Richelson E: "Organic Causes of Mania." *Mayo Clinic Proceedings* 63:906–912, 1988. Used with permission.

Lithium is dialyzable and is therefore given to patients on renal dialysis *after* their dialysis treatments; the usual dose is 300–600 mg/day (Stoudemire et al. 1993). Serum levels of lithium are tested several hours after dialysis because plasma levels may actually rise in the postdialysis period when equilibration between blood and tissue stores occurs (Bennett et al. 1980). Dialysis is the treatment of choice in cases of life-threatening lithium toxicity.

TABLE 6-3. Antimanic medications

Generic name	Trade name	Starting dose (mg)[a]	Usual dose range (mg)[a]
Lithium	Lithobid	300 bid	600–1,200
Carbamazepine	Tegretol	200 bid	600–1,600
Valproate	Depakote, others	250 bid	625–3,800
Gabapentin	Neurontin	300 qd	900–1,800
Lamotrigine	Lamictal	50 qd[b]	300–500[b]
Topiramate	Topamax	25–50 qd	200–400

Note. bid = twice a day; qd = every day.
[a]Doses for elderly and medically ill patients are often lower.
[b]If patient is also taking valproate, starting dose is 25 mg qd and maximum dose is 150 mg/day.
Source. Adapted from Jachna JS, Lane RD, Gelenberg AJ: "Psychopharmacology," in *The American Psychiatric Press Textbook of Consultation-Liaison Psychiatry.* Edited by Rundell JR, Wise MG. Washington, DC, American Psychiatric Press, 1996, p. 980. Used with permission

Adverse effects. In healthy individuals, the side effects of lithium are usually mild, generally well tolerated, and often transient. The most common side effects are tremor, nausea, vomiting, diarrhea, polyuria, and polydipsia. Hypothyroidism, rashes, nephrogenic diabetes insipidus, interstitial nephritis, and weight gain are less frequent. Nonspecific ST segment and T-wave changes are commonly seen on the electrocardiogram (ECG); conduction defects and arrhythmias are rare. At a minimum, the clinician should obtain a baseline ECG, electrolyte measurements, thyroid function tests, weight, and renal function tests before starting lithium administration.

Sodium and lithium are reabsorbed competitively by the kidney in the proximal tubules. However, only sodium is reabsorbed in the distal tubules. Patients taking diuretics that act on the distal tubule, such as thiazides, are at higher risk for lithium toxicity because they will excrete more sodium and retain lithium. If polyuria is distressing or clinically significant, it can often be effectively managed by lowering the dose or changing to carbamazepine. An alternative strategy to manage distressing polyuria is to add a thiazide diuretic to decrease lithium elimination, which allows a reduction in the lithium dose.

Lithium toxicity markedly affects the central nervous system (CNS) and can be a life-threatening emergency in consultation-liaison settings. Symptoms of lithium-induced CNS toxicity include ataxia, slurred speech, and nystagmus and can proceed to convulsions, coma, and death if lithium levels are greater than 2.5 mEq/L. The threshold for more serious side effects is lower in predisposed or medically ill patients.

Anticonvulsant Mood Stabilizers

Both carbamazepine and valproic acid are effective treatments of mania, particularly in patients with secondary mania (see Table 6–3). Carbamazepine is a compound structurally similar to tricyclic antidepressants. Although the precise mechanism of action of carbamazepine in affective illness is not clearly known, it inhibits norepinephrine release at synapses and appears to decrease γ-aminobutyric acid (GABA) turnover in animals (Post 1982). Valproic acid, a widely used anticonvulsant, enhances GABA activity in the brain (Bernstein 1991).

A third generation of anticonvulsants is entering clinical use: lamotrigine, gabapentin, and topiramate (Post et al. 1998). These medications have not yet been established by randomized trials as effective treatments of secondary mania. Anecdotal case reports and open trials are encouraging.

Adverse effects.   When prescribing carbamazepine to medically ill patients, its potential hematological toxicity, quinidine-like effects on cardiac conduction, antidiuretic actions, and enzyme induction that can alter the effects of other drugs must be considered. Particularly common problems in the consultation-liaison setting are carbamazepine's interaction with the calcium channel blockers diltiazem and verapamil, two agents that may elevate carbamazepine levels into the toxic range (Stoudemire et al. 1993). Two different hematological reactions to carbamazepine may occur. One is a predictable and usually transient decline in both red and white blood cell counts when treatment is initiated; the other is aplastic anemia—a rare side effect that can occur at any time after initiation of therapy. The latter occurs in approximately 1 in 575,000 treated patients per year (Seetharam and Pellock 1991).

Hepatic side effects related to carbamazepine are usually limited to a benign, asymptomatic elevation of alanine aminotransferase or aspartate aminotransferase, usually less than twice the upper limit of normal values. This benign reaction is seen in no more than 5% of patients (Jeavons 1983). However, a rare, idiosyncratic, and life-threatening hepatotoxicity is reported to occur in fewer than 1 in 10,000 patients (Jeavons 1983), usually within the first month of therapy. Because carbamazepine is a potent inducer of cytochrome P450 IIIA4, it influences the metabolism of many drugs that rely on this enzyme. Thus, the blood levels of some drugs may decrease if carbamazepine is added to a patient's medication regimen. Carbamazepine induces its own metabolism, necessitating gradual increases in dosage over the first few weeks of treatment to maintain a steady blood level.

When valproate is prescribed for medically ill patients, the clinician should be alert to gastrointestinal side effects, hepato-toxicity, coagulation effects, and possible drug-drug interactions. In most patients, the most troublesome side effect of valproate is nausea, often accompanied by vomiting. Although hepatic toxicity is a concern when prescribing valproate, it is relatively rare. Hepatic necrosis, a major risk factor for children younger than 2 years, is an uncommon complication in adults, occurring in 1 in 10,000 patients (Eadie et al. 1988). Aside from this rare hepatic complication, a more common and benign hepatic effect of valproate is an increase in serum ammonia levels resulting from valproate's inhibition of urea synthesis. Although this elevation in serum ammonia usually causes no difficulties in most patients, it is potentially problematic for patients with preexisting liver disease, especially those prone to hepatic encephalopathy. Therefore, significant liver disease is a relative contraindication to valproate therapy. In contrast to carbamazepine, which induces P450 IIIA4, valproate inhibits P450 IIC enzymes that metabolize drugs. For example, prolonged and elevated benzodiazepine levels can result in increased sedation and ataxia.

Medical Psychotherapy

A manic patient frequently resists medications that will decrease euphoria. A strong alliance can help with compliance. The clinician should offer relief for symptoms that are most bothersome to the patient. Family therapy in the clinic and hospital settings can comfort the patient and family, particularly as they attempt to cope with both the stress of underlying medical illness and the manic syndrome.

■ REFERENCES

American Psychiatric Association: Diagnostic and Statistical Manual of Mental Disorders, 4th Edition. Washington, DC, American Psychiatric Association, 1994

Bennett WM, Muther RS, Parker RA: Drug therapy in renal failure: dosing guidelines for adults, part II: sedatives, hypnotics, and tranquilizers; cardiovascular, antihypertensive, and diuretic agents; miscellaneous agents. Ann Intern Med 93:286–325, 1980

Bernstein JG: Psychotropic drug prescribing, in Massachusetts General Hospital Handbook of General Hospital Psychiatry, 3rd Edition. Edited by Cassem NH. St. Louis, MO, Mosby-Year Book, 1991, pp 527–570

Clayton PJ: Bipolar illness, in The Medical Basis of Psychiatry. Edited by Winokur G, Clayton PJ. Philadelphia, PA, WB Saunders, 1986, pp 39–59

Eadie MJ, Hooper WD, Dickinson RG: Valproate-associated hepatotoxicity and its biochemical mechanisms. Medical Toxicology and Adverse Drug Experience 3:85–106, 1988

Jeavons PM: Hepatotoxicity in antiepileptic drugs, in Chronic Toxicity in Antiepileptic Drugs. Edited by Oxley J, Janz D, Meinardi H. New York, Raven, 1983, pp 1–46

Kessler RC, Rubinow DR, Holmes C, et al: The epidemiology of DSM-III-R bipolar disorder in a general population survey. Psychol Med 27:1079–1089, 1997

McDaniel JS, Johnson KM, Rundell JR: Mania, in The Essentials of Consultation-Liaison Psychiatry. Edited by Rundell JR, Wise MG. Washington, DC, American Psychiatric Press, 1999, pp 149–163

Post RM: Use of the anticonvulsant carbamazepine in primary and secondary affective illness: clinical and theoretical implications. Psychol Med 12:701–704, 1982

Post RM, Frye MA, Denicoff KD, et al: Beyond lithium in the treatment of bipolar illness. Neuropsychopharmacology 19:206–219, 1998

Seetharam MN, Pellock JM: Risk-benefit assessment of carbamazepine in children. Drug Saf 6:148–158, 1991

Starkstein SE, Robinson RG: Neuropsychiatric aspects of cerebrovascular disorders, in The American Psychiatric Press Textbook of Neuropsychiatry. Edited by Yudofsky SC, Hales RE.
Washington, DC, American Psychiatric Press, 1992, pp 449–472

Stoudemire A, Fogel BS, Gulley LR, et al: Psychopharmacology
in the medical patient, in Psychiatric Care of the Medical Patient. Edited by Stoudemire A, Fogel BS. New York, Oxford
University Press, 1993, pp 155–206

■ ADDITIONAL READINGS

Grisaru N, Chudakov B, Yaroslavsky Y, et al: Transcranial magnetic stimulation in mania: a controlled study. Am J Psychiatry
155:1608–1610, 1998

Krauthammer C, Klerman GL: Secondary mania: manic syndromes
associated with antecedent physical illness or drugs. Arch Gen
Psychiatry 35:1333–1339, 1978

Pope HG, Katz DL: Affective and psychotic symptoms associated
with anabolic steroid use. Am J Psychiatry 145:487–490, 1988

Pope HG, McElroy SL, Keck PE, et al: Valproate in the treatment
of acute mania: a placebo-controlled study. Arch Gen Psychiatry 48:62–68, 1991

Robinson RG, Boston JD, Starkstein SE, et al: Comparison of mania with depression following brain injury: causal factors. Am J
Psychiatry 145:172–178, 1988

Rundell JR, Wise MG: Causes of organic mood disorder. J Neuropsychiatry Clin Neurosci 1:398–400, 1989

Wehr TA, Sack DA, Rosenthal NE: Sleep reduction as a final common pathway in the genesis of mania. Am J Psychiatry 144:
201–204, 1987

7

ANXIETY AND INSOMNIA

■ ANXIETY AND ANXIETY DISORDERS

In medically ill patients, anxiety, panic, or insomnia may be a reaction to the stress of illness or hospitalization, a manifestation of a medical or psychiatric disorder, or an adverse effect of medication. Anxiety accounts for 10% of all visits to physicians (Colón and Popkin 1999). Anxiety symptoms are easily mistaken for cardiac arrhythmia, asthma, coronary disease, vertigo, cerebrovascular disease, or an endocrine disorder. Consequently, patients with anxiety disorders are frequently referred for expensive and unnecessary examinations, such as ambulatory electrocardiogram (ECG) monitoring, cardiac catheterization, and pheochromocytoma testing (Simon and Walker 1999). Most anxiety seen in the general hospital is not pathological. Mild anxiety syndromes (normal situational anxiety and adjustment disorder with anxious mood) usually resolve with disappearance of the stressor. However, more severe anxiety, or even mild anxiety in patients with respiratory or cardiac compromise, can cause acute distress, interfere with the medical evaluation, interfere with treatment, or increase morbidity. Anxiety severity also correlates with health care use and length of hospital stay, even when accounting for illness severity (Colón and Popkin 1999; Saravay et al. 1991).

Epidemiology

Anxiety disorders are among the most common of all psychiatric disorders. Lifetime prevalence of anxiety disorders is estimated to be 10%–20% (Colón and Popkin 1999). Women are at higher risk for anxiety disorders than are men (about 2:1). Of patients with chronic medical conditions, 18% have a lifetime prevalence of an anxiety disorder, compared with 12% of patients without chronic medical conditions (Wells et al. 1988). Eighteen percent of patients in an outpatient primary care setting (Spitzer 1995) and 5%–20% of general medical inpatients have a current anxiety disorder (Strain et al. 1981). Panic disorder is present in 3–14 times more patients in medical settings than in the general population (Rosenbaum and Pollack 1991). When panic disorder is treated in these patients, hospitalization rates decline (Katon 1984). Hospitalized patients identified as highly anxious have longer hospital stays and higher hospitalization costs than other hospitalized patients (Levenson et al. 1992).

Biology of Anxiety

Basic science and clinical research implicate noradrenergic, serotonergic, and γ-aminobutyric acid (GABA) systems, and possibly neuropeptides, in the genesis of normal and pathological anxiety. Patients with anxiety disorders appear to have unstable autonomic nervous systems, hypersensitive respiratory control mechanisms, and hypersensitive central nervous system (CNS) carbon dioxide (CO_2) chemoreceptors (Colón and Popkin 1999). Pharmacological challenge studies and functional CNS imaging suggest that key CNS structures important in producing normal and pathological anxiety include the locus coeruleus, amygdala, hippocampus, temporal lobes, and frontal lobes.

Clinical Characteristics

Anxiety Disorder Due to a General Medical Condition and Substance-Induced Anxiety Disorder

Pathological anxiety that is an integral part of the pathophysiology of the medical illness is called "anxiety disorder due to a general medical condition." Secondary panic and obsessive-compulsive symptoms are also included in this diagnosis.

Substance-induced anxiety disorder is reserved for instances in which a clinical constellation of generalized anxiety, panic attacks, or obsessive-compulsive symptoms is linked to substance intoxication or withdrawal. The symptoms must emerge within a month of substance use or withdrawal and are not better accounted for by another anxiety disorder. Medical conditions and substances associated with anxiety and panic are listed in Table 7–1.

Panic Disorder

Panic disorder in DSM-IV (American Psychiatric Association 1994) is classified as with or without agoraphobia. These disorders entail recurrent, unexpected panic attacks followed by worry, concern, and behavior changes related to the attacks. The attacks are not due to a general medical condition or the direct effects of a substance. Panic disorder is underrecognized, underdiagnosed, and undertreated in outpatient medical settings. In one series of panic disorder patients, 70% were seen by 10 or more primary care practitioners before the panic disorder was finally diagnosed (Sheehan et al. 1980). Panic disorder was present in 33%–43% of the patients with chest pain whose cardiac catheterizations revealed normal coronary arteries (Katon 1990).

Agoraphobia Without Panic Disorder

Patients with agoraphobia are not seen in medical-surgical settings for the simple reason that they rarely leave home unless there is a life-threatening emergency or unless the family or a community outreach program brings them to medical attention.

Acute Stress Disorder and Posttraumatic Stress Disorder

Acute stress disorder involves exposure to a life-threatening traumatic event that produces dissociative symptoms, reexperiencing of the trauma, avoidance of associated stimuli, increased arousal, and significant distress or social/occupational impairment. Symptoms must last for more than 2 days but less than 4 weeks and emerge within a month of the trauma. The condition is not substance induced or the result of a general medical condition. Acute

TABLE 7–1. **Medical and toxic causes of anxiety and panic**

Cardiovascular conditions

  Angina pectoris

  Cerebral insufficiency

  Congestive heart failure

  Coronary insufficiency

  Dysrhythmia

  Hypovolemia

  Intra-aortic balloon pump

  Myocardial infarction

  Paroxysmal atrial tachycardia

  Syncope

  Valvular disease, especially mitral valve prolapse

Endocrine conditions

  Carcinoid syndrome

  Hyperadrenalism

  Hyperparathyroidism

  Hyperthyroidism

  Hypocalcemia

  Hypoparathyroidism

  Hypothyroidism

  Ovarian dysfunction

  Pancreatic tumor

  Pheochromocytoma

  Pituitary disorders

  Pseudohyperparathyroidism

Immunological/collagen vascular conditions

  Anaphylaxis

  Polyarteritis nodosa

  Rheumatoid arthritis

  Systemic lupus erythematosus

  Temporal arteritis

(continued)

TABLE 7–1.   **Medical and toxic causes of anxiety and panic**
(continued)

Metabolic conditions

Anemia

Heavy metal toxicity

Hyperkalemia

Hyperthermia

Hypoglycemia

Hyponatremia

Insulinoma

Porphyria

Vitamin deficiency states

Wilson's disease

Drugs

Alcohol and its withdrawal

Aminophylline

Amphetamine

Anticholinergics

Antidepressants, especially fluoxetine and bupropion

Antihypertensives: reserpine, hydralazine

Antituberculous agents

β-Blockers (withdrawal)

Caffeine

Calcium channel blockers

Cannabis

Cocaine

Digitalis (toxicity)

Dopamine

Ephedrine

Epinephrine

Estrogen

Hallucinogens

(continued)

TABLE 7–1. **Medical and toxic causes of anxiety and panic** *(continued)*

Drugs *(continued)*

  Heavy metals

  Hydralazine

  Insulin

  Levodopa

  Lidocaine

  Methylphenidate

  Monosodium glutamate (MSG)

  Neuroleptics (akathisia)

  Nicotinic acid

  Nonsteroidal anti-inflammatory agents

  Phenylephrine

  Phenylpropanolamine

  Procaine

  Procarbazine

  Pseudoephedrine

  Salicylates

  Sedative-hypnotics (and withdrawal)

  Steroids

  Sympathomimetics

  Theophylline

  Thyroid preparations

  Yohimbine

Respiratory conditions

  Asthma

  Chronic obstructive pulmonary disease

  Pneumonia

  Pneumothorax

  Pulmonary edema

  Pulmonary embolus

(continued)

TABLE 7–1.	**Medical and toxic causes of anxiety and panic** *(continued)*

Respiratory conditions *(continued)*
  Respirator dependence
Gastrointestinal conditions
  Crohn's disease
  Peptic ulcer disease
  Ulcerative colitis
Neurologic conditions
  Encephalitic and postencephalitic disorders
  Essential tremor
  Huntington's disease
  Multiple sclerosis
  Myasthenia gravis
  Neurosyphilis
  Postconcussion syndrome
  Restless legs syndrome
  Seizure disorder, especially temporal lobe epilepsy
  Stroke
  Subarachnoid hemorrhage
  Transient ischemic attacks
  Vascular headaches
  Vertigo (e.g., Meniere's disease)

stress disorder identifies patients at risk for posttraumatic stress disorder (PTSD) because 50% of those with acute stress disorder go on to develop PTSD.

A diagnosis of PTSD requires that a life-threatening trauma is "persistently reexperienced," that the duration of the symptoms is longer than 1 month, that emotional numbing and increased arousal are present, and that stimuli linked to the trauma are avoided. The experience of hospitalization or severe illness can trigger reexperiencing phenomena, nightmares, strong emotions, and autonomic arousal. A PTSD diagnosis should alert the clinician to the potential presence of comorbid psychiatric disorders, especially substance-related disorders, mood disorders, and panic disorder.

Generalized Anxiety Disorder

Generalized anxiety disorder (GAD) is characterized by excessive anxiety plus apprehensive expectations about events or activities. A patient's incessant worry is difficult to control and commonly evokes restlessness, fatigue, irritability, muscle tension, and sleep dysfunction. When encountered in consultation-liaison psychiatry, GAD is often an established condition that is exacerbated or unmasked in the general hospital setting. Patients with GAD usually have other psychiatric disorders. Motor tension is a routine part of GAD and may include trembling and twitching. Age at onset is usually in the 20s or 30s.

Obsessive-Compulsive Disorder

Ego-dystonic obsessions and irresistible compulsive behaviors can produce somatic manifestations. For example, patients can develop dermatoses from frequent hand washing. Obsessive-compulsive disorder is highly comorbid with major depressive disorder. Primary obsessive-compulsive disorder, when it appears or recurs during a hospitalization or an outpatient workup for a new medical problem, is possibly related to the stress, uncertainty, and loss of control experienced by patients. Secondary obsessive-compulsive syndromes occur in several neuropsychiatric conditions, including Gilles de la Tourette's syndrome, epilepsy, and after head injury.

Phobias

Specific and social phobias are usually hidden by the patient and are seldom identified by the primary physician (Colón and Popkin 1999), unless the degree of impairment is pronounced or interferes with clinical care, as when a claustrophobic patient cannot tolerate the magnetic resonance imaging procedure or when phobias involve blood, infection, or injury. Patients usually delay seeking medical attention because of avoidance associated with specific phobias.

Adjustment Disorder With Anxiety

Adjustment disorder is a maladaptive response to an identifiable stressor. For many patients, the stressors are the medical illness, the clinic or hospital environment, and the treatment.

Differential Diagnosis

Medical or Psychiatric Etiology

When pathological anxiety is present, the symptoms may be due to 1) situational stress, 2) a primary psychiatric disorder, 3) long-standing character pathology, or 4) a medical or toxic etiology (Table 7–1). Two important questions must be answered when attempting to differentiate among causes of pathological anxiety: 1) What past and family historical data are present? Past or family history of a primary anxiety disorder increases the probability that current signs and symptoms are manifestations or recurrences of a primary anxiety disorder. 2) Is there an identifiable potential medical or toxic cause for the anxiety? The differential diagnosis of anxiety disorders includes a wide range of physical illnesses and psychoactive substances. Evaluation directed toward the body system most prominently affected by anxiety symptoms (e.g., gastrointestinal, respiratory) may provide the most diagnostic evidence for the etiology (Rosenbaum and Pollack 1991).

Psychiatric Differential Diagnosis

Anxiety disorders are sometimes mistaken for other psychiatric disorders, especially agitated depression. Anxiety disorders usually have an earlier age at onset and are less episodic than mood disorders. The mental status examination differentiates agitated delirium and psychotic disorders from anxiety disorders. The akathisia that occasionally occurs with neuroleptics can resemble anxiety. Substance-related disorders are an underdiagnosed cause of anxiety. Anxiety disorders frequently coexist with other psychiatric disorders. More than half of the patients with panic disorder have had at least one major depressive episode (Breier et al. 1984).

Patients with untreated panic disorder have high rates of substance-related disorders (Rosenbaum and Pollack 1991).

Treatment and Management

Anxiety Disorder Due to a General Medical Condition or Substance

When a remediable etiology for an anxiety syndrome is found, the clinician should reverse it, unless medically impossible or contraindicated. Unless anxiety symptoms are reversible or self-limited, consider pharmacological treatment. Symptoms are usually undertreated, and concerns about iatrogenic addiction are overstated.

Acute and Generalized Anxiety Disorder

Benzodiazepines.   Benzodiazepines are effective anxiolytics. Few features make them potentially dangerous in the medically ill, especially for short-term use. However, tolerance, dependence, and accident proneness present severe limitations to long-term use of benzodiazepines. Benzodiazepines are structurally divided into three classes (see Table 7–2).

1. *2-Keto-benzodiazepines* are metabolized (oxidized) in the liver and have long elimination half-lives. The duration of clinical effects is subject to the activity of hepatic enzymes, which is affected by liver disease and other medications. Differences between drugs of this class are determined by absorption rates, distribution rates, and active metabolites. Desmethyldiazepam and desmethylchlordiazepoxide are the two active compounds formed by this class (Table 7–2).
2. *Triazolo-benzodiazepines* are oxidized but have fewer active metabolites and therefore have shorter half-lives than 2-keto compounds. They are also sensitive to the status of hepatic enzymes, especially cytochrome P450 3A4 (see Chapter 10).

TABLE 7–2. Benzodiazepines: oral compounds, dosages, absorption rates, and pharmacokinetics

Name	Oral dose range (mg/day)	Oral absorption	Major active metabolites	Half-life[a]
2-Keto-benzodiazepines				
Diazepam	2–40	Very rapid	Diazepam	40
			Desmethyldiazepam	60
Chlordiazepoxide	15–80	Rapid	Chlordiazepoxide	20
			Desmethylchlordiazepoxide	30
			Demoxepam	Unknown
Clonazepam	1–4	Very rapid		40
Clorazepate	5–60	Very rapid	Desmethyldiazepam	60
Halazepam	40–140	Rapid	Desmethyldiazepam	60
Prazepam	20–60	Very slow	Desmethyldiazepam	60
Triazolo-benzodiazepines				
Alprazolam	1–6	Rapid	Alprazolam	12
3-Hydroxy-benzodiazepines				
Lorazepam	1–6	Intermediate	Lorazepam	12
Oxazepam	30–120	Slow	Oxazepam	12

[a]Approximate elimination half-life in hours based on half-lives reported in healthy young volunteers.

3. *3-Hydroxy-benzodiazepines* are metabolized by direct conjugation, a process more rapid and direct than oxidation, resulting in shorter elimination half-lives. Use of these medications is of less potential medical consequence in patients with liver disease or taking multiple medications than use of 2-keto- and triazolo-benzodiazepines.

Agents with longer half-lives (e.g., diazepam, clorazepate) can be administered less frequently and may be easier to taper after prolonged use than agents with shorter half-lives. However, they are more likely to accumulate in patients who have impaired hepatic function or who are taking multiple medications. Agents with shorter elimination half-lives reach steady state much more rapidly and are eliminated more quickly, making them reasonable options for the short-term management of anxiety (Rickels and Schweizer 1987). Lorazepam and oxazepam have no active metabolites and are better suited for patients with liver impairment or patients taking multiple medications. Among benzodiazepines, only lorazepam is reliably absorbed when administered intramuscularly.

Adverse effects.   The most common benzodiazepine side effect is sedation. Dizziness, weakness, anterograde amnesia (correlated with decreasing duration of action), nausea, and impaired motor performance are also reported. After chronic use, tolerance can develop. Withdrawal syndromes occur when dosage is reduced too rapidly.

Buspirone.   The mechanism of action of buspirone, a nonbenzodiazepine antianxiety agent, is related to its actions on serotonin-1A receptors. Buspirone is attractive because of its apparent lack of abuse potential and sedative effects. Considerable evidence indicates that buspirone is as effective an antianxiety agent in GAD as benzodiazepines. Buspirone may be a particularly desirable choice in treating chronic anxiety in patients with pulmonary conditions; it may be associated with an actual increase in respiratory drive (Garner and Eldridge 1989). Buspirone is not useful in the treatment of acute anxiety because its onset of therapeutic response requires 2 or more weeks; buspirone is also not effective as a primary treatment for panic disorder. Average daily dosage is 30 mg.

Adverse effects.   The adverse effects of buspirone include nausea, vomiting, headache, and dizziness.

Antidepressants.   Antidepressants, especially selective serotonin reuptake inhibitors (SSRIs) and serotonin/norepinephrine reuptake inhibitors (SNRIs), are effective in the treatment of GAD and other anxiety disorders (Gorman and Kent 1999).

Neuroleptics.   Low-dose neuroleptics are particularly beneficial in the medical setting when fear, agitation, or delirium is present. For example, 2 mg of perphenazine or 0.5 mg of haloperidol two or three times per day can markedly reduce the extreme fear that patients sometimes experience when they are being weaned from a respirator. Combining neuroleptics such as haloperidol with benzodiazepines such as lorazepam is increasingly popular in treating delirium. The clinical synergism provides additional sedation and lowers the likelihood of extrapyramidal side effects (Menza et al. 1988). In addition, neuroleptics are particularly useful in treating secondary anxiety disorders and other secondary psychiatric disorders resulting from high-dose steroids. Patients who are medically ill and have severe, refractory anxiety or panic or those in whom sedation from benzodiazepine agents cannot be tolerated also may benefit from a cautious trial of neuroleptics.

Adverse effects.   The treating physician must observe the patient for acute dystonia, akathisia, and early signs of neuroleptic malignant syndrome.

β-Blockers.   Propranolol helps control some sympathetic nervous system symptoms of anxiety, such as palpitations and sweating. The psychological components of anxiety may remain.

Adverse effects.   The adverse effects of β-blockers include bradycardia, hypotension, and fatigue.

Clonidine.   Clonidine, a presynaptic α_2 receptor agonist, can blunt narcotic withdrawal symptoms and has potential uses as an antianxiety agent. Clonidine is also available in transdermal form. Tolerance may develop to the antianxiety effects.

Adverse effects.   The adverse effects of clonidine include dry mouth, fatigue, and hypotension.

Medical psychotherapy.   Supportive psychotherapy can help patients cope with the acute stressors during a hospitalization or series of clinic visits. Attention has focused on the potential efficacy of cognitive-behavioral therapy for anxiety disorders (Welkowitz et al. 1991). Cognitive psychotherapy involves active exploration, clarification, and testing of the patient's perceptions and beliefs. Common psychodynamic themes in anxious patients are loss, real and metaphorical physical threats, and lack of control.

Behavioral management.   Behavior therapies provide an opportunity for reduction of acute anxiety, enhancement of the patient's sense of mastery, and clarification of measurable goals. Behavioral interventions commonly used in consultation-liaison psychiatry include relaxation techniques, systematic desensitization, biofeedback, meditation, hypnosis, and establishing graded goals with simple reinforcement schedules.

Panic Disorder

Antidepressants.   Most antidepressants exert antipanic effects (Ballenger 1991). Two SSRI antidepressants (paroxetine and sertraline) received U.S. Food and Drug Administration (FDA)–approved indications for panic disorder. After a 2-week single-blind, placebo lead-in, one group of 168 research patients experienced an 88% decrease in mean number of panic attacks per week, compared with a decrease of 53% in the placebo-treated group (Pohl et al. 1998). SSRI doses used for panic are similar to those used for depression, although higher doses are frequently necessary for complete control of panic attacks, including the elimination of limited symptom panic attacks. Tricyclic antidepressants, trazodone, nefazodone, and monoamine oxidase inhibitors (MAOIs) are also efficacious. Bupropion is not effective in treating panic disorder. Chapter 5 describes normal antidepressant doses and potential adverse effects.

Benzodiazepines.   Alprazolam and clonazepam have potential usefulness for panic disorder, usually when rapid control of attacks is necessary. A significant limitation of alprazolam in treating panic is the potential for dependence, withdrawal, and rebound symptoms on discontinuation and between doses. Discontinuation of alprazolam should be *very* gradual. Clonazepam has a longer half-life than alprazolam (24–48 hours); it is quite sedating to many patients.

Neuroleptics.   Neuroleptics are effective for rapid relief of acute panic attacks that endanger life or medical status. Parenteral haloperidol, 4–10 mg (or higher doses if needed), can help control attacks.

Other medications.   Propranolol blocks some peripheral manifestations of panic attacks. Clonidine is effective in decreasing symptoms in some patients.

Medical psychotherapy.   Explaining panic disorder to the patient as a part of supportive psychotherapy is helpful and reassuring. Behavioral, cognitive-behavioral, and relaxation therapies are effective primary or adjunctive treatments of panic disorder. Cognitive-behavioral approaches emphasize the combination of symptom control (especially breathing) and cognitive restructuring to give physical symptoms a noncatastrophic interpretation. Use of medication and psychotherapy together is particularly efficacious, especially for patients with severe panic disorder.

Specific and Social Phobia

The treatment of choice for specific phobia is graded exposure. In the hospitalized patient, exposure treatments do not have to be in vivo. Imagery-based exposure that uses a graded hierarchy of anxiety-producing stimuli is also effective (Hollander et al. 1988). SSRIs and SNRIs are increasingly used to treat social phobias (Gorman and Kent 1999) and are superior to placebo, although overall, fewer than half of the patients taking SSRIs respond favorably (Stein et al. 1999).

Obsessive-Compulsive Disorder

Clomipramine is a potent serotonin reuptake blocker but is not well tolerated because of side effects. Two-thirds of patients with obsessive-compulsive disorder can expect significant symptomatic improvement; some patients have an almost complete remission (Hollander et al. 1988). SSRIs are also effective for obsessive-compulsive symptoms, and they lack anticholinergic and sedating side effects. Successful obsessive-compulsive disorder treatment is enhanced when medication is combined with behavioral treatments, such as graded exposure and response prevention techniques.

Acute Stress Disorder and Posttraumatic Stress Disorder

It is important to remember that traumatic events often result in hospitalization (e.g., motor vehicle accidents) and can occur in medical facilities (e.g., cardiac arrests). The development of significant anxiety and dissociative symptoms after exposure to an extreme stressor identifies an individual as "at risk" for PTSD. The mainstay of PTSD treatment is group and individual psychotherapy. Many case reports and series have described successful treatment of PTSD with antidepressant medications. Benzodiazepines also provide symptomatic relief for some PTSD patients, but caution is advised because of the high risk of comorbid substance-related disorders. Other psychiatric disorders that frequently accompany PTSD, such as major depression, are sometimes more treatment responsive than the actual PTSD symptoms.

■ INSOMNIA

Mild, transient sleep disturbance secondary to anxiety or physical discomfort is the most common form of insomnia seen in hospitalized or severely ill patients. The most common DSM-IV insomnia subtype is sleep disorder due to a general medical condition, insomnia type (American Psychiatric Association 1994). To make this diagnosis, a specific medical disorder must produce a significant, new sleep disturbance and/or related daytime distress (Weilburg and Winkelman 1999). Insomnias secondary to psychiatric disorders, primary sleep disorders (e.g., primary or idiopathic insomnia), sleep apnea, and narcolepsy are not included in this category.

Patients in hospitals or nursing homes may have disrupted sleep in any of three ways: decreased total sleep time, disrupted day/night or circadian cycles, and disrupted sleep architecture (Weilburg and Winkelman 1999). In particular, patients in the intensive care unit have periods of sleep that are brief and distributed fairly evenly throughout the 24-hour day rather than consolidated at night. Intensive care unit patients also tend to have frequent awakenings and to spend very little time in rapid eye movement (REM) and delta sleep. Insomnia has many individual toxic and medical causes. A vigorous evaluation of sleep complaints, sometimes including a full-scale sleep study, will yield a treatable psychiatric, neurological, or medical etiology in most cases (Coleman et al. 1982).

Treatment of Insomnia

Reverse Causes

The psychiatrist must determine whether potentially reversible psychiatric or medical illnesses are present that could disrupt sleep—consider depression, delirium, mania, psychoactive substance dependence, anxiety disorders, pain, and psychosis. Several medications can interfere with sleep. The treatment of obstructive sleep apnea has evolved from tracheostomy to a variety of options that include weight loss, nasal continuous positive airway pressure (N-CPAP), pharyngeal surgery, and medications. Myoclonic sleep disorders such as restless legs syndrome are difficult to treat. Dopaminergic agents, such as levodopa, pergolide, and bromocriptine, offer some benefit; reports indicate that pramipexole is particularly effective (Montplaisir et al. 1999).

Behavioral and Environmental Manipulations

Changing a patient's surroundings by recommending different
lighting, altering the schedule of medications (especially those
known to interfere with sleep), modifying vital sign requirements,
and preventing daytime naps frequently can resolve or improve insomnia. Caffeine appears to increase insomnia in hospitalized patients, so simply removing coffee, tea, and cola from the diet
of patients complaining of insomnia may be of practical utility
(Weilburg and Winkelman 1999).

TABLE 7–3. **Sedative-hypnotic medications**

	Clonaze-pam	Estazo-lam	Fluraze-pam	Loraze-pam	Quaze-pam
Onset of action	Interme-diate	Interme-diate	Rapid–inter-mediate	Interme-diate	Rapid–inter-mediate
Duration of action	Long	Interme-diate	Long	Interme-diate	Long
Half-life (hours) (includes metabo-lites)	15–50	10–24	24–150	10–20	35–150
Excretion/metabo-lism	Oxidation/hydrox-ylation	Oxidation/hydrox-ylation	Oxidation/hydrox-ylation	Conjuga-tion	Oxidation/hydrox-ylation
Adult dose (mg)	0.5–1.0	1–2	15–30	1	15
Elderly dose (mg)	0.25–0.5	0.5	15	0.25–0.5	7.5

Source.   Adapted from Weilburg JB, Winkelman JW: "Sleep Disorders," in
Edited by Rundell JR, Wise MG. Washington, DC, American Psychiatric Press,
sion.

Sedative-Hypnotic Medications

Once remediable causes of insomnia are corrected and behavioral and environmental manipulations attempted, the consulting psychiatrist must decide if a patient could benefit from a hypnotic agent. Table 7–3 summarizes the most commonly used sedative-hypnotic medications in general hospital and outpatient settings.

Use benzodiazepine hypnotic agents at the lowest effective dose and only for a brief period. In general, drugs with a rapid onset of action, such as diazepam, triazolam, and zolpidem, help

Temazepam	Triazolam	Zolpidem	Diphenhydramine	Hydroxyzine
Slow–intermediate	Rapid	Rapid	Intermediate	Rapid
Intermediate	Short	Short	Intermediate	Intermediate
8–20	1.5–6	2.4–3	3.5–9.5	6–24
Conjugation	Oxidation/ hydroxylation	Oxidation/ hydroxylation	Oxidation/ hydroxylation	Oxidation/ hydroxylation
15	0.125–0.5	10	50	25
15	0.125	5	25	25

patients who have trouble falling asleep; medications with a somewhat delayed onset of action, such as clonazepam, temazepam, and quazepam, are recommended for patients who have sleep interruption (Weilburg and Winkelman 1999). Discontinuation of a benzodiazepine sedative-hypnotic, especially a shorter-acting agent used for more than a few nights, may lead to rebound insomnia. If this occurs, the clinician should reassure the patient that it is temporary and substitute an antihistamine (e.g., diphenhydramine 25–50 mg orally) for a few nights. Short-acting benzodiazepine sedative-hypnotics, such as triazolam, sometimes cause anterograde amnesia. For outpatients who have long-standing insomnia or who are taking activating medications (e.g., bupropion, fluoxetine), many clinicians have success with low-dose trazodone (25–100 mg nightly). The use of trazodone avoids problems with tolerance and anterograde amnesia, but some patients may report mild "hangover," orthostatic dizziness, or, very rarely, priapism.

■ REFERENCES

American Psychiatric Association: Diagnostic and Statistical Manual of Mental Disorders, 4th Edition. Washington, DC, American Psychiatric Association, 1994

Ballenger JC: Long-term pharmacologic treatment of panic disorder. J Clin Psychiatry 52 (suppl):18–23, 1991

Breier A, Charney DS, Heninger GR: Major depression in patients with agoraphobia and panic disorder. Arch Gen Psychiatry 41:1129–1135, 1984

Coleman RM, Roffwarg HP, Kennedy SJ, et al: Sleep-wake disorders based on a polysomnographic diagnosis: a national cooperative study. JAMA 247:997–1003, 1982

Colón EA, Popkin MK: Anxiety and panic, in The Essentials of Consultation-Liaison Psychiatry. Edited by Rundell JR, Wise MG. Washington, DC, American Psychiatric Press, 1999, pp 189–206

Garner SJ, Eldridge FL: Buspirone, an anxiolytic drug that stimulates respiration. Am Rev Respir Dis 139:945–950, 1989

Gorman JM, Kent JM: SSRIs and SNRIs: broad spectrum of efficacy beyond major depression. J Clin Psychiatry 60 (suppl 4):33–38, 1999

Hollander E, Liebowitz MR, Gorman JM: Anxiety disorders, in The American Psychiatric Press Textbook of Psychiatry. Edited by Talbott JA, Hales RE, Yudofsky SC. Washington, DC, American Psychiatric Press, 1988, pp 443–491

Katon W: Panic disorder and somatization: review of 55 cases. Am J Med 77:101–106, 1984

Katon W: Chest pain, cardiac disease and panic disorder. J Clin Psychiatry 51:27–30, 1990

Levenson JL, Hamer RM, Rossiter C: Psychopathology and pain in medical inpatients: predict resource use during hospitalization but not rehospitalization. J Psychosom Res 36:585–592, 1992

Menza MA, Murray GB, Holmes VF, et al: Controlled study of extrapyramidal reactions in the management of delirious, medically ill patients: intravenous haloperidol versus intravenous haloperidol plus benzodiazepines. Heart Lung 17:238–241, 1988

Montplaisir J, Nicolas A, Denesle R, et al: Restless legs syndrome improved by pramipexole: a double-blind randomized trial. Neurology 52:938–943, 1999

Pohl RB, Wolkow RM, Clary CM: Sertraline in the treatment of panic disorder: a double-blind multicenter trial. Am J Psychiatry 155:1189–1195, 1998

Rickels K, Schweizer EE: Current pharmacotherapy of anxiety and panic, in Psychopharmacology: The Third Generation of Progress. Edited by Meltzer HY. New York, Raven, 1987, pp 1193–1203

Rosenbaum JF, Pollack MH: Anxiety, in Massachusetts General Hospital Handbook of General Hospital Psychiatry, 3rd Edition. Edited by Cassem NH. Boston, MA, Mosby Year Book, 1991, pp 159–190

Saravay SM, Steinberg MD, Weinschel B, et al: Psychological comorbidity and length of stay in the general hospital. Am J Psychiatry 148:324–329, 1991

Sheehan DV, Ballenger J, Jacobsen E: Treatment of endogenous anxiety with phobic, hysterical, and hypochondriacal symptoms. Arch Gen Psychiatry 37:51–59, 1980

Simon GE, Walker EA: The consultation psychiatrist in the primary care clinic, in The Essentials of Consultation-Liaison Psychiatry. Edited by Rundell JR, Wise MG. Washington, DC, American Psychiatric Press, 1999, pp 513–520

Spitzer RL, Kroenke K, Linzer M, et al: Health-related quality of life in primary care patients with mental disorders: results from the PRIME-MD 1000 Study. JAMA 274:1511–1517, 1995

Stein MB, Fyer AJ, Davidson JRT, et al: Fluvoxamine treatment of social phobia (social anxiety disorder): a double-blind, placebo-controlled study. Am J Psychiatry 156:756–760, 1999

Strain JJ, Leibowitz MR, Klein DF: Anxiety and panic attacks in the medically ill. Psychiatr Clin North Am 4:333–350, 1981

Weilburg JB, Winkelman JW: Sleep disorders, in The Essentials of Consultation-Liaison Psychiatry. Edited by Rundell JR, Wise MG. Washington, DC, American Psychiatric Press, 1999, pp 241–256

Welkowitz LA, Papp LA, Cloitre M, et al: Cognitive-behavior therapy for panic disorder delivered by psychopharmacologically oriented clinicians. J Nerv Ment Dis 179:472–476, 1991

Wells KB, Golding JM, Burnham MA: Psychiatric disorder in a sample of the population with and without chronic medical conditions. Am J Psychiatry 145:976–981, 1988

■ ADDITIONAL READINGS

Goldberg RJ: Anxiety in the medically ill, in Principles of Medical Psychiatry. New York, Grune & Stratton, 1987, pp 177–203

Nierenberg AL, Adler EA: Trazodone for antidepressant-associated insomnia. Am J Psychiatry 151:1069–1072, 1994

Popkin MK, Callies AL, Colón EA, et al: Adjustment disorders in medically ill inpatients referred for consultation in a university hospital. Psychosomatics 31:410–414, 1990

Salzman C, Miyawake EK, le Bars P, et al: Neurobiologic basis of anxiety and its treatment. Harv Rev Psychiatry 1:197–206, 1993

Wheatley D: Use of anti-anxiety drugs in the medically ill. Psychother Psychosom 49:63–80, 1988

Wise MG, Rundell JR: Anxiety and neurologic disorders. Seminars in Clinical Neuropsychiatry: Anxiety in the Medically Ill 4:98–102, 1999

8

SOMATOFORM AND RELATED DISORDERS

Between 60% and 80% of people in the general population experience somatic complaints during any given week, and physicians cannot find an organic cause in 20%–84% of these patients (Kellner 1985). Physicians have certain expectations of patients who have physical complaints, according to Lipowski (1988): "A patient should complain in reasonable proportion to demonstrative pathology, report physical distress in bodily terms and emotional distress in psychological terms, and accept a doctor's opinion and advice compliantly" (p. 1361). When a physiological cause cannot be found for a symptom or when the physician feels that a significant disparity exists between the patient's subjective complaints and objective findings, a psychiatric consultation is sometimes requested. A typical consult asks for psychiatric evaluation of a "functional," "psychogenic," or "psychosomatic" symptom.

The amplification or magnification of somatic sensations varies widely among somatizing patients. This amplification process has both trait and state characteristics. Barsky (1992) reported that amplification is influenced by the patient's cognition (information, beliefs, opinions, and attribution), context of the symptom (feedback from others and expectations), amount of attention to the symptom (when attention is increased, the symptom is amplified; if decreased, the symptom is diminished), and mood (anxiety and depression amplify symptoms). A large differential diagnosis must be considered in a patient who has physical symptoms (Table 8–1). Patients who amplify somatic symptoms (somatizers) are a heterogeneous group and defy simple categorization or explanation. Not all somatizers have a somatoform disorder. In this chapter, we review somatization and then review DSM-IV (American Psychiatric Association 1994) somatoform disorders and the three related conditions: psychological factors affecting medical condition, factitious disorder, and malingering.

TABLE 8–1.   **Differential diagnosis of physical complaints**

No diagnosis

Unknown or undiagnosed medical or psychiatric condition(s)

General medical disorder

Somatizer whose conditions do not meet criteria for a somatoform disorder

Somatoform disorder

   Somatization disorder

   Undifferentiated somatoform disorder

   Hypochondriasis

   Conversion disorder

   Body dysmorphic disorder

   Pain disorder

   Somatoform disorder not otherwise specified

Mood disorder, especially major depressive disorder

Anxiety disorder, especially generalized anxiety disorder and panic disorder

Psychotic disorder, especially delusional disorder, somatic type

Substance-related disorder

Dissociative disorder

Dementia or other cognitive disorder

Personality disorder

Factitious disorder with predominantly physical symptoms

Malingering

■ SOMATIZATION

Definitions and Theoretical Concepts

Somatization is the tendency to experience, communicate, and amplify psychological and interpersonal distress in the form of somatic distress and medically unexplained symptoms (Abbey 1999). Kirmayer and Robbins (1991) identified three types of somatization in a study of 685 family practice patients. Most patients fall into one of these categories:

1. *Medically unexplained symptoms*—somatic symptoms not explained after appropriate medical and psychiatric assessment
2. *Hypochondriacal somatization*—bodily preoccupation and a tendency to worry about the possibility of or vulnerability to serious physical illness
3. *Somatic presentation of psychiatric disorder*—nonsomatoform psychiatric disorders, such as major depressive disorder, generalized anxiety disorder, and panic disorder, that often present with somatic symptoms as the most prominent part of the clinical picture

Illness versus disease.   The distinction between *illness* and *disease* (Eisenberg 1977) is a useful one for consultation-liaison psychiatrists. Illness is the response of the individual and his or her family to symptoms. In contrast, disease is a pathophysiological process associated with documentable physical lesions or diagnosed by a physician. A patient can have a disease without an illness and an illness without a disease. Mismatches are common and are at the root of many management problems. For example, a patient with hypertension may not experience symptoms and thus not believe he or she is ill; nonadherence to treatment soon follows. In contrast, the somatizing patient believes that he or she is ill despite the lack of evidence of a disease; or if evidence of disease is present, the patient's reaction is exaggerated.

Illness behavior. *Illness behavior* refers to the manner in which individuals interpret their symptoms, take remedial action, and use sources of help (Mechanic 1986).

Abnormal illness behavior. *Abnormal illness behavior* is "an inappropriate or maladaptive mode of perceiving, evaluating or acting in relation to one's own health status" (Pilowsky 1987, p. 89). This behavior pattern persists despite the fact that a health care provider has offered an accurate explanation of the nature of the disease and the appropriate course of management.

Evaluation

Abbey (1999) recommends a comprehensive approach to evaluating patients who are identified by primary care physicians or specialists as potential somatizers. Although the patient may not have a somatoform or other psychiatric disorder, data gathering is similar to that of a typical psychiatric consultation. Table 8–2 summarizes the evaluation process for a potentially somatizing patient.

■ EPIDEMIOLOGY

Epidemiological and demographic characteristics are included in the discussions of each individual somatoform and related disorder. Somatization accounts for about 10% of total direct health care costs (Ford 1983). Somatizing patients have higher average health costs than other patients: total charges 9 times greater, hospital charges 6 times greater, and physician services 14 times greater. Somatizing patients spend up to 7 days per month sick in bed compared with the general population average of half a day (Smith et al. 1986).

■ CLINICAL CHARACTERISTICS AND SPECIFIC MANAGEMENT STRATEGIES

The common feature shared by the somatoform disorders is the presence of physical symptoms that suggest a general medical con-

---

TABLE 8–2. **Psychiatric evaluation of a patient referred for somatization**

Collaborate with referral sources: Understand clearly the reason for referral and what the patient was told about the consultation/evaluation.

Review the medical records: Review records before the consultation appointment.

Collaborate with family and friends: Gain an accurate assessment of the patient's history, current and past functional capacity, and current or past psychosocial stressors.

Build an alliance with the patient: Address ambivalence about seeing a psychiatrist early, take the patient's symptoms seriously, and ask "how has this illness affected your life?"

Perform a mental status examination: Look for mental status examination findings suggestive of a psychiatric disorder. Pay particular attention to the range and depth of emotional response to issues raised during the examination, level of denial, meaning of symptoms and normal test results to the patient, and evidence of unwarranted hostility toward physicians.

Complete a physical examination: Provide an objective physical and laboratory examination of the patient (the referring physician already believes the patient has no medical condition). Conduct relevant portions of a physical and neurological examination, which is likely to improve the alliance with the patient.

Use psychometric tests: Assess patients with the Minnesota Multiphasic Personality Inventory (MMPI), which is particularly useful for patients who may be malingering and/or who have severe characterological problems, and the Symptom Checklist—90 (SCL-90), which is brief and can be scored in the office.

Source.   Adapted from Abbey SE: "Somatization and Somatoform Disorders," in *The American Psychiatric Press Textbook Consultation-Liaison Psychiatry.* Edited by Rundell JR, Wise MG. Washington, DC, American Psychiatric Press, 1996, pp. 368–401. Copyright 1996, American Psychiatric Press. Used with permission.

dition and are not fully explained by a general medical condition, by the direct effects of a substance, or by another mental disorder. The physical symptoms are not intentional and cause significant disruption in social or occupational functioning (American Psychiatric Association 1994). DSM-IV somatoform disorder diagnoses include somatization disorder, undifferentiated somatoform disorder, hypochondriasis, conversion disorder, body dysmorphic disorder (BDD), pain disorder, and somatoform disorder not otherwise specified. Epidemiology, clinical and associated features, clinical course and prognosis, and specific treatment and management strategies are discussed for each disorder.

Somatization Disorder (Briquet's Syndrome)

Epidemiology.   The general population lifetime prevalence of somatization disorder is estimated at 0.1%–1%, depending on the criteria used (Regier et al. 1988). The prevalence in medical settings is obviously higher—as high as 5% in some outpatient primary care clinics (deGruy et al. 1987). Somatization disorder is perhaps 10 times more common in women than in men. Symptom onset is usually in the teens, often with menarche. Of first-degree female relatives of women with somatization disorder, 20% have somatization disorder, and male relatives have a higher than expected rate of alcohol abuse and antisocial personality disorder (Golding et al. 1992).

Clinical features.   The typical patient with somatization disorder is a woman who describes herself as "always sickly." She began to experience medically unexplained symptoms in early adolescence and has, over the years, continued to have repeated unexplained physical complaints involving multiple organ systems. To make the diagnosis, DSM-IV requires a history at some time of at least four pain symptoms, two gastrointestinal symptoms, one sexual symptom, and one pseudoneurological symptom, all unexplained medically.

Associated features.   As many as 75% of patients with somatization disorder have comorbid Axis I diagnoses (Katon et al. 1991), most commonly major depressive disorder, dysthymic disorder, panic disorder, simple phobia, and substance abuse. As many as two-thirds of patients with somatization disorder have symptoms that meet criteria for one or more personality disorders (Rost et al. 1992), most frequently avoidant, paranoid, obsessive-compulsive, and histrionic.

Clinical course and prognosis. The psychiatric consultant first must ensure that patients receive an appropriate diagnosis. Somatization disorder is a chronic but fluctuating disorder that rarely remits completely. The diagnosis of somatization disorder influences how physicians and the medical system respond to a patient. These patients are at risk for iatrogenic complications from numerous repetitive tests, procedures, and medications; the cost of the disorder is staggering.

Management. Appropriate management of somatization disorder is not easily implemented. It is a lifelong disorder, and most patients resist psychiatric consultation. The consultant must identify and treat comorbid psychiatric conditions. Table 8–3 contains a recommended management plan for patients with somatization disorder. To complicate management further, patients with somatization disorder also have primary and iatrogenically (often surgically) induced medical disorders, particularly as they grow older. When a patient with Briquet's syndrome also has a chronic medical illness, the primary physician is often reluctant to curtail medical evaluations. It is helpful in this situation to suggest to the primary physician that only complaints that have objective findings should be further evaluated and treated.

Undifferentiated Somatoform Disorder

Definition. Undifferentiated somatoform disorder is a residual category for individuals not yet meeting criteria for somatization disorder or another somatoform disorder but who nevertheless have significant dysfunction caused by unexplained medical symptoms.

Epidemiology. No studies of undifferentiated somatoform disorder have been done, but studies of subsyndromal somatization disorder have attempted to identify a group of patients with

TABLE 8–3.	Management of somatization disorder

1. Establish one physician who can develop a doctor-patient relationship (usually a primary care physician, a physician with combined psychiatry–primary care training, or a medically oriented psychiatrist).

2. Maintain regular appointments. Even if the patient is doing well, continue regular appointments.

3. Gradually reduce the frequency of appointments. If physical symptoms recur in response to fewer appointments, reestablish more frequent appointments and try tapering appointments more slowly at a later date.

4. Perform regular physical examinations and offer reassurance.

5. Do not pursue somatic complaints with further evaluations or treatment unless objective evidence of disease is present.

6. Gradually shift the emphasis from listening to somatic complaints to talking about psychosocial stressors ("how is this illness affecting your life" often answers the question "how is your life affecting this illness?").

7. Work with the family or significant others to verify history and to monitor the patient's contacts with the health care system.

8. Anticipate that the patient will receive prescription drugs or diagnostic procedures from other physicians; watch for drug misuse.

9. Protect the patient from iatrogenic problems, especially nonindicated surgical procedures.

sociodemographic and clinical characteristics similar to patients meeting the full criteria for somatization disorder (Escobar et al. 1989). Further support for this diagnosis comes from the study of distressed high utilizers of medical care; these studies documented significantly increased health care utilization by patients with functional somatic symptoms who have too few symptoms to meet DSM-IV criteria (Katon et al. 1991). As many as 4%–11% of the population have multiple medically unexplained symptoms consistent with a subsyndromal form of somatization disorder (Escobar et al. 1989).

Clinical features.   Undifferentiated somatoform disorder is diagnosed when the patient has one or more unexplained physical symptoms but does not meet the full criteria for somatization disorder. Most clinicians believe the same principles of assessment and management hold for patients with this diagnosis (see Tables 8–2 and 8–3).

Clinical course and prognosis.   Individuals with this disorder are probably quite a heterogeneous group. DSM-IV notes that the "course of individual unexplained physical complaints is unpredictable. The eventual diagnosis of a general medical condition or another mental disorder is frequent" (American Psychiatric Association 1994, p. 451).

Management.   See the earlier discussion of management in the "Somatization Disorder" section and Table 8–3.

Hypochondriasis

Definition.   Hypochondriasis is the fear or the belief that one has a serious disease based on the misinterpretation of bodily symptoms. Anxiety and fear about the disease persist despite normal medical evaluations and reassurance (American Psychiatric Association 1994).

Epidemiology.   The prevalence of hypochondriasis depends on the diagnostic criteria used (Barsky et al. 1986). A broad definition estimates that 50% of all patients seeing a physician have hypochondriacal symptoms or overlay (often not a mental disorder); a narrow definition estimates a 1%–3% rate of hypochondriasis among various ethnic groups. Hypochondriasis is equally common in men and women (American Psychiatric Association 1994). The typical age at onset is in early adulthood.

Clinical features.   The core feature of hypochondriasis is fear of disease or conviction that one has a disease despite normal physical examination findings and physician reassurance. Bodily preoccupation (i.e., increased observation of and vigilance toward bodily sensations) is common. Hypochondriasis patients believe that good health is a relatively symptom-free state, and they are more likely than control patients to believe that symptoms mean disease (Barsky et al. 1993). Concern about the feared illness "often becomes a central feature of the individual's self-image, a topic of social discourse, and a response to life stressors" (American Psychiatric Association 1994, p. 463). Central clinical features of hypochondriasis are summed up by the four Ds: **d**isease conviction, **d**isease fear, **d**isease preoccupation, and **d**isability. According to DSM-IV, 6 months of symptoms are required before making the diagnosis.

Associated features. Barsky et al. (1992) found that 88% of hypochondriacal patients in a general medical outpatient clinic had one or more concurrent Axis I diagnoses; the most common were generalized anxiety disorder (71.4%), dysthymia (45.2%), major depression (42.9%), somatization disorder (21.4%), and panic disorder (16.7%). Patients with hypochondriasis have high medical use and the potential for iatrogenic damage from repeated investigations (Abbey 1999). Interestingly, research has shown that relatives of patients with hypochondriasis do not have a greater frequency of hypochondriasis than in the general population (Noyes et al. 1997).

Clinical course and prognosis. Hypochondriasis is often a chronic condition; thus, one might argue that it is better understood as a personality style or anxiety disorder (Barsky et al. 1992).

Treatment and management. Hypochondriasis often remits or improves with resolution of underlying major life stressors, interpersonal situations, or mood and anxiety disorders. Three diagnoses to rule out are depression, anxiety disorders (particularly panic disorder), and somatization disorder (Briquet's syndrome). The clinician should reassure patients frequently—even though it does not change their behavior—and should protect them from iatrogenic harm, especially nonindicated surgical procedures. The family and significant others should be educated about the nature of hypochondriasis, which may help decrease anxiety and stress at home. In one study of pharmacological treatment of hypochondriasis, high-dose fluoxetine improved conditions of 10 of 16 patients who did not have marked depressive features (Fallon et al. 1993).

Conversion Disorder

Definition. Conversion disorder is a loss of or alteration in function that suggests a physical, usually neurological, disease, although one is not present. The initiation or exacerbation of the symptom is associated with a meaningful stressor.

Epidemiology. The prevalence of conversion disorder varies among studies. Toone (1990), in a review of several studies, estimated rates of 0.3% in the general population, 1%–3% in medical outpatient settings, and 1%–4.5% in inpatient neurological and medical settings. Women outnumber men with the disorder by a ratio varying from 2:1 to 10:1 (Murphy 1990). Onset is typically in adolescence or early adulthood, although cases occur throughout the life cycle.

Clinical features. Common presentations of conversion include motor symptoms (e.g., paralysis, disturbances in coordination or balance, localized weakness, akinesia, dyskinesia, aphonia, urinary retention, and difficulty swallowing), sensory symptoms (e.g., blindness, double vision, anesthesia, paresthesia, deafness), and seizures or convulsions that may have voluntary motor or sensory components (Abbey 1999). When unilateral conversion symptoms occur in women they are more likely to occur on the left side of the body. The reasons for this are unknown, but the same is true for somatoform pain and hypochondriasis symptoms (Toone 1990).

Persons with a conversion symptom frequently have a psychological "bind." For example, a teenager has perfectionistic parents who constantly pressure her to do numerous chores. When she does the chores, they always criticize her for inadequate performance. The teenager is in a "no-win" bind and must endure criticism whether or not the chores are done. She develops a "pain in the sacrum," which gives her a medical "out." She does not have to do the chores and avoids the usual criticism. The association between her symptom and the fact that her parents are "pains in the butt" is obvious to the consultation-liaison psychiatrist but not in conscious awareness for the teenager or her parents.

Conversion means that a conflict is converted by the unconscious to a physical symptom; this process is sometimes referred to as *primary gain*. The unconscious nature of conversion helps distinguish it from the consciously planned manipulative behaviors associated with malingering and factitious disorders. The consultation psychiatrist must exercise caution before diagnosing conversion. In follow-up studies, 13%–50% of cases later reveal evidence of an actual disease process that retrospectively explains the "conversion" symptom (Ford and Folks 1985; Lazare 1981).

Associated features.   Protracted conversion reactions are sometimes associated with secondary physical changes (e.g., disuse atrophy). Patients frequently have a model for the symptom in a family member or close friend.

Clinical course and prognosis.   Individual episodes of conversion usually are short, have a sudden onset, and resolve when the associated psychosocial stressor (bind) remits (American Psychiatric Association 1994; Murphy 1990). Factors reported to predispose to conversion disorder are 1) prior physical disorders in the individual or a close contact who provides a model for the conversion symptoms and 2) severe social stressors, including bereavement, rape, incest, warfare, and other forms of psychosocial trauma (Toone 1990). A better prognosis is linked to 1) acute and recent onset, 2) traumatic or stressful life event at onset, 3) good premorbid health, and 4) absence of other major medical or psychiatric disorders (Lazare 1981).

Treatment and management.   A wide variety of successful treatments are reported. Spontaneous remission is common. Suggestion that the symptom will rapidly resolve and hypnosis are usually helpful and potentially curative; most conversion disorder patients are quite suggestible. When a clear relation between a conflict and a conversion symptom is identified, short-term focused or supportive therapy is indicated. Effective treatment focused on suggestion, combined with identifying and resolving unconscious psychological binds, will help the patient rapidly resolve the conversion symptom. Direct confrontation usually does not help and may worsen the symptom. Most patients show a rapid response to treatment, but some do not. Pseudoseizures, tremor, and amnesia are least likely to have a rapid and good outcome (Toone 1990).

Body Dysmorphic Disorder (BDD)

Definition. The hallmark of BDD is a preoccupation with an imagined defect in appearance (if a slight physical anomaly is present, the individual's concern with it is markedly excessive) that is accompanied by significant distress or impairment in social or occupational functioning (American Psychiatric Association 1994).

Epidemiology. Onset is typically in adolescence (Phillips et al. 1993), although the range is from ages 6 through 33 years. Many years may pass before diagnosis because of the patient's reluctance to reveal symptoms (American Psychiatric Association 1994). With structured interviews, 3.2% of psychiatric patients met criteria for BDD (Zimmerman et al. 1988).

Clinical features. The patient with BDD has an obsession or preoccupation with an imagined physical body defect or flaw. The most common complaints involve facial appearance (e.g., wrinkles, nose, mouth), and less common complaints are about hair, breasts, genitalia, or other body parts. A minor flaw may exist, but the patient's concern is grossly excessive, and he or she may seek medical attention from a plastic surgeon or dermatologist. It is sometimes difficult to determine whether the patient's complaint is an overvalued idea or a somatic delusion (Hollander et al. 1992).

Associated features.   In a study of 30 patients with BDD, the current prevalence of major depression was 50% and the lifetime prevalence was 60%, the current prevalence of bipolar disorder was 27% and the lifetime prevalence was 33%, the current prevalence of dysthymia was 7%, and the lifetime history of psychotic symptoms was 77% (Phillips et al. 1993). Psychosocial dysfunction is often profound, with social withdrawal and functioning below expected occupational capacity. Phillips et al. (1993) found that 97% of BDD patients avoid usual social and occupational activities; 30% were housebound, and 17% reported suicide attempts.

Clinical course and prognosis.   BDD is usually chronic, with few symptom-free intervals, although the intensity of the symptoms often varies over time.

Treatment and management.   Surgical alteration of the perceived defect usually offers only temporary relief, if even that, and may create a real defect. Similarities are found between BDD and obsessive-compulsive disorder, so a trial of a serotonin reuptake blocker is warranted if symptoms persist (Abbey 1999). If the disorder is of psychotic proportion, pimozide is recommended (see section "Delusional Disorder, Somatic Type" later in this chapter). Successful pharmacotherapy of small series of patients with BDD was also reported with imipramine and doxepin (Brotman and Jenike 1984), clomipramine (Hollander et al. 1989), fluoxetine (Phillips et al. 1993), and tranylcypromine (Jenike 1984).

Pain Disorder

Definition.   Pain disorder in DSM-IV evolved from the previous concepts of somatoform pain disorder (DSM-III-R; American Psychiatric Association 1987) and psychogenic pain disorder (DSM-III; American Psychiatric Association 1980). In pain disorder, psychological factors are important in the onset, severity, exacerbation, or maintenance of the pain, or if a medical disorder is also present, psychological factors exacerbate the pain. Some patients also have a medical condition; but psychological factors play a key role in the way the condition's pain-related illness behaviors are played out.

Epidemiology.   The prevalence of pain disorder is unknown.

Clinical features.   Chronic pain patients who were given the previous diagnoses of psychogenic or somatoform pain disorder were described as having "the disease of the *D*s": 1) **d**isability, 2) **d**isuse and **d**egeneration of functional capacity secondary to pain behavior, 3) **d**rug misuse, 4) **d**octor shopping, 5) **d**ependency (emotional), 6) **d**emoralization, 7) **d**epression, and 8) **d**ramatic accounts of illness (Brena and Chapman 1983). DSM-IV has three forms of this diagnosis: pain disorder associated with psychological factors, pain disorder associated with both psychological factors and a general medical condition, and pain disorder associated with a general medical condition.

Associated features.   Depression is diagnosed frequently in patients with chronic pain syndromes. Estimates range widely from 8% to 80%; most studies find that at least half of their chronic pain sample is depressed (Smith 1991).

Clinical course and prognosis.   Iatrogenic complications are likely common and include dependence on narcotic analgesics and benzodiazepines and unnecessary surgical interventions (Abbey 1999).

Treatment and management.   Management of pain syndromes is complex. The most effective treatment, especially when the pain is chronic and complicated by emotional issues and suffering, is provided by a multidisciplinary team that uses many modes of therapy. Chapter 12 discusses pain management in more detail.

Somatoform Disorder Not Otherwise Specified

Somatoform disorder not otherwise specified is the diagnosis used for patients with somatoform symptoms that do not meet diagnostic criteria for any of the specific somatoform disorders. Examples include pseudocyesis and hypochondriacal and other unexplained physical symptoms lasting less than 6 months.

Psychological Factors Affecting Medical Condition

To diagnose psychological factors affecting medical condition, a temporal relationship between a stressor(s) and the initiation or exacerbation of a physical condition must exist. The physical condition is either tissue pathology (e.g., gastric ulcer) or a recognized physiological process (e.g., migraine headache). Common examples of physical conditions that can be exacerbated by psychological stress are tension or migraine headaches, hypertension, gastric and duodenal ulcers, asthma, and ulcerative colitis. The consultant must rule out a somatoform disorder during the patient's evaluation. A neutral way of uncovering stressors is to inquire, "How has this [*state the patient's somatic complaint in his or her own words*] affected your life?" The patient will frequently reveal what part of his or her life is most related to the symptom.

Factitious Disorders

Definition.   Patients with factitious disorders intentionally feign or induce diseases or symptoms.

Epidemiology.   Demographic analyses of factitious disorder patients suggest two general patterns. Patients with chronic factitious disorder (Munchausen syndrome) are usually middle-aged men, usually unmarried, and estranged from their families. Patients with more acute forms of factitious disorder are usually women, ages 20–40, who work in medical occupations such as nursing and medical technology (Ford and Feldman 1996). Gault and colleagues (1988) used an interesting mechanism for estimating factitious disorder frequency. They analyzed material submitted by patients as "kidney stones"; 3.5% of the "stones" were obviously nonphysiological and artifactual.

Clinical features.   Patients with factitious disorder are aware of their behaviors, although their underlying motivations are often unconscious. Factitious disorder may occur with predominantly physical symptoms, predominantly psychological symptoms, or combined physical and psychological symptoms. In chronic factitious disorder, or Munchausen syndrome, self-production of dramatic illnesses allows the patient to achieve the goal of multiple hospitalizations. In factitious disorder by proxy (Munchausen by proxy), signs and symptoms are created in another person, usually a child or an elderly relative (Ford and Feldman 1996). In factitious disorder by proxy, the perpetrators were the mothers in almost all reported cases. A number of factitious behaviors are reported (Table 8–4).

Clinical course and prognosis.   Factitious disorders are associated with considerable morbidity and mortality. Few patients accept treatment and even fewer are cured. If confronted, some patients may deny but stop behavior, a very few may acknowledge it and enter treatment, and most will transfer their medical care elsewhere and continue factitious behavior (Wise and Ford 1999).

Treatment and management.   Recent changes in medical practice in the United States emphasize patient rights and informed consent. As a result, many practices, such as clandestine searches of personal articles, are not acceptable and are probably illegal (Feldman and Ford 1994). Thus, when a patient is suspected of having a factitious disorder, it is prudent to take the steps outlined in Table 8–5.

Confrontation of the patient's behavior is best accomplished by having the primary physician and consulting psychiatrist approach the patient in a noncondemning but firm manner (Hollender and

Hersh 1970). The patient is told that he or she is contributing to the illness and that this behavior must reflect a high degree of emotional distress and difficulty in directly communicating needs. The psychiatrist then offers therapeutic assistance. A small minority of patients will accept treatment, which preferably will occur initially on an inpatient psychiatric unit.

TABLE 8–4. **Some signs, symptoms, and diseases simulated in or caused by factitious behavior**

More common	Less common
Cancer	AIDS
Chronic diarrhea	Anaplastic anemia
Epilepsy	Cushing's disease
Fever of unknown origin	Diabetes mellitus
Hematuria	Goodpasture's syndrome
Hypoglycemia	Hemiplegia
Intestinal bleeding	Hypersomnia
Iron deficiency anemia	Hypertension
Renal stones	Hyperthyroidism
	Hypotension
	Myocardial infarction
	Pheochromocytoma
	Pupillary dysfunction
	Reflex sympathetic dystrophy
	Septic arthritis
	Thrombocytopenia
	Torsion dystonia
	Uterine bleeding
	Ventricular tachycardia

Source. Reprinted from Ford CV, Feldman MD: "Factitious Disorders and Malingering," in *The American Psychiatric Press Textbook Consultation-Liaison Psychiatry.* Edited by Rundell JR, Wise MG. Washington, DC, American Psychiatric Press, 1996, pp. 532–544. Copyright 1996, American Psychiatric Press. Used with permission.

TABLE 8–5.	**Steps to take when factitious disorders are suspected**

1. Involve the hospital administration from the start.
2. Seek legal advice from the hospital's risk management department and/or the physician's own attorney.
3. Consult early on with the hospital ethics committee.
4. Maintain confidentiality to the extent specified by law. The "blacklists" of Munchausen patients advocated and maintained by some institutions are not legally acceptable in the United States.

Source. Reprinted from Ford CV, Feldman MD: "Factitious Disorders and Malingering," in *The American Psychiatric Press Textbook Consultation-Liaison Psychiatry.* Edited by Rundell JR, Wise MG. Washington, DC, American Psychiatric Press, 1996, pp. 532–544. Copyright 1996, American Psychiatric Press. Used with permission.

Malingering

Definition.   Malingering is grossly exaggerating, lying, or faking physical or psychological symptoms for the purpose of a concrete, recognizable gain (often called *secondary gain*). Individuals who have malingering are motivated by specific external incentives (Gorman 1982), including deferment from military service, avoidance of hazardous work assignments, receipt of financial rewards such as disability payments, escape from incarceration, or procurement of controlled substances (Ford and Feldman 1996).

Epidemiology.   Malingering occurs when illness brings tangible gains. It is common in prisons, courtrooms, military settings, and settings where disability evaluations are performed. This behavior adds considerably to the cost of insurance coverage (Gorman 1982).

Clinical features.   The following illustrates a case of malingering:

A 24-year-old man en route to a trial for auto theft complains of excruciating low back pain. Medical evaluation is equivocal for disc disease. During his evaluation in the hospital, he requests and is given a pass to visit a "dying aunt." That night he is observed dancing at a disco. The secondary gain for the individual was his avoidance of prosecution.

Malingering is likely if more than one of the following factors is present: medicolegal presentation, marked disparity between the patient's claimed disability and objective findings, lack of cooperation with psychiatric or medical evaluation and treatment, and antisocial personality disorder. Psychological testing is often helpful in identifying malingering patients. The Minnesota Multiphasic Personality Inventory—2 (MMPI-2) is a useful test for patients who distort their presentations.

Treatment and management. Malingering is a legal rather than a medical or psychiatric issue. With this fact in mind, the clinician must be circumspect in his or her approach to the patient. Every note should be written with the expectation that it will likely become a courtroom exhibit (Ford and Feldman 1996). The patient suspected of malingering usually is not confronted with a direct accusation. Instead, subtle communication indicates that the physician is "onto the game" (Kramer et al. 1979).

■ DIFFERENTIAL DIAGNOSIS

Other Somatoform and Related Disorders

Patients may have more than one somatoform or related disorder simultaneously. These disorders are distinguished from one another by the diagnostic criteria and clinical characteristics described earlier in this chapter.

Medical Disorder

The consultant's first task is to rule out a medical disorder. Consultants should not assume that the referring physician has eliminated this possibility. The patient's personality or inappropriate behavior may have decreased the primary physician's index of suspicion for medical diagnoses. In addition, these patients are often medically complex. Therefore, the psychiatrist must thoroughly review current and past charts (often a time-consuming task) and perform physical, neurological, and mental status examinations.

Secondary Psychiatric Disorders

Patients with dementia, delirium, or other cognitive disorders may present with increased physical complaints, particularly when anxious. For example, a 69-year-old woman presents to the emergency room with hyperventilation, shaking, crying, and obvious anxiety. She is given a diagnosis of an "anxiety neurosis" by the emergency room physician, and psychiatric consultation is requested. Her mental status examination shows significant cognitive impairment (i.e., a Mini-Mental State Exam score of 9 out of 30). Symptoms started acutely when she could not understand how to operate an answering machine at her husband's business. This is an example of a catastrophic reaction in a person with dementia.

Adjustment Disorder

If the symptom (e.g., fatigue, headache, backache) occurs acutely as a reaction to significant stress(es), it is often self-limited and can be diagnosed as an adjustment disorder (unspecified type). Identification of the stressor and its significance to the individual is the first and most important step to planning treatment. Short-term supportive, cognitive, focused insight-oriented, and group therapy are all potentially effective treatments.

Anxiety Disorders

A high correlation exists between anxiety, anxiety disorders, and the development of somatic symptoms (Simon and VonKorff 1991), sometimes called *secondary hypochondriasis*. Patients with an anxiety disorder, especially panic disorder, are hyperaware of body sensations and usually have increased sympathetic arousal. Those with panic disorder or generalized anxiety disorder have numerous somatic symptoms (see also Chapter 7).

Depressive Disorder

Depressed patients typically have numerous somatic symptoms, including neurovegetative signs of depression such as sleep disturbance, decreased energy, anorexia, decreased libido, and other associated physical complaints (e.g., headache, tinnitus, dizziness, fatigue). Anxiety is a common feature of depression. Hypochondriacal preoccupation during depressive episodes increases with age (Cassem and Barsky 1991).

Substance-Related Disorders

Alcohol abuse and dependence, alcohol withdrawal, and the medical sequelae of chronic alcohol use are seen commonly by psychiatrists in the general hospital. Patients who abuse other drugs also have physical symptoms associated with active use or withdrawal. These patients will commonly report physical symptoms (e.g., sleep disturbance, palpitations, gooseflesh, tremor, irritability, dysthymia, gastrointestinal complaints).

Psychotic Disorder

Patients who are actively psychotic are easily recognized because the somatic symptoms reported are usually bizarre. The psychiatric consultant plays an important role in such cases. The consultant must ensure that physical symptoms are not ignored simply because the patient has a chronic psychotic disorder. On the other hand, the consultant must discourage unnecessary pursuit of bizarre physical symptoms that are secondary to psychosis. For example, a patient reported a "terrible buzzing sound in my head." Examination by an otolaryngologist showed no abnormalities. On further questioning, the patient stated that the buzzing was a result of a CIA photon transmitter aimed at his head.

Delusional Disorder, Somatic Type

Delusional disorder, somatic type, is also called *monosymptomatic hypochondriasis* or *monosymptomatic hypochondriacal psychosis.* The three most common delusions are delusions of infestation (e.g., parasites, insects, worms, or foreign bodies on or under the skin), olfactory delusions (e.g., a foul odor from skin, mouth, rectum, or vagina), and dysmorphophobia (i.e., the belief that one's body is ugly or misshapen) (Munro and Chmara 1982). Pimozide (a neuroleptic) is the drug of choice for delusional disorder, somatic type. This medication should be begun at 2 mg in the morning and increased in 2-mg increments every 3 days. Doses rarely need to exceed 12 mg/day, and an 80% rate of improvement has been reported.

■ ADDITIONAL TREATMENT AND MANAGEMENT CONSIDERATIONS

Approach to the Patient

Specific management strategies for individual somatoform and related disorders are detailed in the specific discussions about those disorders earlier in this chapter. The key to the clinical management of the somatizing patient is to adopt "caring" rather than "curing" as a goal. "Management" is a much more realistic goal than "treatment." Abbey (1999) suggested the following fundamental principles of managing the somatoform disorders:

1. *Emphasize explanation.* In order to engage in treatment, patients require a sense that their primary physician and consultation-liaison psychiatrist are taking them seriously, appreciate the magnitude of their distress, and have a rationale for the proposed management plan.

2. *Arrange for regular follow-up.* Regular follow-up results in decreased health care use. The best choice for most patients is management by their primary care practitioner in consultation with a consultation-liaison psychiatrist.

3. *Treat mood or anxiety disorders.* Mood and anxiety disorders have significant morbidity in their own right and interfere with participation in rehabilitation and psychotherapy. These disorders may fuel the somatization process or heighten somatic amplification.

4. *Minimize polypharmacy.* Polypharmacy may cause iatrogenic complications. Taper and withdraw unnecessary medications. This process is often long and complicated, so it is important to take a staged approach with small, realistic, achievable steps.

5. *Provide specific therapy when indicated.* A variety of specific therapies are suggested for the somatoform disorders. They are discussed elsewhere in this chapter.

6. *Change social dynamics.* Many patients' lives revolve around their symptoms and the health care system. When possible, important members of the patient's social support system should be persuaded to consistently reward nonillness-related behaviors.

7. *Recognize and control negative reactions and countertransference.* Somatizing patients evoke powerful negative emotional responses in physicians. This usually results in less than optimal clinical care. The range of emotions experienced by physicians may include guilt for failing to help, fear that the patient will make a complaint (or sue), and anger at the patient.

Physical Reactivation and Physical Therapy

Physical reactivation via a gradually escalating program of exercise (e.g., walking, swimming) often improves the quality of life in patients with a variety of somatoform disorders (Abbey 1999). Although it is often difficult to engage patients with somatoform disorders in exercise, once they become more active, they often find it pleasurable and report feelings of accomplishment, reduced stress, and greater confidence in their body. Physical therapy is helpful for patients with conversion disorder and is sometimes the only treatment required.

Relaxation Therapies, Meditation, and Hypnotherapy

Various forms of relaxation therapies, biofeedback, meditation, and hypnotherapy are used in patients with somatoform disorder. Relaxation therapies aim to modulate somatic sensations and give patients a sense of self-empowerment.

Cognitive Therapy

Cognitive therapy is used in both individual and group formats for somatoform disorders. A cognitive model directs attention to factors maintaining preoccupation with worries about health, including attentional factors, avoidant behaviors, beliefs and misinterpretation of symptoms, signs, and medical communications (Salkovskis 1989). Cognitive therapy is a particularly valuable adjunct for pain disorders. It helps the patient identify and replace inappropriate negative beliefs or attributions with more appropriate ideas or coping strategies (Benjamin 1989). For chronic pain syndromes, cognitive therapy is reported to produce a greater reduction in pain complaints than do other forms of treatment (Benjamin 1989).

Group Psychotherapy

Group therapy is particularly useful in the management of somatoform patients. With the gratification of social and affiliative needs via the group, the need to somatize to establish or maintain relationships may be reduced (Ford 1984). Confrontation by fellow group members regarding primary or secondary gain is usually better tolerated than that from an individual's therapist (Abbey 1999). Anger at physicians and family and dependency needs are better tolerated in the group setting, which tends to diffuse intense affects. Group therapy is also useful in increasing interpersonal skills and in enhancing more direct forms of communication (Ford 1984).

■ REFERENCES

Abbey SE: Somatization and somatoform disorders, in Essentials of Consultation-Liaison Psychiatry. Edited by Rundell JR, Wise MG. Washington, DC, American Psychiatric Press, 1999, pp 165–187

American Psychiatric Association: Diagnostic and Statistical Manual of Mental Disorders, 3rd Edition. Washington, DC, American Psychiatric Association, 1980

American Psychiatric Association: Diagnostic and Statistical Manual of Mental Disorders, 3rd Edition, Revised. Washington, DC, American Psychiatric Association, 1987

American Psychiatric Association: Diagnostic and Statistical Manual of Mental Disorders, 4th Edition. Washington, DC, American Psychiatric Association, 1994

Barsky AJ, Wyshak G, Klerman GL: Medical and psychiatric determinants of outpatient medical utilization. Med Care 24: 548–560, 1986

Barsky AJ, Wyshade G, Klerman GL: Psychiatric comorbidity in DSM-III-R hypochondriasis. Arch Gen Psychiatry 49:101–108, 1992

Benjamin S: Psychological treatment of chronic pain: a selective review. J Psychosom Res 33:121–131, 1989

Brena SF, Chapman SL (eds): Management of Patients With Chronic Pain. New York, Spectrum, 1983

Brotman AW, Jenicke MA: Monosymptomatic hypochondriasis treated with tricyclic antidepressants. Am J Psychiatry 141: 1608–11609, 1984

Cassem NH, Barsky AJ: Functional somatic symptoms and somatoform disorders, in Massachusetts General Hospital Handbook of General Hospital Psychiatry, 3rd Edition. Edited by Cassem NH. Boston, MA, Mosby Year Book, 1991, pp 131–157

deGruy F, Columbia L, Dickinson P: Somatization disorder in a family practice. J Fam Pract 25:45–51, 1987

Eisenberg L: Disease and illness: distinctions between professional and popular ideas of sickness. Cult Med Psychiatry 1:9–23, 1977

Escobar JI, Manu P, Matthews D, et al: Medically unexplained physical symptoms, somatization disorder and abridged somatization: studies with the Diagnostic Interview Schedule. Psychiatric Developments 3:235–245, 1989

Fallon BA, Liebowitz MR, Salman E, et al: Fluoxetine for hypochondriacal patients without major depression. J Clin Psychopharmacol 13:438–441, 1993

Feldman MD, Ford CV: Patients or Pretenders?: The Strange World of Factitious Disorders. New York, Wiley, 1994

Ford CV: The Somatizing Disorders: Illness as a Way of Life. New York, Elsevier, 1983

Ford CV: Somatizing disorders, in Helping Patients and Their Families Cope With Medical Problems. Edited by Roback HB. Washington, DC, Jossey-Bass, 1984, pp 39–59

Ford CV, Feldman MD: Factitious disorders and malingering, in The American Psychiatric Press Textbook of Consultation-Liaison Psychiatry. Edited by Rundell JR, Wise MG. Washington, DC, American Psychiatric Press, 1996, pp 532–544

Ford CV, Folks DG: Conversion disorders: an overview. Psychosomatics 26:371–383, 1985

Gault MH, Campbell NR, Aksu AE: Spurious stones. Nephron 48:274–279, 1988

Golding JM, Rost K, Kashner TM, et al: Family psychiatric history of patients with somatization disorder. Psychiatr Med 10:33–47, 1992

Gorman WF: Defining malingering. J Forensic Sci 27:401–407, 1982

Hollander E, Liebowitz MR, Winchel R, et al: Treatment of body dysmorphic disorder with serotonin reuptake blockers. Am J Psychiatry 146:768–770, 1989

Hollander E, Neville D, Frenkel M, et al: Body dysmorphic disorder: diagnostic issues and related disorders. Psychosomatics 33:156–165, 1992

Hollender MH, Hersh SP: Impossible consultation made possible. Arch Gen Psychiatry 23:343–345, 1970

Jenike MA: A case report of successful treatment of dysmorphophobia with tranylcypromine. Am J Psychiatry 141: 1463–1464, 1984

Katon W, Lin E, Von Korff M, et al: Somatization: a spectrum of severity. Am J Psychiatry 148:34–40, 1991

Kellner R: Functional somatic symptoms and hypochondriasis. Arch Gen Psychiatry 42:821–833, 1985

Kirmayer LJ, Robbins JM: Three forms of somatization in primary care: prevalence, co-occurrence, and sociodemographic characteristics. J Nerv Ment Dis 179:647–655, 1991

Kramer KK, LaPiana FG, Appleton B: Ocular malingering and hysteria: diagnosis and management. Surv Ophthalmol 24: 89–96, 1979

Lazare A: Current concepts in psychiatry: conversion symptoms. N Engl J Med 305:745– 748, 1981

Lipowski ZJ: Somatization: the concept and its clinical application. Am J Psychiatry 145:1358–1368, 1988

Mechanic D: The concept of illness behaviour: culture, situation and personal predisposition. Psychol Med 16:1–7, 1986

Munro A, Chmara J: Monosymptomanic hypochondriacal psychosis: a diagnostic checklist based on 50 cases of the disorder. Can J Psychiatry 27:374–376, 1982

Murphy MR: Classification of the somatoform disorders, in Somatization: Physical Symptoms and Psychological Illness. Edited by Bass C. Oxford, England, Blackwell Scientific, 1990, pp 10–39

Noyes R, Holt CS, Happel RL, et al: A family study of hypochondriasis. J Nerv Ment Dis 185:223–232, 1997

Phillips KA, McElroy SL, Keck PE, et al: Body dysmorphic disorder: 30 cases of imagined ugliness. Am J Psychiatry 150: 302–308, 1993

Pilowsky I: Abnormal illness behavior. Psychiatr Med 5:85–91, 1987

Regier DA, Boyd JH, Burke JD, et al: One-month prevalence of mental disorders in the United States based on five Epidemiologic Catchment Area sites. Arch Gen Psychiatry 45: 977–986, 1988

Rost KM, Akins RN, Brown FW, et al: The comorbidity of DSM-III-R personality disorders in somatization disorder. Gen Hosp Psychiatry 14:322–326, 1992

Salkovskis PM: Somatic problems, in Cognitive Behaviour Therapy for Psychiatric Problems. Edited by Hawton K, Salkovskis PM, Kirk J, et al. Oxford, England, Oxford University Press, 1989, pp 235–276

Simon GE, VonKorff M: Somatization and psychiatric disorder in the NIMH Epidemiologic Catchment Area study. Am J Psychiatry 148:1494–1500, 1991

Smith GR: Somatization Disorder in Medical Settings. Washington, DC, American Psychiatric Press, 1991

Smith GR, Monson RA, Ray DC: Psychiatric consultation in somatization disorder: a randomized controlled study. N Engl J Med 314:1407–1413, 1986

Toone BK: Disorders of hysterical conversion, in Somatization: Physical Symptoms and Psychological Illness. Edited by Bass C. Oxford, England, Blackwell Scientific, 1990, pp 207–234

Wise MG, Ford CV: Factitious disorders. Primary Care 26:315–326, 1999

Zimmerman M, Mattia JI: Body dysmorphic disorder in psychiatric outpatients: recognition, prevalence, comorbidity, demographics, and clinical correlates. Comprehensive Psychiatry 39:265–270, 1998

■ ADDITIONAL READINGS

Cloninger CR, Martin RL, Guze SB, et al: A prospective follow-up and family study of somatization in men and women. Am J Psychiatry 143:873–878, 1986

Derogatis LR, Lipman RS, Rickels K, et al: The Hopkins Symptom Check List (HSCL): a self-report symptom inventory. Behav Sci 19:1–15, 1974

Eisendrath SJ: Factitious physical disorders: treatment without confrontation. Psychosomatics 30:383–387, 1989

Ewald H, Rogne T, Ewald K, et al: Somatization in patients newly admitted to a neurological department. Acta Psychiatr Scand 89:174–179, 1994

Folks DG, Houck CA: Somatoform disorders, factitious disorders, and malingering, in Psychiatric Care of the Medical Patient. Edited by Stoudemire A, Fogel BS. New York, Oxford University Press, 1993, pp 267–287

Goldberg D, Gask L, O'Dowd T: The treatment of somatization: teaching techniques of reattribution. J Psychosom Res 33: 689–695, 1989

Hahn SR, Thompson KS, Wills TA, et al: The difficult doctor-patient relationship: somatization, personality and psychopathology. J Clin Epidemiol 47:647–657, 1994

Lipowski ZJ: Somatization and depression. Psychosomatics 31: 13–21, 1990

9

SUBSTANCE-RELATED DISORDERS

Between 25% and 50% of general hospital patients have current alcohol abuse or dependence (Curtis et al. 1989; Gerke et al. 1997). Unfortunately, clinicians underrecognize substance-related disorders. Although psychiatrists positively identify alcohol abuse two-thirds of the time, other physicians recognize and diagnose the disorder only 10% of the time (Moore et al. 1989). Only 22% of people who develop substance use disorders ever receive any addiction treatment during their lifetime; of these, about half receive treatment from specialty mental health/addiction professionals, and the other half receive treatment from general medical providers (Regier et al. 1993).

Consultation-liaison psychiatrists are in unique positions to identify and intervene in medically ill patients with substance-related disorders. There is a window of opportunity in patients while they are sick; they are often more open to treatment recommendations. Effective treatment or referral of patients who abuse substances requires close collaboration between the consultant and the referring physician. Both must communicate to the patient the medical, psychological, and social consequences of continued alcohol or drug use.

■ DSM-IV SUBSTANCE-RELATED DISORDERS

Substance-related disorders are divided into *substance use disorders* and *substance-induced disorders*. Substance use disorders include alcohol and drug abuse and dependence. Substance-induced disorders include intoxication, withdrawal, delirium, dementia, amnestic, psychotic, mood, sexual dysfunction, anxiety, and sleep disorders. Table 9–1 summarizes DSM-IV criteria for substance abuse and dependence (American Psychiatric Association 1994).

TABLE 9–1.   **DSM-IV substance abuse and dependence**

Substance abuse

At least one of the following at any time during a 12-month period:

1. Recurrent substance use resulting in a failure to fulfill major role obligations at work, school, or home.
2. Recurrent substance use in situations in which it is physically hazardous.
3. Recurrent substance-related legal problems.
4. Continued substance use despite having persistent or recurrent social or interpersonal problems.

Substance dependence

At least three of the following at any time during a 12-month period:

1. Marked tolerance (at least 50% increase needed).
2. Characteristic withdrawal symptoms or substance taken to avoid withdrawal problems.
3. Substance often taken longer or in larger amounts than the person intended.
4. Persistent desire or unsuccessful efforts to cut down or control use.
5. Large amount of time spent obtaining, using, or recovering from the substance.
6. Impaired social, recreational, or occupational functioning.
7. Persistent use despite knowledge of medical, psychological, or social problems.

Source.   Adapted from American Psychiatric Association: *Diagnostic and Statistical Manual of Mental Disorders,* 4th Edition. Washington, DC, American Psychiatric Association, 1994. Copyright 1994, American Psychiatric Association. Used with permission.

■ ALCOHOL-RELATED DISORDERS

Introduction

Alcohol is the most frequently abused substance. Sixty-seven percent of Americans drink, and 14% of men and 4% of women are heavy drinkers (Liskow and Goodwin 1986). Lifetime prevalence for alcohol dependence or abuse is 19.1%–28.9% for men and 4.2%–4.8% for women (Craig 1986). Alcohol-related problems usually begin between ages 16 and 30. Alcoholism runs in families. Children of alcoholic parents have alcoholism four to five times more often than children of nonalcoholic parents (Goodwin 1985). That this ratio holds even if the children are adopted away is evidence that the familial association is largely hereditary.

Classification, Diagnosis, and Management

Alcohol Abuse and Dependence

Several brief diagnostic screens are available to assist with diagnosis of alcohol abuse and dependence (Soderstrom 1997). One of these diagnostic aids, the CAGE screen, is particularly useful and is summarized in Table 9–2 (Ewing 1984). The clinician should also look for chronic anxiety or dysphoria, job loss, financial problems, legal problems, and absenteeism.

Several laboratory tests are highly suggestive, although not diagnostic, of alcohol abuse (e.g., uric acid, aspartate aminotransferase [AST] or serum glutamic-oxaloacetic transaminase [SGOT], red blood cell [RBC] count, mean corpuscular volume [MCV], and γ-glutamyl transpeptidase [GGTP]). Because alcohol abuse progressively damages many different organs, many laboratory test results become abnormal. A very high blood alcohol level (>200 mg/dL) found on routine clinical examination in a nonintoxicated patient is pathognomonic.

TABLE 9–2.   **CAGE screen for diagnosis of alcoholism**

---

2 or 3 = high index of suspicion   4 = pathognomonic

Have you ever:

C thought you should **CUT** back?

A felt **ANNOYED** by people criticizing your drinking?

G felt **GUILTY** or bad about your drinking?

E had a morning **EYE-OPENER** to relieve hangover or nerves?

Reprinted from Ewing J: "Detecting Alcoholism—The CAGE Questionnaire." *Journal of the American Medical Association* 25:1905–1907, 1984. Copyright 1984, American Medical Association. Used with permission.

Medical complications of chronic alcohol abuse include dementia, anemia, pancreatitis, cirrhosis, gastritis, insomnia, impotence, peripheral neuropathy, myopathy, cardiomyopathy, and Wernicke-Korsakoff syndrome. Physical examination may find bruises, rib tenderness due to old or new fractures, spider angiomata, abdominal tenderness, muscle wasting, peripheral neuropathy, abducens nerve deficit, nystagmus, ataxia, and hypertension. Head imaging may reveal cerebral atrophy and/or subdural hematomas.

Management.   It is foolish to recommend drinking in moderation to a medically ill alcoholic patient. After the patient is medically stabilized, the clinician should encourage the patient and family to become involved in community resources, especially Alcoholics Anonymous. Seventy percent of patients who seriously commit to AA improve. Inpatient alcohol rehabilitation, day programs, or intensive outpatient alcohol rehabilitation also should be considered. In patients who have regular follow-up, a history of abstinence that culminates with impulsive drinking, and no hepatic impairment, the clinician should consider disulfiram. Also remember and instruct the patient on disulfiram that many over-the-counter and pharmacological agents contain alcohol.

Alcohol Intoxication

Alcohol activates γ-aminobutyric acid (GABA) chloride ion channels, inhibits *N*-methyl-D-aspartate (NMDA)–activated ion channels, and potentiates serotonin type 3 receptor (5-HT3)– activated ion channels (Franklin and Frances 1999). The body metabolizes alcohol at a rate of 100 mg/kg/hour. It takes approximately 1.5 hours to metabolize one shot of whiskey. Unless the person is alcohol-tolerant, blood levels of 30–50 mg/dL will cause mild euphoria; at 100 mg/dL, significant ataxia is present. Disorientation and stupor can occur at 200 mg/dL, and coma and death may occur at 400 mg/dL. Table 9–3 summarizes the salient features of alcohol intoxication and its management.

Management.　The behavior associated with intoxication is managed by decreasing external stimuli, interrupting alcohol ingestion, and protecting individuals from harming themselves or others until the toxic effects of alcohol disappear. Unless medically contraindicated, food and/or coffee should be offered. The clinician should obtain a blood alcohol level and a toxic screen to look for other drug use. If the patient is severely agitated, see pharmacological treatments listed in Table 9–3.

Alcohol Overdose

Unfortunately, the lethal level of alcohol does not increase as tolerance develops (Mebane 1987). The LD_{50} of alcohol (a lethal dose in 50% of patients) is 500 mg/dL. Signs of life-threatening alcohol overdose are nonresponsiveness, slow and shallow breathing, and cardiac dysrhythmia.

Management.　The clinician should immediately intubate the patient if he or she has respiratory compromise, hydrate the patient, monitor the patient's cardiac status, and provide other indicated emergency supportive measures. Hemodialysis is an option in potentially life-threatening alcohol overdoses.

TABLE 9-3. Substance intoxication and its management

Substance	Signs and symptoms	Management
Alcohol	Alcohol smell, disinhibition, mood lability, impaired judgment, ataxia, dysarthria, nystagmus	If severely agitated, have security present, prevent more ingestion, provide a quiet room, reduce stimuli, offer food and/or coffee, use restraints if needed, sedate with lorazepam (1–2 mg iv/im every hour prm) or haloperidol (1–5 mg iv every half-hour until calm). Administer thiamine (100 mg/day im for 5 days) and folate (1 mg po four times a day).
Sedatives, hypnotics, anxiolytics	Disinhibition, mood lability, dysarthria, ataxia, hyporeflexia, nystagmus	Observe for respiratory depression. Move to ICU if patient becomes stuporous, hypoxic, or unresponsive. If agitated, give haloperidol (1–5 mg iv/im) or lorazepam (1–2 mg iv/im) if there is no respiratory depression.
Opiates	Apathy, dysphoria or euphoria, drowsiness, dysarthria, pinpoint pupils. If severe, respiratory depression. Nystagmus is rare.	Observe for respiratory depression. Give naloxone (0.4 mg iv every 3–5 minutes) until symptoms clear; may have to repeat frequently.
Amphetamines/ Cocaine	Euphoria, heightened self-esteem, grandiosity, suspiciousness, perspiration, hypervigilance, paranoia, delusions, miosis, hypertension, tachycardia, nausea, anxiety, psychomotor agitation	Obtain ECG and watch for dysrhythmias. Try to "talk the patient down." Watch for violent and suicidal behavior. Give lorazepam (1–3 mg hourly iv/im) to manage agitation and haloperidol (1–5 mg iv/po) for psychotic symptoms.

Note. iv = intravenously; im = intramuscularly; prm = as needed; po = orally; ICU = intensive care unit; ECG = electrocardiogram.

Alcoholic-Induced Psychotic Disorder

Diagnosis of alcoholic-induced psychotic disorder is based on a history of recent heavy alcohol use and the absence of schizophrenia or mania. Auditory hallucinations are more prominent than other withdrawal symptoms, last at least 1 week, and occur while the patient has a clear sensorium.

Management. When patients develop alcoholic-induced psychotic disorder during detoxification, a potent antipsychotic such as haldoperidol, 2–5 mg orally twice a day, is typically needed to control agitation and hallucinations. After symptoms cease, neuroleptics should be discontinued.

Uncomplicated Alcohol Withdrawal

Within 6–48 hours after cessation of or reduction in prolonged alcohol use, withdrawal symptoms often appear (i.e., coarse tremor, nausea, weakness, autonomic hyperactivity, anxiety, irritability, mild transient illusions or hallucinations, insomnia, numbness, and/or paresthesias) (Table 9–4). The tremors typically peak 24–48 hours after the last drink and subside after 5–7 days of abstinence. Vital signs should be monitored during the abstinence syndrome, which is prevented by treatment with benzodiazepines.

Management. The choice of an inpatient versus outpatient setting to manage withdrawal depends on the severity of symptoms, stage of withdrawal, medical and psychiatric complications, presence of polysubstance abuse, patient cooperation, ability to follow instructions, social support systems, patient history, and, increasingly, insurance or managed care reimbursement policies. For outpatient alcohol withdrawal (Franklin and Frances 1999), 25–50 mg of chlordiazepoxide is prescribed orally four times a day on the first day, followed by a 20% decrease in dose every day over a 5-day period. Thiamine, 100 mg/day, should be given orally for 5 days. A standard inpatient detoxification regimen is chlordiazepoxide, 25–100 mg orally four times a day, and an additional 25–50 mg every 2 hours, as needed. The total amount given over the first 24 hours is given each day and tapered over 5–7

TABLE 9–4. **Substance withdrawal syndromes and their management**

Substance	Signs and symptoms	Management
Alcohol	Coarse tremor, nausea, autonomic hyperactivity, anxiety, irritability, insomnia. *DTs:* disorientation, agitation, visual/tactile hallucinations, fever, dilated pupils, further autonomic hyperactivity	Monitor vital signs. Give thiamine (100 mg/day im for 5 days) and folic acid (1 mg four times a day). Watch for fluid/electrolyte imbalances. Give chlordiazepoxide (25–100 mg qid) or oxazepam (15–45 mg every 4–6 hours); taper over 5–7 days. For psychotic symptoms, use haloperidol po/im/iv. Watch for seizures.
Sedatives, hypnotics, anxiolytics	Nausea, tremor, hyperreflexia, hyperphagia, tachycardia, dilated pupils, diaphoresis, irritability, insomnia, restlessness, anxiety. Seizures and delirium can occur in severe cases. Can be life-threatening.	Taper agent 10% daily. If agent is short-acting (i.e., lorazepam, alprazolam), use longer-acting agent such as clonazepam.
Opiates	Rarely life-threatening but uncomfortable: dilated pupils, piloerection, rhinorrhea, fever, yawning, hypertension, tachycardia, cramps, craving, irritability, insomnia	Methadone in dose equivalent to that of opiate patient is taking. Taper by 20% daily; slower taper in medically ill patients (10%/day) and over the last 10–20 mg.
Amphetamines/ Cocaine	Depression, irritability, fatigue, anxiety, insomnia or hypersomnia, craving, psychomotor agitation	Watch for suicidal and drug-seeking behavior. Give desipramine in antidepressant doses for depression and lorazepam (1–2 mg every 2–5 hours po/im/iv) for severe anxiety/agitation.

days; the 24-hour dose is equally divided during the day. Diazepam is recommended in patients with cross-addiction to other depressants or with a history of seizures. Thiamine, 100 mg/day, should be given intramuscularly for 5 days. Fluid and electrolyte imbalances, hypoglycemia, fever, and hypomagnesemia must be monitored and treated.

Alcohol Withdrawal Seizures

Withdrawal seizures typically occur 7–38 hours after last alcohol use, with peak frequency at about 24 hours (Adams and Victor 1981). Hypomagnesemia, respiratory alkalosis, hypoglycemia, increased intracellular sodium, and upregulation of NMDA receptors all potentially contribute to alcohol withdrawal seizures. One-third of patients who have withdrawal seizures go on to develop alcohol withdrawal delirium (delirium tremens [DTs]).

Management. Benzodiazepines are the treatment of choice for alcohol withdrawal seizures, but intramuscular administration should be avoided because of variable absorption (lorazepam is an exception). Diazepam, 2–10 mg intravenously, is a good choice if immediate seizure control is needed. For underlying seizure disorders, phenytoin maintenance is necessary. The most effective way to prevent alcohol withdrawal seizures is to detoxify the patient adequately with appropriate doses of benzodiazepines.

Alcohol Withdrawal Delirium (Delirium Tremens)

DTs begin 2–7 days after cessation of drinking. The risk for DTs is highest when the patient has a long history (>10 years) of heavy drinking and a major medical illness, especially liver disease, infection, trauma, poor nutrition, and metabolic disorders (Frances and Franklin 1987). Clinical signs and symptoms of DTs are disorientation, agitation, visual or tactile hallucinations, autonomic hyperactivity, tremor, ataxia, fever, and dilated pupils. Alcohol withdrawal delirium is life-threatening. Up to 40% of patients die if untreated (Miller 1991). Fortunately, mortality in hospitalized patients is less than 5% (Yost 1996). When patients die during DTs, the cause of death is usually heart failure, infection, or traumatic injury.

Management. The management of alcohol withdrawal delirium is the same as that for uncomplicated alcohol withdrawal, except more medications are required. The clinician should administer thiamine, reverse fluid and electrolyte imbalances, and correct hypoglycemia, if present. The addition of high-potency neuroleptics, such as haloperidol, is sometimes necessary if benzodiazepines do not adequately control confusion, delusions, hallucinations, or agitation.

Alcohol-Induced Persisting Amnestic Disorder (Wernicke-Korsakoff Syndrome)

Alcohol-induced persisting amnestic disorder (Wernicke-Korsakoff syndrome) begins with an abrupt onset of truncal ataxia, ophthalmoplegia (usually third nerve palsy), and delirium (Wernicke's encephalopathy). Ataxia may precede the mental status change. The clinician should not wait for all three signs; the presence of two suggests the disorder (Brew 1986). The etiology of the disorder is thiamine deficiency. Long-term and short-term memory impairment (Korsakoff's syndrome) usually develops if Wernicke's encephalopathy is unrecognized and goes untreated. The symptoms and signs are caused by lesions in the medial dorsal nucleus of the thalamus, the hippocampus, and the mamillary bodies. In Korsakoff's syndrome, memory losses are profound, but other cognitive functions are relatively spared.

Management. Give thiamine, 100 mg/day intramuscularly for at least 7 days, to treat alcohol-induced persisting amnestic disorder. Ocular findings improve first, followed by motor improvement, and, finally, resolution of mental status abnormalities. Many patients are left with residual ataxia or confusion. Up to three-fourths of patients with Korsakoff's syndrome will show some improvement if they are given intramuscular thiamine and remain sober (Victor et al. 1971).

■ SEDATIVE-, HYPNOTIC-, OR ANXIOLYTIC-RELATED DISORDERS

Introduction

All sedative-hypnotics and benzodiazepines induce tolerance to some degree. Unfortunately, even though the dose necessary for intoxication increases, the lethal dose does not. Whereas the opiate-dependent patient may double the dose and still not experience respiratory depression, barbiturate-addicted patients can develop potentially fatal respiratory depression with a dose only 20%–25% higher than the usual daily dose. Benzodiazepines have a much higher LD_{50} than barbiturates.

Classification, Diagnosis, and Management

Sedative, Hypnotic, or Anxiolytic Abuse and Dependence

Barbiturate and benzodiazepine abuse and dependence may develop secondary to street abuse or medical use. Table 9–1 summarizes DSM-IV criteria for abuse and dependence diagnoses. An effective diagnostic aid is a "positive shopping bag sign"; the clinician asks the patient's family to bring in all the patient's medications. Benzodiazepines are frequently present in the bag.

Management. Although sedative-hypnotic dependence in medical patients caused by polypharmacy or the involvement of multiple physicians is uncommon, simplification of medication regimens may be all that is required. If the patient has a positive "shopping bag sign," his or her medication needs should be reassessed and unnecessary medications thrown away. After medically supervised tapering and "dryout," any concurrent psychiatric disorders should be treated. The clinician should watch for drug-seeking behavior among patients and on the patient's behalf by friends and family members.

Sedative, Hypnotic, or Anxiolytic Intoxication

The most common features of intoxication are disinhibition, mood lability, dysarthria, ataxia, hyporeflexia, nystagmus, and impaired attention (Table 9–3). The symptoms and signs are similar to those of alcohol intoxication. Accidental, iatrogenic, or suicidal overdose may cause respiratory depression. There is cross-reactivity between alcohol, benzodiazepines, and sedative-hypnotics.

Management. Because barbiturate withdrawal is life-threatening, close observation of anyone with barbiturate intoxication is necessary. Move the patient to the intensive care unit if stupor, hypoxia, or unresponsiveness occurs. When agitation threatens medical status, give low doses of lorazepam (1–2 mg) intravenously or intramuscularly, and observe the patient for respiratory compromise. An alternative is haloperidol, 1–5 mg orally intramuscularly or intravenously. In life-threatening overdose situations, the clinician should consider hemodialysis. Benzodiazepine antagonists, such as flumazenil, can reverse coma in some individuals with hepatic coma or benzodiazepine overdose.

Sedative, Hypnotic, or Anxiolytic Withdrawal

The features of sedative, hypnotic, or anxiolytic withdrawal are similar to those of alcohol withdrawal; the time of onset and duration of sedative-hypnotic withdrawal vary with the half-life of the drugs (see Chapter 7). The most common withdrawal features are hyperreflexia, nausea, tremulousness, tachycardia, dilated pupils, diaphoresis, irritability, insomnia, restlessness, and anxiety (Table 9–4). Seizures and delirium occur in severe cases. As in alcohol withdrawal, sedative-hypnotic withdrawal is potentially life-threatening. Withdrawal is sometimes missed in hospitalized patients because of a low index of suspicion or because symptoms can occur 7–10 days after admission. Changes in mental status in a hospitalized elderly patient taking many medications should alert the clinician to the possibility of sedative-hypnotic withdrawal, especially if accompanied by fever, autonomic hyperactivity, seizures, insomnia, or tremor.

Management.   Because of potential medical complications during detoxification, especially among high-dose abusers, inpatient treatment is preferred (Franklin and Frances 1999). The clinician can construct a withdrawal regimen with the same medication the patient is taking. If, however, the drug's half-life is too short to permit comfortable tapering, as is sometimes the case with lorazepam or alprazolam, use longer-acting agents.

Sedative, Hypnotic, or Anxiolytic Amnestic Disorder

Long-term and short-term memory impairment may occur after prolonged and heavy use of a sedative-hypnotic agent. The clinical findings are equivalent to those of Korsakoff's syndrome.

Management.   The sedative, hypnotic, or anxiolytic amnestic disorder usually gradually reverses. The clinician should attend to nutritional needs.

■ OPIATE (NARCOTIC)-RELATED DISORDERS

Introduction

Narcotics are used to relieve pain, cough, diarrhea, agitation, and severe anxiety in the intensive care unit. Unfortunately, tolerance begins within days, so narcotics' potential effectiveness in long-term treatment is limited. Psychiatrists are frequently consulted to examine patients in pain who do not respond to an "adequate" narcotic regimen or to evaluate a patient's "overuse" of narcotics. In the course of such consultations, underuse rather than abuse of narcotic analgesics is often found.

It is sometimes difficult to determine whether a patient has crossed the line between "appropriate" and "excessive" use of narcotics. At least 19% of patients who have chronic pain syndromes use opiates chronically, and 27% of those have symptoms that meet three or more of DSM-III-R (American Psychiatric Association 1987) criteria for abuse (Chabal et al. 1997). A careful examination includes psychiatric history, family psychiatric history, personality style, pattern of medical resources use, and physical and laboratory examination. More than 90% of opiate-addicted patients have at least one other diagnosable psychiatric disorder, most commonly, depression, alcoholism, or antisocial personality disorder (Khantzian and Treece 1985). Mebane (1988) described a number of warning signs for potential opiate/narcotic abuse (Table 9–5).

Psychiatric effects such as euphoria, paranoia, psychomotor agitation, and sedation can occur because of occupation of an opiate receptor site. There are several subtypes of opioid receptors (i.e., mu, delta, kappa, lambda, iota, and epsilon). Opiates that occupy different receptor types have little cross-tolerance. The mu receptor mediates analgesia, euphoria, sedation, meiosis, and respiratory depression (Kosten et al. 1990) and has selective affinity for heroin, meperidine, hydromorphone, and methadone. The mu receptor is also sensitive to the opioid antagonist naloxone. Neuroadaptive changes at receptor sites are hypothesized to produce dependence and tolerance, especially tolerance to respiratory depression (Franklin and Frances 1999). Once neuroadaptation occurs, removal of the opioid from receptors produces withdrawal symptoms.

Classification, Diagnosis, and Management

Opiate Abuse and Dependence

Tables 9–1, 9–3, and 9–4 detail DSM-IV requirements for a diagnosis of opiate abuse and dependence as well as signs of clinical toxicity and withdrawal to watch for.

Management.   After medical stabilization and drug detoxification, the patient should be referred for treatment. Both inpatient and outpatient treatment programs are available. In general, success and retention rates of methadone programs exceed those of programs that require abstinence.

Opiate Intoxication

Cardinal features of opiate intoxication include apathy, dysphoria or euphoria, psychomotor retardation, drowsiness, dysarthria, im-

TABLE 9–5. **Clinical cues that warn of possible narcotic abuse or dependence in general medical patients**

History	Exaggerated pain complaints in relation to physical findings
	Drug-seeking behavior
	Multiple medical visits for pain complaints requiring a narcotic prescription
	"Allergic" to every analgesic except meperidine
Physical examination	Pupillary constriction
	Withdrawal signs: hyperthermia, hypertension, tachycardia, diaphoresis, nausea
	Hyperpigmentation over veins or tourniquet areas, tattoos, abscesses
	Jaundice
Laboratory	Positive toxic screen
	Increased transaminases
	Decreased globulins
Hospital course	Demanding, unruly, or agitated
	Threatens to leave against medical advice
	Delirium accompanying other withdrawal signs or symptoms

Source. Adapted from Mebane AH: "Drug Abuse Issues in Critically Ill Patients," in *Problems in Critical Care.* Edited by Wise MG. Philadelphia, PA, JB Lippincott, 1988, pp. 63–85. Used with permission.

paired attention, and pinpoint pupils; with more severe toxic states, respiratory depression, stupor, or coma can occur (Table 9–3). Pupils are pinpoint unless respiratory depression or meperidine caused dilation. Suspect an opiate overdose in any patient who presents in a coma, especially when associated with respiratory depression, pupillary constriction, and/or the presence of needle marks.

Management. Observe patients for respiratory depression, pulmonary edema, and seizures. In a comatose patient suspected of opiate overdose, naloxone, 0.4 mg, should be given immediately and repeated every 3–5 minutes until symptoms clear significantly. Naloxone is administered repeatedly because of its short duration of action relative to the opiate.

Opiate Withdrawal

Narcotic or opiate withdrawal is uncomfortable but not life-threatening; opiate overdose, alcohol withdrawal, barbiturate overdose, and barbiturate withdrawal are potentially life-threatening. The course and presentation of symptoms for opiate withdrawal vary with the half-life of the agent and hepatic status. Classic features include pupillary dilation, yawning, piloerection, rhinorrhea, nausea, fever, hypertension, tachycardia, cramps, drug craving, insomnia, restlessness, irritability, and seizures (Table 9–4). Untreated symptoms can last 2–3 weeks.

Management.   Methadone is an excellent treatment of withdrawal because of its long half-life. In opioid-dependent patients hospitalized on a general medical unit, methadone is started at 30–40 mg/day in divided doses (Franklin and Frances 1999). Based on signs of withdrawal, 5 mg may be added twice a day. The amount given the first day is divided into two doses on the second day, then tapered by 10%–20% per day. Methadone in medically ill patients is tapered more slowly. Observe patients closely for oversedation or undertreatment. An average daily maintenance dose is 60–80 mg; 80–120 mg is occasionally needed. Because of meperidine's short duration of action, methadone is sometimes too difficult to use for detoxification—slow tapering of meperidine itself is often necessary.

■ AMPHETAMINE-RELATED DISORDERS

Introduction

Amphetamines block the reuptake of dopamine, serotonin, and norepinephrine and profoundly affect dopamine storage release. Amphetamines are especially abused by night workers, students, dieters, persons who work long hours, and persons who are chronically dysphoric. Legitimate medical uses of amphetamines include treatment of depression, attention-deficit/hyperactivity disorder, and narcolepsy; doses range from 5 to 25 mg/day. On the street, daily doses reach 100 mg or more. Higher doses can cause psychosis or delirium. Repeated use leads to postintoxication depression, which can perpetuate further abuse (Mebane 1988).

Classification, Diagnosis, and Management

Amphetamine Abuse and Dependence

Table 9–1 summarizes DSM-IV criteria for substance abuse and dependence. The clinician should obtain a toxic screen because polydrug abuse is common. Poor nutrition may lead to anemia.

Management. The patient must discontinue amphetamine use. If postamphetamine depression occurs, consider antidepressants and psychiatric hospitalization. Individuals who abuse amphetamines daily or intravenously require inpatient hospitalization to treat violence, psychosis, and depression as well as suicidal ideation during withdrawal.

Amphetamine Intoxication

Symptoms and signs of mild amphetamine intoxication include euphoria, heightened self-esteem, grandiosity, suspiciousness, miosis, tachycardia, nausea, perspiration, hypertension, and anxiety (Table 9–3). More severe intoxication leads to hypervigilance, paranoia, psychomotor agitation, delirium, arrhythmias, and convulsions.

Management. Amphetamine-intoxicated patients should be "talked down." The clinician should watch for hypertension, hyperpyrexia, seizures, violence, and suicidal ideation. A urine toxic screen is necessary to check for concurrent drug use. Benzodiazepines, such as lorazepam (1–3 mg hourly), should be used to treat severe anxiety or agitation and to help prevent seizures in patients with a seizure history. In an amphetamine overdose, the urine should be acidified with vitamin C to speed elimination. Treat paranoid or delusional symptoms with antipsychotic medications, such as haloperidol.

Amphetamine Delirium

An agitated confusional state may develop within 24 hours of amphetamine use. Hallucinations, delusions, and signs of autonomic hyperactivity are frequently present.

Management. Administer haloperidol, 2–10 mg every half-hour, as needed for agitation and psychosis. Watch for violence and hyperpyrexia, obtain a toxic screen to rule out other drug use, and acidify the urine to enhance excretion.

Amphetamine Delusional Disorder

Amphetamines can induce paranoia that can last several days in a patient with a clear sensorium. Amphetamine psychosis resembles acute paranoid schizophrenia.

Management. Haloperidol, 2–10 mg every half-hour, should be administered. The clinician should obtain a toxic screen to rule out other drug use and acidify the urine to enhance excretion.

Amphetamine "Withdrawal"

Although amphetamines are abruptly discontinued, several treatable postintoxication findings can occur, including depression, especially if the patient is at risk for depression already; irritability; anxiety; fatigue; insomnia or hypersomnia; psychomotor agitation; and hyperphagia (Table 9–4).

Management. The drug should not be restarted; postintoxication symptoms are usually self-limited or treatable. Use benzodiazepines (lorazepam or diazepam) as needed for severe anxiety or agitation. Neuroleptics are occasionally required if agitation is accompanied by psychosis or delirium. Observe the patient carefully for postwithdrawal depression. If depression appears, the patient may need antidepressant medications or a transfer to the psychiatry unit.

■ COCAINE-RELATED DISORDERS

Introduction

Cocaine blocks the reuptake of neuronal dopamine, serotonin, and norepinephrine. Cocaine has a fairly specific activating effect on mesocortical and mesolimbic dopaminergic pathways (Franklin and Frances 1999). Dopamine is an important neurotransmitter in limbic pleasure centers, including those related to food and sex. A patient's inability to control cocaine intake is probably related to the highly rewarding properties of the drug. With repeated cocaine use, tolerance develops secondary to decreased reuptake inhibition and altered receptor sensitivity. Cocaine also causes cortical kindling (Stripling and Russel 1984). *Kindling* is the process by which brief bursts of central nervous system stimulation at regular intervals and constant intensity result in lasting changes in brain excitability. Limbic areas of the brain are uniquely sensitive to kindling and its neuropsychiatric consequences.

Classification, Diagnosis, and Management

Cocaine Abuse and Dependence

Table 9–1 includes DSM-IV diagnostic criteria for abuse and dependence. The chronic cocaine user may have severe financial problems because of the large amounts of the drug needed (often several times hourly) to stave off the cocaine "crash."

   Management.   When a patient who abuses cocaine is admitted to the hospital, the staff should watch for drug-seeking behavior, depression, suicidal behavior, and insomnia. A toxic screen can help make the diagnosis and rule out potential contributions by other drugs of abuse. Periodic toxic screens are often needed.

After the patient is medically stabilized, he or she should be referred for treatment. Inpatient drug rehabilitation is indicated when outpatient treatment has failed, when the patient is unmotivated, when concurrent psychiatric illness is present, or when a complicating psychosocial situation exists.

Cocaine Intoxication

Features of cocaine intoxication vary but may include euphoria, grandiosity, hypervigilance, increased libido, psychomotor agitation, tachycardia, miosis, hypertension, perspiration, nausea, delirium, and hallucinations (Table 9–3). Sudden death has been reported with acute cocaine intoxication; death is usually the result of cardiac arrest or ventricular fibrillation. Cocaine binges can last a few hours to several days. Tolerance to the euphoric effects develops rapidly during the course of a binge.

Management. Agitation and anxiety associated with cocaine intoxication are treated with diazepam or lorazepam. Reassurance and the constant presence of family or friends are frequently enough to help the patient get through the acute phase. The clinician should observe the patient for suicidality, arrhythmias, and psychotic symptoms. Because cocaine is rapidly metabolized, symptoms of acute intoxication usually clear within hours. Life-threatening levels fall quickly, so airway support and cardiac monitoring are required only for a few hours. Prolonged cocaine use is usually followed by a severe dysphoric syndrome ("crash"), which, if persistent, may require antidepressant medication or a transfer to the psychiatry ward.

Cocaine Delirium

An agitated confusional state may appear within 24 hours of cocaine use.

Management. Obtain a toxic screen immediately. Cocaine delirium usually disappears rapidly as the serum level decreases. Violence is common, so restraints should be ready (both physical and chemical—lorazepam or haloperidol, 1–4 mg intravenously, intramuscularly, or orally as needed). Watch for seizures.

Cocaine Delusional Disorder

Paranoid delusions can appear shortly after cocaine use. Unlike the confusional state, psychosis is often prolonged, lasting weeks or months in an occasional patient.

Management. Cocaine delusional disorder requires neuroleptics (haloperidol, 1–5 mg intravenously, intramuscularly, or orally, every 6 hours). Psychiatric hospitalization is often required. The clinician should obtain a toxic screen and watch for seizures.

Cocaine "Withdrawal"

Although abrupt discontinuation of cocaine is medically safe, postintoxication sequelae can occur after prolonged use. A profound dysphoria ("crash") frequently occurs and may last 2 weeks or longer. It is typically accompanied by strong drug craving and insomnia (Table 9–4). After several weeks of improvement, a second period of craving and depression may occur, which resolves slowly over weeks to months (Gawin and Kleber 1986). Episodic craving, often triggered in response to environmental stimuli, can continue indefinitely.

Management. Persistent depression that meets criteria for major depressive episode should be treated pharmacologically. Gawin et al. (1989) conducted a double-blind, random-assignment, 6-week comparison of desipramine and placebo in outpatient cocaine abusers. Cocaine craving and use were significantly reduced in the group given desipramine (40% relapse to cocaine use after 6 weeks, compared with 80% relapse among placebo recipients). The consultant should make the patient and hospital staff aware of the phases of abstinence and watch for suicidal and drug-seeking behavior.

■ REFERENCES

Adams RD, Victor M: Principles of Neurology. New York, McGraw-Hill, 1981

American Psychiatric Association: Diagnostic and Statistical Manual of Mental Disorders, 3rd Edition, Revised. Washington, DC, American Psychiatric Association, 1987

American Psychiatric Association: Diagnostic and Statistical Manual of Mental Disorders, 4th Edition. Washington, DC, American Psychiatric Association, 1994

Brew BJ: Diagnosis of Wernicke's encephalopathy. Aust N Z J Med 16:676–678, 1986

Chabal C, Erjavec MK, Jacobson L, et al: Prescription opiate abuse in chronic pain patients: clinical criteria, incidence and predictors. Clin J Pain 13:150–155, 1997

Craig TJ: Epidemiology of psychiatric illness, in The Medical Basis of Psychiatry. Edited by Winokur G, Clayton PJ. Philadelphia, PA, WB Saunders, 1986, pp 541–561

Curtis JR, Geller G, Stokes EG, et al: Characteristics, diagnosis, and treatment of alcoholism in elderly patients. J Am Geriatr Soc 37:310–316, 1989

Ewing J: Detecting alcoholism—the CAGE questionnaire. JAMA 25:1905–1907, 1984

Frances RJ, Franklin JE: Alcohol-induced organic mental disorders, in The American Psychiatric Press Textbook of Neuropsychiatry. Edited by Hales RE, Yudofsky SC. Washington, DC, American Psychiatric Press, 1987

Franklin JE, Frances RJ: Substance-related disorders, in The Essentials of Consultation-Liaison Psychiatry. Edited by Rundell JR, Wise MG. Washington, DC, American Psychiatric Press, 1999, pp 207–228

Gawin FH, Kleber HD: Abstinence symptomatology and psychiatric diagnosis in cocaine abusers. Arch Gen Psychiatry 43:107–113, 1986

Gawin FH, Kleber H, Buck R, et al: Desipramine facilitation of initial cocaine abstinence. Arch Gen Psychiatry 46:117–121, 1989

Gerke P, Hapke U, Rumpf HJ, et al: Alcohol-related diseases in general hospital patients. Alcohol Alcohol 32:179–184, 1997

Goodwin DW: Alcoholism and genetics. Arch Gen Psychiatry 42:171–174, 1985

Khantzian IF, Treece C: DSM-III psychiatric diagnoses of narcotic addicts. Arch Gen Psychiatry 42:1067–1071, 1985

Kosten TR, Gawin FH, Morgan C: Evidence for altered desipramine disposition in methadone-maintained patients treated for cocaine abuse. Am J Drug Alcohol Abuse 16:329–336, 1990

Liskow B, Goodwin DW: Alcoholism, in The Medical Basis of Psychiatry. Edited by Winokur G, Clayton PJ. Philadelphia, PA, WB Saunders, 1986, pp 190–211

Mebane AH: Drug abuse issues in critically ill patients, in Problems in Critical Care. Edited by Wise MG. Philadelphia, PA, JB Lippincott, 1988, pp 623–85

Miller NS: Alcohol and drug dependence, in Comprehensive Review of Geriatric Psychiatry. Edited by Sadavoy J, Lazarus LW, Farvik LF. Washington, DC, American Psychiatric Press, 1991, pp 387–401

Moore RD, Bone LR, Geller G, et al: Prevalence, detection and treatment of alcoholism in hospitalized patients JAMA 261: 403–407, 1989

Regier DA, Narrow WE, Rae DS, et al: The de facto US Mental and Addictive Disorders Service System: Epidemiologic Catchment Area prospective 1-year prevalence rates of disorders and services. Arch Gen Psychiatry 50:85–94, 1993

Soderstrom CA, Smith GS, Kufera JA, et al: The accuracy of the CAGE, the Brief Michigan Alcoholism Screening Test, and the Alcohol Use Disorder Identification Test in screening trauma center patients for alcoholism. J Trauma 43:962–969, 1997

Stripling JS, Russel RD: Effect of cocaine and pentylenetetrazol on cortical kindling. Pharmacol Biochem Behav 23:573–581, 1984

Victor M, Adams RD, Collins GH (eds): The Wernicke-Korsakoff Syndrome. Philadelphia, PA, FA Davis, 1971

Yost DA: Alcohol withdrawal syndrome. American Family Physician 54:657–664, 1996

■ ADDITIONAL READINGS

Daley DC, Salloum IM, Zuckoff A, et al: Increasing treatment adherence among outpatients with depression and cocaine dependence: results of a pilot study. Am J Psychiatry 155: 1611–1613, 1998

Fischman MU, Foltin RW, Nestadt G, et al: Effects of desipramine maintenance on cocaine self-administration by humans. J Pharmacol Exp Ther 253:760–770, 1990

Selzer ML: The Michigan Alcoholism Screening Test: the quest for a new diagnostic instrument. Am J Psychiatry 127:1653–1658, 1971

Taylor JR, Helzer JE: The natural history of alcoholism, in The Biology of Alcoholism, Vol. 6. Edited by Kissin B, Begleiter H. New York, Plenum, 1983, pp 85–101

Walsh DC, Ringson RW, Merrigan DM, et al: A randomized trial of treatment options for alcohol abusing workers. N Engl J Med 325:775–782, 1991

Weisner C, Schmidt L: Gender disparities in treatment for alcohol problems. JAMA 268:1872–1876, 1992

10

IMPORTANT PHARMACOLOGICAL ISSUES

■ ADHERENCE TO PHARMACOLOGICAL TREATMENT

Forming an alliance with the patient is fundamental to achieving the best possible outcome. It is unnerving to take a medication that changes how your brain works. In addition, a patient's use of the medication and perceived response, besides the well-known placebo effect, is affected by feelings of failure about needing a "chemical crutch," fear of addiction, magical hopes for cure, transference feelings toward the physician, and other personal beliefs about the medication (Jachna et al. 1999). Patients benefit from education about target symptoms and basic pharmacology, potential adverse reactions, how to properly take the medication, and expected time until response. Educational discussions that consider the patient as a partner facilitate formation of the doctor-patient alliance.

Make the medication regimen as simple as possible. The consultant should always obtain and document informed consent. Clinicians can use these principles to improve adherence (Table 10–1).

■ DRUG ACTIONS

Drug Absorption

Absorption rates differ among administration routes, although absorption from different forms of oral medications (capsule, pill, liquid) is generally similar (Jachna et al. 1999). Parenteral admin-

TABLE 10-1.	**Medication treatment principles in the consultation-liaison setting**

Stopping or tapering a medication is often more valuable than adding another.

Whenever possible, avoid using medications prn.

If prn medications are required, monitor frequency of use to establish a standing dosage.

Use the minimum dose of medication necessary to obtain the desired response.

Change one medication at a time.

Whenever possible, use only one medication to treat a symptom or disorder.

Keep the medication regimen simple.

Do not treat prophylactically unless a clear rationale exists.

Use a medication that has worked in the past.

Serum drug levels are only one indicator of effect, not a certification of efficacy or toxicity.

Generic drugs are cost-effective, but bioavailability can vary.

Each patient is unique!

Source. Adapted from Jachna JS, Lane RD, Gelenberg AJ: "Psychopharmacology," in *The American Psychiatric Press Textbook of Consultation-Liaison Psychiatry.* Edited by Rundell JR, Wise MG. Washington, DC, American Psychiatric Press, 1996, pp. 958–1005. Copyright 1996, American Psychiatric Press. Used with permission.

istration generally results in more rapid effects, although the erratic absorption of some medications given intramuscularly, such as diazepam, makes their clinical benefits less predictable. Gastric absorption increases when the stomach is empty, and emptying into the jejunum is more rapid. Aluminum or magnesium antacids can impair absorption and clinical efficacy of psychotropic medications. Cholestyramine, an exchange resin used to decrease cholesterol, can significantly impair absorption of several drugs (e.g., doxepin), even when the medications are ingested several hours apart (Geeze and Wise 1988).

Drug Distribution

With the exception of lithium, psychotropic medications are lipophilic and drawn to fatty tissues. Thus, psychotropic medications also generally have large volumes of distribution. In addition, most psychiatric medications are bound to plasma proteins, such as albumin and glycoprotein. When medication is bound to proteins, it is not available for biological activity, such as occupying receptors in the brain (Jachna et al. 1999). Protein binding complicates removal of toxic levels of medications. With aging and chronic medical illness, albumin levels decrease and the proportion of unbound (free) drug generally increases. Some medications compete with psychotropic medications for protein binding. For example, warfarin is greater than 90% plasma protein bound. If the patient taking warfarin is then prescribed chloral hydrate for insomnia, a metabolite of chloral hydrate (trichloroacetic acid) may displace warfarin from plasma proteins (Csernansky and Whiteford 1987). This can increase the amount of active anticoagulant several-fold and place the patient at risk for complications, including death.

Drug Receptors

Receptors are the site of action for medications in the central nervous system (CNS). A medication's receptor activity can be modified in several ways: 1) competitive inhibition, 2) alteration of the receptor, or 3) activation of multiple receptor sites by several drugs. The latter activation may produce side, additive, or opposite effects.

Competitive inhibition.   A patient who develops a severe hypotensive reaction to chlorpromazine is given epinephrine. The epinephrine, which normally stimulates both α-adrenergic and β-adrenergic receptors, cannot stimulate the α-adrenergic receptor because it is blocked by chlorpromazine. As a result, epinephrine's unopposed β-adrenergic stimulation further lowers blood pressure. Competitive inhibition also can have a desired response, such as the administration of naloxone hydrochloride to reverse the effects of an opioid overdose.

Alteration of the receptor. Alteration of the receptor by a neuromodulator may influence drug efficacy. Thyroid medication (particularly triiodothyronine) or lithium in some patients appears to increase the effectiveness of antidepressant medication. In addition, continued stimulation of a receptor by an agonist generally results in downregulation, such that subsequent exposure to the same agonist has a diminished effect.

Activation of multiple receptor sites. Activation of multiple receptor sites by one or several medications can produce unwanted side effects, additive effects (e.g., CNS depression), unpredictable effects, or opposite effects. The effect of multiple drugs on receptors is often integrated through second messenger pathways (Gilman et al. 1990).

Drug Metabolism

Absorbed drugs first pass through the liver before entering the systemic circulation ("first-pass effect"). Liver enzymes act on these drugs; the metabolites are inactive or active psychopharmacological compounds. Once in the liver, a medication, whether on a first or subsequent pass, is exposed to two main groups of metabolizing enzymes. The oxidative process occurs via the monooxygenase or cytochrome P450 (CYP) enzyme system. Conjugation is usually the second catabolic enzymatic process; the medication or its metabolites are coupled with other compounds to form more easily excreted (i.e., more hydrophilic) compounds. The metabolism rate, especially the oxidative process, is affected by many factors and disease states, which are discussed later in this chapter.

Drug Elimination

A medication and its metabolites are usually excreted by the kidneys, as well as into the bile or feces. Small amounts are also lost through sweat, saliva, or tears. Water-soluble drugs (e.g., lithium) are readily excreted by the kidneys. Biological or elimination half-life measures the amount of time needed to excrete half of the medication from the body. This is usually expressed as plasma half-life, which is how long it takes to remove half of the medication from the plasma. Frequency of drug administration is established by the length of its half-life. A "steady-state" drug level is generally achieved after four to five half-lives of a drug; at this point, meaningful serum medication levels are obtained.

Lithium clearance.   Administration of a medication that inhibits the synthesis of renal prostaglandins, such as nonsteroidal anti-inflammatory drugs, can impair renal clearance of lithium. Thus, lithium clearance is decreased by indomethacin, ibuprofen, diclofenac, piroxicam, and phenylbutazone. Renal disease can also impair lithium clearance.

Renal failure.   The adjustment of psychotropic medications in patients with renal failure is not too cumbersome, because almost all psychotropics and their active metabolites are eliminated by hepatic metabolism (Bennett et al. 1999). Lithium is the exception. The lithium dose should be decreased to 50%–75% of normal for a glomerular filtration rate (GFR) of 10–50 mL/min and 25%–50% for a GFR less than 10 mL/min. Antidepressants do not usually require dosage adjustment as GFR declines. The dosage of the longer-acting benzodiazepines, such as diazepam, chlordiazepoxide, and flurazepam, may need to be lowered by up to 50% in patients whose GFR is less than 10 mL/min. The use of chloral hydrate, nomifensine, and ethchlorvynol should be avoided in patients with renal failure.

■ DRUG INTERACTIONS

Drugs Being Taken by the Patient

Recognizing drug interactions is a crucial part of consultation work (Table 10–2). The effect of one drug on another can be *pharmacokinetic* (i.e., affecting the absorption, distribution, biotransformation, and excretion of the other drug) or *pharmacodynamic* (i.e., changing the effect of the drug at its point of action)

TABLE 10–2. **Important drug interactions**

Drug interactions	Effect
Antipsychotics	
Alcohol	Intensifies CNS depression
Amphetamines	Antagonizes efficacy
Antacids	Decreases neuroleptic absorption
Anticholinergics	Additive anticholinergic effects
Antihypertensives[a]	Hypotension
Barbiturates	Decreases neuroleptic levels
Epinephrine[a]	Hypotension
Levodopa	Antagonizes levodopa efficacy
Lithium	Increases neurotoxicity
MAOIs[a]	Hypotension
TCAs	Increases TCA plasma levels
BZs	
Alcohol (& other CNS depressants)	Intensifies CNS depression
Alcohol (acute)	Increases BZ levels
Alcohol (chronic)	Decreases BZ levels
Antacids	Decreases BZ levels
Cimetidine[b]	Increases BZ levels
Disulfiram[b]	Increases BZ levels
SSRIs	Increases BZ levels
Isoniazid[b]	Increases BZ levels
Oral contraceptives[b]	Increases BZ levels
Rifampin[b]	Decreases BZ levels
Tobacco/nicotine[b]	Decreases BZ levels
Carbamazepine (induces CYP450 3A3/3A4)	
Alprazolam	Decreases alprazolam levels
Cimetidine	Increases carbamazepine levels
Clonazepam	Decreases clonazepam levels
Diltiazem, verapamil	Increases carbamazepine levels

(continued)

TABLE 10–2. **Important drug interactions** *(continued)*

Drug interactions	Effect
Carbamazepine (induces CYP450 3A3/3A4) *(continued)*	
Erythromycin	Increases carbamazepine levels
Isoniazid	Increases carbamazepine levels
Phenobarbital	Decreases carbamazepine levels
Phenytoin	Decreases carbamazepine levels
Primidone	Decreases carbamazepine levels
Propoxyphene	Increases carbamazepine levels
SSRIs	Increases carbamazepine levels
Valproate	Decreases valproate levels
Lithium	
Acetazolamide	Decreases lithium levels
Antipsychotics	Increases neurotoxicity
β-Blockers	Decreases tremor
Carbamazepine	Increases lithium effects
Captopril, Enalapril	Increases lithium levels
Cyclosporine	Markedly increases lithium levels
Diltiazem, verapamil	Increases lithium toxicity
Methyldopa	Increases lithium toxicity
Potassium iodide	Enhances hypothyroid effects
Tetracycline	Increases lithium levels
Thiazide diuretics	Increases lithium levels
SSRIs (See Table 10–4 for specific enzyme inhibition)	
BZs[b]	Increases BZ levels
Carbamazepine	Increases carbamazepine levels
Antipsychotics	Increases neuroleptic levels
TCAs	Increases TCA levels
MAOIs	
Alcohol	Additive CNS depression

(continued)

TABLE 10–2.	**Important drug interactions** *(continued)*

Drug interactions	Effect
MAOIs *(continued)*	
Clomipramine	Serotonin syndrome
SSRIs	Serotonin syndrome
Meperidine	Serotonin syndrome
Phenothiazine	Hypotension
Succinylcholine	Prolongs muscle relaxation
Tyramine	Potential hypertensive crisis
Sympathomimetic drugs (amphetamine, cocaine, dopamine, ephedrine, epinephrine, metaraminol, norepinephrine, phenylpropanolamine, phenylephrine)	Potential hypertensive crisis
TCAs	
Alcohol	Additive CNS depression
Anticholinergics	Additive anticholinergic effects
Antihypertensives (guanethidine, clonidine, debrisoquin)	Increases hypertension
Antipsychotics	Increases TCA plasma levels
BZs	Additive CNS depression
Class I antiarrhythmics (disopyramide, lidocaine, quinidine, procainamide)	Prolongs cardiac conduction
Liothyronine	Enhances antidepressant action

Note. CNS = central nervous system; MAOI = monoamine oxidase inhibitor; TCA = tricyclic antidepressant; BZ = benzodiazepine; SSRI = selective serotonin reuptake inhibitor; CYP450 = cytochrome P450.
[a]Phenothiazines (chlorpromazine, thioridazine, mesoridazine).
[b]Except oxazepam, lorazepam, alprazolam, and temazepam.

(Jachna et al. 1999). The clinician should obtain a complete medication list, including medications recently discontinued, over-the-counter medications used, and herbal or other alternative drug preparations used, from the patient or from the chart if the patient is hospitalized. The clinician should ask a family member to bring in all medications from the patient's house; he or she must watch for the "shopping bag sign," in which the family member brings in massive quantities of current and expired medications that will only fit into a sizable bag or box.

Monoamine Oxidase Inhibitors and Diet

Tyramine in the diet can interact with a monoamine oxidase inhibitor (MAOI) to cause a hypertensive crisis. If the patient ingests food containing significant amounts of tyramine, the catecholamine produced can cause severe hypertension. Reasonable dietary restraint is the best prevention. It is recommended that patients carry 10 mg of nifedipine with them to take in the unlikely event of a hypertensive event (Stoudemire et al. 1990, 1991).

Other Drug Interactions

Other clinically significant drug interactions can occur with psychotropic drugs. Many of them are summarized in Table 10–2. Psychiatrists may find it helpful to have this list with them when performing psychiatric consultations.

■ CYTOCHROME P450 SYSTEM

The hepatic CYP enzyme system (vesicles containing the enzymes have a great deal of red pigment, whose wavelength happens to be 450 nm) evolved to eliminate toxic substances from the body. It did not evolve to metabolize medications; it just happens to do so. This helps explain why different ethnic groups and individuals metabolize the same medication at different rates (i.e., have widely different blood levels after an identical dose).

Four CYP enzymes are especially important in the oxidative metabolism of medications: CYP2D6, CYP1A2, CYP2C, and CYP3A3/3A4. These enzymes are subject to inhibition, genetic variation and, in some cases, induction. Table 10–3 lists some of the more common actions of these enzymes on substrates (i.e., medications) of interest to consultation-liaison psychiatrists. Medications are often metabolized by a particular enzyme, can compete for metabolism with other substrates, and/or can inhibit an enzyme without being metabolized by it. Hepatic enzyme inhibition slows metabolism (i.e., increases the half-life) and increases the concentration and toxicity of psychotropic and other drugs. Hepatic enzyme induction can decrease the efficacy of a medication because it increases metabolism (i.e., decreases the half-life).

More becomes known about this important set of enzymes all the time (Ereshefsky et al. 1996). In Caucasians, 5%–10% lack the 2D6 enzyme; they are poor metabolizers of medications oxidized by this enzyme (e.g., poor analgesia from tramadol). Fluvoxamine inhibits several enzymes; the combination of fluvoxamine and clozapine, in particular, should be avoided (Dequardo 1996). It is wise to assume that selective serotonin reuptake inhibitors (SSRIs), except citalopram, raise levels of tricyclic antidepressants. Many consultation-liaison psychiatrists advocate the use of sertraline or citalopram for most consultation-liaison patients. These medications are associated with fewer drug-drug interactions attributable to hepatic enzyme inhibitions; this is particularly important in the consultation-liaison setting where the average inpatient takes eight medications (Adson et al. 1998).

■ NEUROLEPTIC MALIGNANT SYNDROME

Clinical Characteristics

Neuroleptic malignant syndrome (NMS) is a rare, potentially fatal idiosyncratic reaction to rapid alteration in CNS dopamine activity. NMS is typically caused by medications that block dopamine, such as neuroleptics, metoclopramide, and (rarely) clozapine. In

TABLE 10–3. Cytochrome P450 enzyme–drug interactions[a]

2D6	3A3/4	1A2	2C (2C9/2C19)
Substrates of P450 enzymes			
β-Blockers	Alprazolam	Caffeine	Barbiturates
Clomipramine	Astemizole	Clozapine	Diazepam
Codeine	Clozapine	Demethylation of tertiary tricyclics	Demethylation of tertiary tricyclics
Fluoxetine	Carbamazepine	Fluvoxamine	Phenytoin
Haloperidol[b]	Cyclosporine	Haloperidol[b]	Propranolol
Loratadine	Erythromycin	Olanzapine	Tolbutamide
Morphine	Lidocaine	Phenacetin	Warfarin
Paroxetine	Midazolam	Propranolol	NSAIDs
Phenothiazines	Quinidine	Theophylline	
Quetiapine	Pimozide	Verapamil	
Risperidone	Sertraline	Warfarin	
Secondary tricyclic antidepressants	Steroids		
Sertindole	Terfenadine		
Venlafaxine	Demethylation of tertiary tricyclics		
Type 1C antiarrhythmics (flecainide, propafenone)	Triazolam		
	Venlafaxine		
	Verapamil		

(continued)

TABLE 10–3.   Cytochrome P450 enzyme–drug interactions *(continued)*

Inhibitors of P450 enzymes

Amitriptyline	Cimetidine	Fluvoxamine	Fluoxetine
Doxepin	Cyclosporine	Ciprofloxacin	Fluvoxamine
Fluvoxamine	Diltiazem	Grapefruit juice	Sertraline (?)
Fluphenazine	Erythromycin	Tacrine	
Norfluoxetine	Fluoxetine		
Paroxetine	Fluvoxamine		
Quinidine	Grapefruit juice		
Phenothiazines	Ketoconazole		
Methylphenidate	Miconazole		
Quinidine	Nefazodone		
Cimetidine	Nifedipine		
Sertraline	Norfluoxetine		
Tricyclic antidepressants	Protease inhibitors: ritonavir, saquinavir		
	Sertraline		

(continued)

TABLE 10–3. Cytochrome P450 enzyme–drug interactions *(continued)*

Inducers of P450 enzymes

Not induced		
	Carbamazepine	Cigarettes
	Dexamethasone	Caffeine
	Phenobarbital	Cabbage
	Primidone	Charbroiled food
	Phenytoin	Omeprazole
	Rifabutin	Rifampin
	Rifampin	
		Phenobarbital
		Phenytoin

Note. Tricyclic antidepressants are metabolized by cytochrome P450 2D6, 3A, 2C, and 1A2. NSAIDs = nonsteroidal anti-inflammatory drugs; (?) = incomplete or inconsistent data.
aIncludes both in vivo and in vitro data.
bComplex interaction.
Source. Information compiled by M. G. Wise, L. Ereshefsky, and J. R. Rundell.

89% of cases, NMS symptoms start within the first 10 days of neuroleptic treatment or dosage increase. The full syndrome usually develops within 48 hours of initial onset (Shalev 1986). The clinical characteristics of NMS are listed in Table 10–4. The core symptoms of NMS—fever, skeletal muscle rigidity, autonomic instability, and altered mental state—are present in most cases.

Laboratory abnormalities in NMS are elevated creatinine phosphokinase (CPK) in 92% of patients, leukocytosis in 70% of patients, myoglobinemia in 75% of patients, and reduced serum iron levels in 96% of patients during an episode of NMS (Rosebush and Steward 1989). Laboratory values may also reflect dehydration and elevated liver enzymes. Brain scan and computed tomography rarely have abnormal results, and the cerebrospinal fluid may (in 2 of 54 patients [Addonizio et al. 1987]) show elevated protein levels. Electroencephalograms commonly show nonspecific slowing (21 of 45 patients [Addonizio et al. 1987]).

Epidemiology

Various authors have estimated the incidence of NMS in psychiatric inpatients receiving neuroleptics to be .02%–3.23% (Pelonero et al. 1998). If milder variants of NMS are included, the frequency among some populations may be as high as 12.2% (Levinson and Simpson 1986). The prevalence of NMS is unknown. NMS has an estimated mortality of 1%–20%, depending on the population being studied (Caroff 1980). NMS occurs at all ages, with a range from 3 to 78 years (Shalev and Munitz 1986). However, Caroff (1980) summarized 60 NMS cases and noted that nearly 80% were in patients younger than 40. He also noted that young adult men predominated (male-to-female ratio of 2:1). Addonizio et al. (1987), in a review of 115 NMS patients, reported that 63% were male and 37% were female. The mean age was higher (40 years).

Risk factors. The two most significant risk factors for NMS (Table 10–5) are rapid neuroleptization with intramuscular haloperidol and rechallenge with a neuroleptic within 2 weeks after

TABLE 10–4. **Clinical characteristics of neuroleptic malignant syndrome and their frequency (%)**

	Kurlan et al. 1984	Levenson 1985	Rosebush/ Steward 1989
Core features			
Fever	100	98	100
Rigidity	92	89	96
Autonomic instability			
Tachycardia	79	89	100
Diaphoresis	60	67	100
Labile blood pressure	54	74	100
Altered mental state			
Stupor	27		
Coma	27		
Associated features			
Tremor	56	45	92
Akinesia	38		
Dystonia	33		
Sialorrhea	31		
Tachypnea	25		29

NMS. Addonizio and Susman (1991) reported 68 instances of post-NMS patients who were safely restarted on neuroleptics (28 received thioridazine) and 41 who experienced a recurrence. High-potency neuroleptics, such as haloperidol, may be associated with a higher risk for NMS. Shalev and Munitz's (1986) review of 202 patients with NMS found that haloperidol was involved in 49.5% of cases. This association likely reflects haloperidol's popularity; however, it more likely indicates that rapid increases in neuroleptic dosage that occur with haloperidol are an important risk factor (Addonizio and Susman 1991; Keck et al. 1987; Shalev and Munitz 1986). Other risk factors associated with the development of NMS are listed in Table 10–5.

Occurrence in medically ill patients.　No clear association exists between a particular medical illness and NMS. Because dehydration and exhaustion occur in a wide variety of medical diseases, medical disease may increase the risk for NMS. Shalev et al. (1989) found that patients with organic brain disease who develop NMS have a higher mortality rate than patients with NMS who have a normal CNS (i.e., 39% vs. 18.8% for the overall group). Patients with NMS develop secondary medical problems, including pneumonia, pulmonary emboli, and renal failure (secondary to rhadodmyolysis), that are potentially lethal. "Lead-pipe" muscle rigidity leads to muscle contractures, rhabdomyolysis, myoglobinemia, and potentially to acute myoglobinuric renal failure. Chest wall rigidity may decrease pulmonary function. Other medical complications resulting from NMS include dehydration, malnutrition, infections, deep venous thrombosis, exacerbation of preexisting coronary disease, and myocardial infarction.

Differential Diagnosis

Extrapyramidal side effects accompanied by fever.　Extrapyramidal side effects accompanied by fever are very likely to be

---

TABLE 10–5.　**Risk factors for neuroleptic malignant syndrome (NMS)**

Rapid decrease in central nervous system dopamine activity (essential)

Prior episode of NMS within the last few weeks

Treatment with haloperidol (lower mortality)

Intramuscular administration of neuroleptic

Dehydration

Use of lithium

Diagnosis of mood disorder

Male (especially young males)

Brain disorder (increases mortality)

Concurrent medical illness

---

misdiagnosed as NMS. In Levinson and Simpson's examination of 67 NMS patients, 41% of the patients had a medical illness to explain the fever, 23% probably had complicating medical factors, and only 36% of the patients had no medical factors (i.e., had NMS). The lesson seems clear—when a febrile patient who is taking a neuroleptic is examined, the clinician should have a high index of suspicion that the fever is caused by a medical illness.

Neuroleptic-induced catatonia. A patient with neuroleptic-induced catatonia presents with a combination of catatonia and parkinsonian signs. As Gelenberg and Mandel (1977) noted in eight patients, "All [patients] developed posturing, waxy flexibility, negativism, regressive behavior, incontinence of urine, and slowness of response. Parkinsonian features noted in all patients included stiffness, bradykinesia, and lack of associated movements" (p. 949). Significant temperature elevation and autonomic instability were not seen in these patients.

Catatonia. Signs and symptoms of catatonia *predate* neuroleptic treatment, and significant temperature elevation and autonomic instability are absent. Catatonia is treated by *increasing* neuroleptic medication or administering electroconvulsive therapy.

Heatstroke. Heatstroke is a potential complication of neuroleptic agents. Therefore, a neuroleptic-treated patient during hot, humid weather is at risk for heatstroke. Symptoms are fever, tachycardia, hyperventilation, and mental confusion, which may rapidly progress to coma. Sweating is usually not present; vomiting and nausea occur in most patients. The clinician can differentiate heatstroke from NMS by a history of heat exposure, absence of sweating, and flaccid muscle tone.

Malignant hyperthermia. Malignant hyperthermia is caused by a genetic abnormality. Vulnerable individuals, after exposure to inhalation anesthesia (e.g., halothane), skeletal muscle relaxants (e.g., succinylcholine hydrochloride), certain chemicals (e.g., carbon tetrachloride), or even stress, may develop profound muscular rigidity and fever. In malignant hyperthermia, a defect in cellular calcium transport causes muscle contraction and heat generation. Several differences are found between malignant hyperthermia and NMS. Malignant hyperthermia occurs after exposure to anesthetics, and NMS occurs after exposure to neuroleptics. Malignant hyperthermia occurs within minutes to hours, and NMS occurs in hours to days. Both respond well to dantrolene, but only NMS patients show muscular relaxation with curare or diazepam.

Anticholinergic delirium or coma. Anticholinergic delirium or coma can result from treatment with a variety of anticholinergic medications. Signs of toxicity include blurred vision; ileus; urinary retention; tachycardia; dry, flushed skin with absent sweating; mild temperature elevation; disorientation; and hallucinations. Anticholinergic delirium, but not NMS, is briefly relieved by 1–2 mg of intravenous physostigmine infused over 2–3 minutes and repeated in 20–30 minutes if needed (cardiac and vital sign monitoring is recommended, and seizures are possible). In anticholinergic toxicity, muscle rigidity is lacking.

Serotonin syndrome. Characteristics of serotonin syndrome are similar to those of NMS, although differences in etiology, presentation, and treatment are seen. Serotonin syndrome results from excessive serotonin activity in the CNS. NMS is an idiosyncratic reaction but serotonin syndrome is not. Serotonin syndrome is dose related, and any patient, given sufficient serotoninergic activity, will develop serotonin syndrome. Therefore, the risk factors for serotonin syndrome are pharmacologically related, although constitutional factors may alter the threshold. Serotonin syndrome is most closely associated with MAOIs (MAOI overdose, combination of two MAOIs, MAOI plus meperidine, MAOI plus L-tryptophan, and MAOI plus an SSRI). Serotonin syndrome very rarely occurs secondary to a single antidepressant, even in overdose (except an MAOI). Serotonin syndrome typically develops from a combination of medications, each medication augmenting serotoninergic activity by a different mechanism.

Table 10–6 lists the clinical characteristics of serotonin syndrome. Early warning signs for serotonin syndrome include myoclonus,

TABLE 10–6.	Clinical characteristics of serotonin syndrome and their frequency	
Features	**Frequency (%)**
Altered mental state	
Confusion	42
Hypomania	21
Restlessness	45
Myoclonus	34
Hyperreflexia	29
Diaphoresis	26
Shivering	26
Tremor	26
Diarrhea	16
Incoordination	13

Source. Adapted from Sternbach 1991.

clonus, hyperreflexia, shivering, and restlessness. The generalized rigidity ("lead-pipe" rigidity) present in NMS is typically absent in serotonin syndrome, although an individual with serotonin syndrome can experience muscle tension (e.g., clenched jaws, bruxism).

Treatment and Management

Death does not occur from the same mechanism that triggers NMS but is caused by medical complications. Treatment consists of neuroleptic discontinuation, supportive care, and pharmacological therapies such as dantrolene and bromocriptine. When supportive measures (respiratory therapy, external cooling, hydration, physical therapy, nutritional measures) alone are used, the mean time until clinical improvement is 6.8 days. The addition of dantrolene or bromocriptine reduces recovery time to 1.2 and 1.0 days, respectively. Pharmacological treatment with dantrolene is initially given intravenously 2–3 mg/kg over 10–15 minutes (daily total 0.8–10 mg/kg/day intravenously) or is given orally 50–700 mg/day in four divided doses. Bromocriptine is given orally 2.5–10 mg three times a day. Several treatments of NMS are not recommended: electroconvulsive therapy (except for lethal catatonia), benzodiazepines, anticholinergics, and nitroprusside.

The treatment and management of serotonin syndrome is similar to that of NMS, in that all offending agents are discontinued and supportive care is provided. Pharmacological treatment is based on nonspecific blockade of excessive postsynaptic serotonergic activity. Medications used for treatment include cyproheptadine 0.5 mg/kg/day maximum, methysergide 4–8 mg, or propranolol (insufficient experience to recommend a specific dose).

■ REFERENCES

Addonizio G, Susman VL: Neuroleptic Malignant Syndrome: A Clinical Approach. St. Louis, MO, Mosby-Year Book, 1991

Addonizio S, Susman VL, Roth SD: Neuroleptic malignant syndrome: review and analysis of 115 cases. Biol Psychiatry 22: 1004–1020, 1987

Adson DE, Crow SJ, Meller WH, et al: Potential drug-drug interactions on a tertiary care hospital consultation-liaison psychiatry service. Psychosomatics 39:360–365, 1998

Bennett WM, Aronoff GR, Golper TA, et al: Drug Prescribing in Renal Failure, 4th Edition. Philadelphia, PA, American College of Physicians, 1999

Caroff SN: The neuroleptic malignant syndrome. J Clin Psychiatry 41:79–83, 1980

Csernansky JG, Whiteford HA: Clinically significant psychoactive drug interactions, in Psychiatry Update: The American Psychiatric Association Annual Review, Vol 6. Edited by Hales RE, Frances AJ. Washington, DC, American Psychiatric Press, 1987, pp 802–815

Dequardo EA: Elevated clozapine levels after fluvoxamine initiation. Am J Psychiatry 153:840–841, 1996

Ereshefsky L, Riesenman C, Francis LYW: Serotonin selective reuptake inhibitors: drug interactions and the cytochrome P450 system. J Clin Psychiatry 57 (suppl 8):17–25, 1996

Geeze D, Wise MG: Doxepin-cholestyramine interaction. Psychosomatics 29:233–236, 1988

Gelenberg AL, Mandel MR: Catatonic reactions to high-potency neuroleptic drugs. Arch Gen Psychiatry 34:947–950, 1977

Gilman AG, Rall TW, Neis AS, et al: Goodman and Gilman's The Pharmacological Basis of Therapeutics, 8th Edition. New York, Pergamon, 1990

Jachna JS, Lane RD, Gelenberg AJ: Psychopharmacology, in Essentials of Consultation-Liaison Psychiatry. Edited by Rundell JR, Wise MG. Washington, DC, American Psychiatric Press, 1999, pp 523–553

Keck PE, Pope HG, McElroy SL: Frequency and presentation of neuroleptic syndrome: a prospective study. Am J Psychiatry 144:1344–1346, 1987

Kurlan R, Hamill R, Shoulson I: Neuroleptic malignant syndrome. Clinical Psychopharmacology 7:109–120, 1984

Levenson JL: Neuroleptic malignant syndrome. Am J Psychiatry 142:1137–1145, 1985

Levinson DF, Simpson GM: Neuroleptic induced extrapyramidal symptoms with fever—heterogeneity of the neuroleptic malignant syndrome. Arch Gen Psychiatry 43:839–848, 1986

Pelonero AL, Levenson JL, Pandurangi AK: Neuroleptic malignant syndrome: a review. Psychiatric Services 49:1163–1172, 1998

Pope HG Jr, Keck PE, McElroy SL: Frequency of neuroleptic malignant syndrome in a large psychiatric hospital. Am J Psychiatry 143:1227–1233, 1986

Rosebush PI, Steward T: A prospective analysis of 24 episodes of neuroleptic malignant syndrome. Am J Psychiatry 146: 717–725, 1989

Shalev A, Munitz H: The neuroleptic malignant syndrome: agent and host interaction. Acta Psychiatr Scand 73:337–347, 1986

Shalev A, Hermesh H, Munitz H: Mortality from neuroleptic malignant syndrome. J Clin Psychiatry 50:18–25, 1989

Sternbach H: The serotonin syndrome. Am J Psychiatry 148:705–713, 1991

Stoudemire A, Moran MG, Fogel BS: Psychiatric drug use in the medically ill: part I. Psychosomatics 31:377–391, 1990

Stoudemire A, Moran MG, Fogel BS: Psychiatric drug use in the medically ill: part II. Psychosomatics 32:34–46, 1991

■ ADDITIONAL READINGS

Bernstein JG: Psychotropic drug prescribing, and drug interactions, in Massachusetts General Hospital Handbook of General Psychiatry, 3rd Edition. Edited by Cassem NH. St. Louis, MO, Mosby-Year Book, 1991, pp 527–570, 571–610

DeVane CL: Pharmacogenetics and drug metabolism of newer antidepressant agents. J Clin Psychiatry 55 (12 suppl):38–45, 1994

Hales RE: Psychopharmacological side effects and drug interactions of importance in the critical care unit, in Problems in Critical Care. Edited by Wise MG. Philadelphia, PA, JB Lippincott, 1988

Leipzig RM: Psychopharmacology in patients with hepatic and gastrointestinal disease. Int J Psychiatry Med 20:109–139, 1990

Risch SC, Groom GP, Janowski DS: Interfaces of psychopharmacology and cardiology: parts 1 and 2. J Clin Psychiatry 42:23–34, 47–59, 1981

Roose SP, Glassman AH: Antidepressant choice in the patient with cardiac disease: lessons from the Cardiac Arrhythmia Suppression Trial (CAST) studies. J Clin Psychiatry 55:83–100, 1994

Rosebush PI, Mazurek MF: Serum iron and neuroleptic malignant syndrome. Lancet 338:149–151, 1991

Sakkas P, Davis JM, Hua J, et al: Pharmacotherapy of neuroleptic malignant syndrome. Psychiatric Annals 21:157–164, 1991

Sternbach H: The serotonin syndrome. Am J Psychiatry 148:705–713, 1991

11

VIOLENCE AND AGGRESSION

■ EMERGENCY CONSULTATION

Aside from a suicide attempt, few events focus the attention of medical staff and other patients faster than violence or the threat of violence in a hospital. When this situation arises, a "stat" psychiatric consultation is often requested. The psychiatrist usually is faced with one of three situations: 1) a patient is actively violent and combative; 2) a patient is threatening violence; or 3) violence has already occurred, and the patient may or may not now appear acutely violent.

When first contacted about an acute or emergency psychiatric consultation for a potentially violent or violent patient—usually by telephone—the consultant should find out from the referring physician or staff whether the individual is armed with a gun, knife, or other potentially lethal weapon. He or she should inquire about medical and mental state. If the family is available, the staff or referring physician should gather information about the patient's history of violence and recent mental state. They can collect this information while the psychiatrist is en route to the location. When the psychiatrist arrives, a sufficient number of personnel should be ready to restrain the individual if necessary. The organization and instruction of the restraint team are important. When the instruction is properly given, injury to the patient, the members of the restraint team, and the psychiatrist is less likely (Table 11–1).

The Combative, Actively Violent Patient

The combative, actively violent patient needs restraint and sedation. If the patient is armed, restraint is best performed by police or security personnel. Neuroleptic medications (e.g., haloperidol) are

TABLE 11–1.	**Procedure for physical restraint**

1. If the patient is armed, call security or police.

2. If the patient is unarmed, get sufficient help. At least five adults are required.

3. Assign each individual a specific extremity or the head (e.g., "You secure the right arm."). Personnel should wait for the team leader's command for restraint to proceed.

4. Ensure that a nurse has a sedative injection prepared and ready to administer.

5. Ensure that leather restraints are readily available. If the patient is already hospitalized and has intravenous and other lines attached, soft restraints are recommended.

6. Ensure that properly trained personnel who know how to quickly apply the restraints are available.

7. Do not remove the restraints unless adequate force is available to reapply restraints or until it is certain that the patient or staff is not at risk.

8. Evaluate the patient for medical or toxic explanations for the violent episode.

9. Monitor the patient closely for changes in medical status (especially vital signs and circulatory function distal to the restraints) and mental status and the need for medication.

10. Document carefully the reasons for the restraint and the lack of alternatives; ensure that all medical facility operating instructions are adhered to.

frequently used to calm the acutely aggressive patient. The initial dose is 1–2 mg intravenously (if an intravenous line is still in place) or intramuscularly. The dose should be increased by 1 mg every half-hour until aggression is controlled. Young, strong patients often require higher doses (e.g., 5 mg). Neuroleptics are not appropriate long-term management medications (unless the violence is related to a psychotic disorder) and may cause potentially complicating adverse effects, such as dystonias, akathisia, and extrapyramidal signs. Lorazepam is also frequently used in the acute violent setting because it is short-acting and can be administered by several routes. Lorazepam, 1–2 mg, should be administered orally or intramuscularly every hour until control is achieved. If lorazepam is given intravenously, to avoid respiratory depression and laryngospasm, the clinician should push slowly and not exceed 2 mg/minute (Hales et al. 1999).

A Person Who Is Threatening Violence

An individual who is threatening violence requires immediate intervention. A clinician should not knowingly place him- or herself in harms way. However, if the person indicates during an evaluation that he or she is armed, the clinician should ask the individual why he or she needs a weapon. The psychiatrist can then formulate an appropriate request for the person to relinquish the weapon. If he or she refuses, the psychiatrist is advised not to continue the interview and to call police and/or security personnel to disarm the person.

The psychiatrist should use a calm, reassuring voice to let the patient know that he or she will help him or her maintain control. The psychiatrist must avoid angry confrontation and determine the reason for the aggressiveness. Is the patient paranoid, confused, and/or filled with rage? Common psychiatric etiologies are delirium, mania, psychosis, drug or alcohol intoxication, and drug or alcohol withdrawal. Persons with primitive character pathology often become enraged and act out impulsively.

Most patients will respond to an emphatic inquiry, and, in this way, the situation can be defused. Sedation should be offered, but if the patient's behavior escalates and becomes violent, the restraint team should be signaled to restrain the patient and administer sedation. The patient's family is often helpful, particularly if the patient is delirious and paranoid. If a hospitalized patient believes the hospital staff is about to kill him or her, calm reassurance from loved ones is helpful. In some situations, family involvement is not indicated. If the individual has a character disorder or is angry with the family, the family's involvement may escalate the person's anger rather than calm it.

A Person Who Has Already Committed Violence

If violence has already occurred and the patient is now calm, the clinician should immediately try to answer the following:

1. Does the person still have the urge and the means to be violent?
2. What was the reason(s) for the violence, and is that stimulus still present?
3. What is the patient's current mental status, and what was the mental status before and at the time of the violence?
4. What is the environment (physical and social) in which the violence occurred?
5. Is a potentially contributory psychiatric disorder present?

■ PHYSIOLOGICAL BASIS FOR VIOLENCE AND AGGRESSION

Multiple neurotransmitters mediate aggression. Serotonin, dopamine, acetylcholine, and γ-aminobutyric acid (GABA) all play important roles (Hales et al. 1999). Neurotransmitters probably interface with one another to influence aggression. Norepinephrine tracks originate in the locus coeruleus in the lateral tegmental system and terminate in the forebrain. Frontal and temporal lobes of the forebrain, when damaged, are associated with rage and violent behavior. β_1-Adrenergic receptors are also located in the limbic forebrain and are implicated in mediating aggressive behavior (Alexander et al. 1979).

■ DIFFERENTIAL DIAGNOSIS OF VIOLENCE AND AGGRESSION

Many medical and psychiatric disorders are associated with violence and aggression. Neurological conditions such as dementia, epilepsy, stroke, and degenerative conditions (e.g., Parkinson's disease, multiple sclerosis) predispose patients to aggression. Violent behavior is common among psychiatric patients with intermittent explosive disorder, conduct disorder, oppositional defiant disorder, antisocial personality disorder, and borderline personality disorder. It is somewhat less common among patients with psychotic disorders and bipolar disorder, manic. Several psychoactive substances can precipitate or lower the threshold for aggression: alcohol, amphetamines, antianxiety medications, anticholinergic drugs, cocaine, hypnotics, and steroids (Hales et al. 1999).

■ TREATMENT AND PREVENTION OF CHRONIC AGGRESSION

Pharmacological Treatment

Pharmacological treatment is sometimes necessary to help manage chronic aggression. When selecting a medication, consultation-liaison psychiatrists must search for the underlying cause of the chronic aggression. Unless unique and specific indications for other pharmacological agents are present, many clinicians consider β-blockers (e.g., propranolol, nadolol, pindolol) as the first-line treatment of chronic aggression (Greendyke et al. 1986; Hales et al. 1999; Ratey et al. 1992; Yudofsky et al. 1987). Table 11–2 summarizes medications used for chronic aggression, underlying conditions that might lead a clinician to use that medication, and dosage ranges.

Nonpharmacological Treatment

Patients with aggressive syndromes almost always require a multimodal management approach that includes behavioral, psychoeducational, and family approaches. Behavioral treatments are highly effective for patients with aggression related to central nervous system dysfunction. Behavioral strategies include token economy, aggression replacement strategies, and decelerative techniques (Corrigan and Jakus 1994, Corrigan et al. 1993). Patients and their families must learn to identify behaviors (e.g., yelling, cursing, and threatening) that are warning signs that

TABLE 11–2.   **Pharmacological management of chronic aggression**

Medication	Indication	Dosage range
β-Blockers	(Exclude cardiac and pulmonary patients)	
Propranolol	Aggression associated with CNS syndromes	Start at 20 mg tid
		Increase by 60 mg/day every 3–5 days
		Target is symptom control or 12 mg/kg/day
Antianxiety medications		
Buspirone	Traumatic brain injury	10–20 mg tid
Clonazepam	Aggression associated with anxiety or tics	0.5–3.0 mg tid
Anticonvulsants		
Carbamazepine	Aggressive behavior associated with brain disorders	400–1,200 mg/day
Valproic acid	Aggressive behavior associated with brain disorders	1,000–1,500 mg/day
Lithium	Aggressive behavior associated with mania	300–1,800 mg/day
	Traumatic brain injury[a]	
Antidepressants		
SSRIs	Impulsive aggressivity, mental retardation, CNS lesions, depression	See footnote b.
Trazodone	Aggressive behavior associated with depression	50–300 mg/day

(continued)

TABLE 11–2.	**Pharmacological management of chronic aggression** *(continued)*	
Medication	**Indication**	**Dosage range**
Neuroleptics	Psychotic disorders (only)	Depends on drug

Note. CNS = central nervous system; tid = three times a day; SSRIs = selective serotonin reuptake inhibitors.

[a]Although reportedly effective, patients with brain injury may have increased sensitivity to neurotoxic effects of lithium (Hornstein and Seliger 1989).

[b]SSRI treatment for chronic aggression should begin at relatively low doses (e.g., 10 mg fluoxetine, 25 mg sertraline, 10 mg paroxetine). If antiaggression effects are not achieved over several weeks, the dose may be slowly increased at 1- to 2-week intervals toward higher levels (up to 80 mg/day fluoxetine, 200 mg sertraline, 60 mg paroxetine).

Source. Adapted from Hales RE, Silver JM, Yudofsky SC: "Aggression and Agitation," in *The American Psychiatric Press Textbook of Consultation-Liaison Psychiatry.* Edited by Rundell JR, Wise MG. Washington, DC, American Psychiatric Press, 1996, pp. 162–177. Copyright 1996, American Psychiatric Press. Used with permission.

aggression or violence is likely to occur (Hales et al. 1999). Patients and families can then apply alternative behaviors such as sitting quietly or engaging in pleasurable activities. Family therapy may assist families in coping with and more effectively managing aggressive household members.

■ REFERENCES

Alexander RW, Davis JN, Lejkowitz RJ: Direct identification and characterization of beta-adrenergic receptors in rat brain. Nature 258:437–440, 1979

Corrigan PW, Jakus MR: Behavioral treatment, in Neuropsychiatry of Traumatic Brain Injury. Edited by Silver JM, Yudofsky SC, Hales RE. Washington, DC, American Psychiatric Press, 1994, pp 733–769

Corrigan PW, Yudofsky SC, Silver JM: Pharmacological and behavioral treatments for aggressive psychiatric inpatients. Hosp Community Psychiatry 44:125–133, 1993

Greendyke RM, Kanter DR, Schuster DB, et al: Propranolol treatment of assaultive patients with organic brain disease: a double-blind crossover, placebo-controlled study. J Nerv Ment Dis 174:290–294, 1986

Hales RE, Silver JM, Yudofsky SC: Aggression and agitation, in Essentials of Consultation-Liaison Psychiatry. Edited by Rundell JR, Wise MG. Washington, DC, American Psychiatric Press, 1999, pp 53–62

Hornstein A, Seliger G: Cognitive side effects of lithium in closed head injury (letter). J Neuropsychiatry Clin Neurosci 1:446–447, 1989

Ratey JJ, Sorgi P, O'Driscoll GA, et al: Nadolol to treat aggression and psychiatric symptomatology in chronic psychiatric inpatients: a double-blind, placebo-controlled study. J Clin Psychiatry 53:41–46, 1992

Yudofsky SC, Silver JM, Schneider SE: Pharmacologic treatment of aggression. Psychiatric Annals 17:397–407, 1987

■ ADDITIONAL READINGS

Silver JM, Yudofsky SC: The Overt Aggression Scale: overview and guiding principles. J Neuropsychiatry Clin Neurosci 3 (suppl 1):S22–S29, 1991

Yudofsky SC, Silver JM, Hales RE: Pharmacologic management of aggression in the elderly. J Clin Psychiatry 51:1–58, 1990

12

PAIN AND ANALGESICS

Pain is a frequent complaint and commonly prompts patients to seek medical attention. In a random sample of 1,265 people in the general population surveyed for the presence of significant or recurrent pain during a 6-month period, 37% reported no pain, 34% had pain in one location, 20% had pain in two locations, and 9% reported pain in three or more locations (Dworkin et al. 1990).

When pain has an acute onset, is well localized, and fits a recognized pathophysiological pattern, the patient usually receives prompt analgesia and appropriate treatment from the physician. A psychiatrist is rarely consulted in such cases. On the other hand, patients who have pain that is chronic, poorly localized, resistant to treatment, or does not fit into a recognized pathophysiological pattern are often referred to a psychiatrist. The consultation request may read, "Rule out functional pain." Bouckoms and Hackett (1991) correctly pointed out that this "request to separate psyche from soma is often a symbolic write-off" (p. 39). The patient typically does not want to see a psychiatrist and is often angry about the referral. The spoken, or more typically unspoken, thought of the patient is, "I have real pain; it's not in my imagination!"

Pain is not purely "functional" or "organic"; it is a combination of both. Pain has two major components: the sensation (nociception) and the perception of that sensation. The perceptual component is influenced by emotional factors and is as important as, if not sometimes more important than, the sensation. For example, two-thirds of the soldiers shot on the beachhead at Anzio during World War II did not require morphine. Most denied pain despite serious injury (Beecher 1955). The gunshot wound meant immediate relief from combat and an honorable exit from the war for the wounded soldier.

To evaluate a patient who complains of pain continuously and chronically, the physician needs

- A detailed history of the pain complaint(s)
- An understanding of pain characteristics (types of pain and descriptors used) (the patient should complete a pain drawing to obtain a graphic, often dramatic depiction of the pain [Figure 12–1])
- A physical examination
- An analysis of impairment of social, physical, and occupational functioning
- A list of, and response to, current and past treatments
- A thorough understanding of the patient's history (i.e., a review of the often voluminous medical records, as well as psychiatric and psychosocial history)
- An examination of the temporal relationship between significant past events and the onset or exacerbation of pain

■ PAIN TERMINOLOGY

Knowledge of pain terminology and characteristics is essential for differential diagnosis and the selection of treatment modalities. Table 12–1 defines the terms commonly used by physicians to describe pain.

Nociceptive (Peripheral) Versus Central Pain

Nociceptive pain. Nociceptive or peripheral pain is activated by stimulation of specialized nerve endings in the skin, subcutaneous tissues, muscles, bones, or viscera. When skin or underlying tissues are disrupted, the pain produced is well localized and sharp. The source of the lesion is easily found unless the pain is referred to another area of the body. In referred pain, recognition of

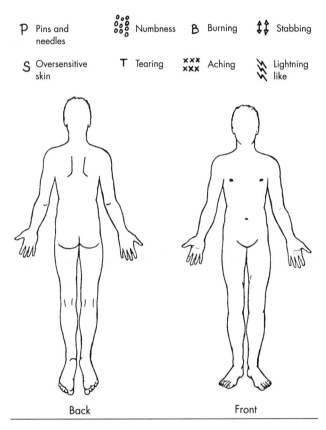

FIGURE 12–1. **Pain drawing.**

the pain pattern is necessary (e.g., angina may be referred to the T1–4 dermatomes, resulting in arm pain). Pain that occurs when viscera are stretched is less well localized. It may be sharp, colicky, or aching in quality.

TABLE 12–1. **Pain terminology**

Nociceptors	Nerve endings in the skin, tissue, and viscera activated by potentially damaging stimuli.
Central (neuropathic) pain	Results from injury to, or changes in, somatosensory pathways. It may persist without demonstrable nociceptive stimuli. (See Table 12–2 for clinical characteristics of central pain.)
Allodynia	The perception of a nonnociceptive stimulus (e.g., light touch) as painful.
Causalgia	A continuous burning pain usually following nerve injury. It may be associated with allodynia, sympathetic dysfunction, and glossy skin.
Deafferentation	Central pain that follows direct injury to the peripheral or central nervous system. Associated sensations include causalgia, dysesthesia, formication, and/or allodynia.
Dysesthesia	An unpleasant sensation (e.g., pins and needles).
Hyperesthesia	An excessive sensitivity to touch, pain, and other sensations.
Hyperalgesia	An exaggerated sensitivity to touch, pain, and other sensations.
Hyperpathia	An increased sensitivity to painful stimuli.
Hypoesthesia	A decreased sensitivity to touch, pain, and other sensations.
Hypoalgesia	A decreased sensitivity to painful stimuli.
Neuralgia	Pain in the distribution of a single nerve, usually the result of trauma or irritation.

Central pain (neuropathic or deafferentation pain). Central pain involves neuronal structures proximal to the nociceptor. Therefore, it can occur without an obvious nociceptive source. Central pain is usually poorly localized, and the patient often has difficulty describing the pain. Examples of central pain include reflex sympathetic dystrophy, phantom limb pain, thalamic pain, posttherapeutic pain, and causalgia. Central nervous system (CNS) or central pain occurs in 20%–50% of chronic pain states (Bouckoms and Hackett 1991). The clinical characteristics of central pain are listed in Table 12–2.

Acute, Continuous, and Chronic Pain

Acute pain. Acute pain is easily recognized. The patient is in obvious discomfort and manifests sympathetic nervous system hyperactivity. For example, a patient with renal colic will cry out in pain and writhe on the gurney. The flank pain is excruciating and often radiates into the groin or testicles. The patient is pale, diaphoretic, and nauseated and often vomits. This clinical picture is recognized by medical students and physicians alike. When acute pain is encountered, the source is identified, treatment is instituted, and analgesics are given.

Continuous pain. Continuous pain occurs in cancer and other chronic disease states. Patients with continuous pain have a recognized nociceptive source, such as metastatic bone lesions from cancer. Narcotics, pain blocks, and ablative surgical procedure

---

TABLE 12–2. **Characteristics of central pain**

Burning sensation

Change in sensory threshold: anesthesia, allodynia, hyperalgesia, or hyperesthesia

Delayed onset for days to weeks following injury

Dysesthesia

Lancinating (paroxysmal exacerbations)

Poor efficacy of narcotics

Nonanatomical distribution (may have trigger zones)

Source. Adapted from Bouckoms A: "Psychiatric Aspects of Pain in the Critically Ill," in *Problems in Critical Care.* Edited by Wise MG. Philadelphia, PA, JB Lippincott, 1988. Copyright 1988, JB Lippincott. Used with permission.

are used as necessary. Hyman and Cassem (1989) offer several helpful management suggestions:

1. Give analgesics on a regular basis, not as needed. Write the order either for a routine regimen or so the patient has the option to decline (e.g., "Offer the patient 10 mg morphine every 4 hours for pain"). In either instance, the patient does not have to "beg" for medication, and the staff is not placed in the position of labeling the patient's regular requests for narcotics as addictive behavior.

2. Observe patients for constipation; 95% of patients taking regular narcotics become constipated. Stool softeners, bulking agents, hydration, and laxatives are usually needed.

3. Monitor patients for tolerance to narcotics, which usually but not always occurs. Although the degree of tolerance that develops is variable, an increase of approximately 50% is sometimes necessary during the first 2 weeks of treatment. Thereafter, smaller incremental increases in the narcotic may be required.

4. Do not consider narcotic addiction in a terminally ill patient. Even in the non–terminally ill patient, the risk of addiction is far less than 1%.

5. Give two to three times the regular narcotic dose at bedtime so that the patient can sleep through the night.

6. If bone or inflammatory pain is present, give antiprostaglandin drugs (e.g., aspirin, nonsteroidal anti-inflammatory drugs such as ibuprofen).

7. Begin narcotics by the oral or suppository route. Later, if the pain worsens, intravenous, epidural, intrathecal, or cerebro-ventricular morphine is sometimes required.

8. Use pain adjuvants, behavioral treatment methods, and exercise to reduce narcotic requirements.

Other medication approaches to analgesia deserve mention: 1) the use of sustained-release morphine preparations, such as MS-Contin and Roxanol-SR, which have a duration of action of 8–12 hours (for breakthrough pain, additional standard morphine preparations should be given); 2) the use of patient-controlled analgesia (PCA) devices, which allow the patient, by pushing a button, to self-administer intravenous analgesics at doses and intervals preset by the physician (patient acceptance is very high, probably higher than efficacy); and 3) the use of epidural anesthesia or narcotics, which are extremely effective.

Chronic pain.   Chronic pain is defined as pain that has persisted for more than 6 months. The original nociceptive stimulus is either gone or cannot account for the continuing pain. The pain has become centralized through mechanisms that are not understood. The mechanisms for the creation and maintenance of chronic pain are complex, involving stress analgesia, endogenous pain inhibition, and psychosocial contributors. The patient with chronic pain accommodates neurophysiologically and psychologically to pain and no longer behaves as if he or she is in acute pain. When this happens, even surgical interruption of specific pain pathways will not eliminate the suffering (Bouckoms and Hackett 1991). Unfortunately, medical personnel apply their knowledge and experience with acute pain to the patient who has chronic pain. The staff become suspicious because the patient with chronic pain reports severe distress but does not behave as if he or she has severe pain. The nurses see the patient laughing during a television show or engaging in a lively discussion with a hospital roommate. The staff conclude that the patient does not have "real" pain. To "prove" the pain is "functional," a misguided physician may give the patient a saline injection (placebo) instead of a narcotic. Unfortunately, such a trial destroys any hope of developing a doctor-patient alliance, although it may establish that the patient is a placebo responder.

■ PAIN BEHAVIOR, SUFFERING, AND PSYCHIATRIC DIAGNOSES

Pain, because it is a symptom, is imperceptible to the observer; it is experienced only by the patient. Pain behaviors, on the other hand, are "signs" that the physician can use to assess the patient's status.

Nociception is the stimulus from the damaged tissue, and pain is the perceived sensation (the "Owwww!"). For some patients, particularly those with chronic pain, a suffering component develops (a moaning "Ohhhhhhhh!" or "Oyyyyyyyy!"). Suffering is the negative emotional response to the pain. Psychiatric diagnoses frequently accompany pain behavior and suffering. Depression, somatoform disorders, and anxiety disorders especially should be considered.

Psychiatric diagnoses to look for in chronic pain patients are listed in Table 12–3. Patients with psychotic disorders also may present with pain. The bizarre nature of the pain and the patient's thought processes will indicate whether psychosis is present. Malingering and factitious disorders also can present with a complaint of pain and associated pain behaviors (see Chapter 8). Personality disorders can present with pain behavior in the absence of demonstrable pathological problems. The patient with an antisocial personality disorder may use pain to evade prosecution or to manipulate for narcotics and other drugs (malingering). Patients with borderline personality disorder may involve physicians in pathological relationships in which pain relief is the overt goal. Engle (1959) described these patients as "pain-prone."

Depression

Major depressive disorder is present in 30% or more of chronic pain patients. Some authors, such as Lindsay and Wyckoff (Hyman and Cassem 1989), reported that as many as 87% of 300 patients referred to a pain center were depressed (Feighner diagnostic criteria). These authors also examined 196 patients referred for depression and found that 59% had pain complaints. Patients with depression and pain often will deny depression and depressed mood ("Doc, I'm not depressed. If I didn't have the pain, everything would be fine."). The key to diagnosis is a thorough investigation of the signs and symptoms of depression (depressed mood, anhedonia, sleep disturbance, decreased interest, impaired concentration, anergy, guilt, psychomotor retardation or agitation, and suicidal ideation or preoccupation with death).

TABLE 12–3.	**Psychiatric syndromes to look for in patients with chronic pain**

Major depressive disorder
Dysthymic disorder
Generalized anxiety disorder
Substance abuse or dependence
Psychoactive substance withdrawal (especially narcotics)
Delusional disorder, somatic type
Somatoform disorders
   Somatization disorder
   Pain disorder
   Hypochondriasis
   Conversion disorder
Pain-prone patient (Engle 1959)
Factitious disorder
Malingering

Anxiety

Anxiety or fear intensifies pain. Unfortunately, patients often are not aware of the heightened anxiety and instead report an increase in pain. Low-dose neuroleptics (e.g., 2 mg perphenazine twice a day) or benzodiazepines are sometimes useful adjuvants to pain medications in the highly anxious patient (Drasner et al. 1992). The majority of patients with chronic pain have pain-related anxiety. When present, it predicts a dysfunctional adjustment to chronic pain (McCracken et al. 1999). Cognitive therapy can help patients to identify cause-and-effect misattributions related to their pain and anxiety symptoms. For example, when patients have fearful thoughts about when the next pain flare-up will occur, substituting more adaptive thoughts prevents the fears from becoming self-fulfilling prophecies.

Somatoform Disorders

Patients with somatoform disorders (Chapter 8) periodically complain of chronic pain. In fact, individuals with somatization disorder must have four pain complaints during the course of their disturbance to meet DSM-IV (American Psychiatric Association 1994) diagnostic criteria. Three other somatoform disorders to consider are hypochondriasis, conversion disorder, and pain disorder.

■ AIDS TO DIAGNOSIS

Aids are available to help the psychiatrist identify whether significant psychological issues are present and to delineate the nature of these issues. An appropriate treatment plan can then follow.

Minnesota Multiphasic Personality Inventory

The Minnesota Multiphasic Personality Inventory—2 (MMPI-2; Butcher et al. 1989) is a useful diagnostic aid if used in combination with other information gathered during an examination. It is also helpful if obvious and subtle subscale scores are available. Occasionally, a physician will send a consultation that states, "Give MMPI" (e.g., many orthopedic surgeons make this request for patients with low back pain). The use of psychological tests alone to make psychiatric diagnoses is inappropriate. A blind interpretation of a patient's MMPI score without clinical correlation often leads to misdiagnosis, because the patient with medical illness will endorse items on the MMPI/MMPI-2 that elevate the (Hy) hysteria and (Hs) hypochondriasis scales (Mapou et al. 1996).

Projective Tests

Projective tests such as the Rorschach or Thematic Apperception Test may reveal unconscious issues that play an important role in the perpetuation of pain.

Pain Drawing

A pain drawing (Figure 12–1) offers the patient an opportunity to present the pain graphically. The drawings are clinically valuable and show both the quality and the distribution of a patient's pain complaints. These drawings should be part of the evaluation of a patient with pain.

Visual Analogue Scale

In a visual analogue scale, the patient simply rates his or her pain on a 100-mm horizontal line with a 0 marking the left end of the line (indicating "no pain") and a 10 marking the right end of the line (indicating "the worst pain that you have ever had"). The visual analogue scale is easy for the patient to do and is used repetitively to monitor the patient's response to a therapeutic intervention (Bouckoms and Hackett 1991). When patients are unable or unwilling to use paper and pencil, the clinician can ask: "On a scale from 0 (no pain) to 10 (the worst pain that you have ever had), where is your pain right now?"

Sadomasochistic Index (Pain-Prone)

Engle (1959), in his classic paper "'Psychogenic' Pain and the Pain-Prone Patient," beautifully described patients who are predisposed to develop chronic pain because of their upbringings and personalities. These pain-prone patients share a common trait: a high sadomasochistic index. The histories of these patients are replete with punishing, abusive relationships, and their interpersonal interactions are often angry and bitter. Such patients are not consciously aware of the sadomasochistic nature of their relationships. Therefore, evaluation of patients' past and present relationships for this malignant sadomasochistic quality helps to identify such pain-prone individuals.

■ ANALGESICS

Acute, very severe nociceptive pain, in the absence of a surgically or medically correctable cause, is best relieved by opiates. Opiates are not as efficacious in patients with central or chronic pain (Table

12–4), whereas nonpharmacological treatment and other medications, such as antidepressants, anticonvulsants (e.g., clonazepam), neuropeptides (e.g., calcitonin in the case of phantom limb pain), α-adrenergic blockade, or clonidine, may prove more helpful (Maciewicz et al. 1985). The addition of nonpharmacological and pharmacological pain adjuvants, particularly in the terminally ill patient with continuous pain, may allow a reduction in opiate use and, therefore, decrease side effects such as sedation.

■ OPIATES (NARCOTICS)

Although opiates are efficacious in the treatment of nociceptive pain, they are underused in hospital settings. The reasons for undertreatment are physicians' underestimate of effective doses, overestimate of duration of action, and fears of addiction. Use of more than one narcotic is seldom if ever necessary. Thus, a complicated regimen can almost always be simplified. A consulting psychiatrist who understands opiate pharmacology has the opportunity to improve patient treatment (Table 12–4).

Dependence

Physical dependence and tolerance (i.e., the dosage needed to achieve same effect will increase) may develop within the first weeks of opiate use. Physical dependence is usually manifest by withdrawal symptoms if the drug is discontinued abruptly. The latter is preventable by gradually tapering the opiate. Narcotics that have partial antagonist properties (i.e., butorphanol, nalbuphine, pentazocine) can precipitate withdrawal in a patient taking another opiate.

Addiction

Addiction is a frequently misused term; it is a behavioral disorder. It implies an overwhelming involvement with the use of a drug; extraordinary efforts to secure a supply, such as robbery; and a high

TABLE 12–4.　Comparison of opiate potency and dosage

Drug (trade name)	Equal analgesic dose (mg/im)	Oral equivalent dose (mg)	Duration of analgesic (hours)
Opioid agonists			
Morphine	10	30–60	4–5
Codeine	120	200	4–6
Heroin	4	60	3–5
Hydromorphone (Dilaudid)	1.5	7.5	4–5
Levorphanol (Levo-Dromoran)	2	4	4–5
Meperidine (Demerol)	75–100	300	2–5
Methadone (Dolophine)	10	20	3–8
Morphine, sustained release (MS-Contin)	—	*[a]	8–12
Opioid agonists-antagonists[b]			
Butorphanol (Stadol)	2	—	2.5–3.5
Nalbuphine (Nubain)	12	—	4–6
Pentazocine (Talwin)	60	180	2–3

Note.　im = intramuscular.

[a]Divide total morphine use for 24 hours by 2 or 3, and give that number of milligrams of MS-Contin two or three times a day, respectively. [b]May precipitate withdrawal symptoms if patient has extensive use of pure opioid agonist(s). Abuse possible but potential less.

Source.　Adapted from Jaffe JH, Martin WR: "Opioid Analgesics and Antagonists," in *The Pharmacological Basis of Therapeutics.* Edited by Gilman AG, Rall TW, Nies AS, et al. New York, Pergamon, 1990; Bouckoms A: "Psychiatric Aspects of Pain in the Critically Ill," in *Problems in Critical Care.* Edited by Wise MG. Philadelphia, PA, JB Lippincott, 1988. Copyright 1988, JB Lippincott; Cassem NH: "Pain (Current Topics in Medicine, Vol. 2)," in *Scientific American Medicine.* Edited by Rubenstein E, Federman DD. New York, Scientific American, 1989. All rights reserved. Used with permission.

likelihood of relapse following withdrawal. Porter reported that of 11,882 patients who received narcotics during hospitalization, 4 cases of abuse (a rate of 0.03%) developed in patients with no history of prior problems (Jaffe and Martin 1990). Therefore, fear of abuse does not justify the routine undertreatment of pain. The proper selection of patients for opiate therapy is the key. Opiates should be used judiciously in patients with a history of abuse, an untreated affective illness, or a limited response to opiates in the past. When an acute injury occurs in a patient with a history of drug abuse or addiction, the amount of opiate needed by most patients undergoing a similar trauma should be used, and the medication should be tapered at a normal or typical pace.

Adverse Effects

Few side effects of opiates are serious. The only absolute contraindication is a documented allergy. (Note: many patients will report an allergy to opiates but are not actually allergic. They have experienced a side effect, such as nausea and vomiting or hallucinations, not an allergic response.) Relative contraindications are severe bronchial asthma, increased intracranial pressure, and hypoxia (Bouckoms 1988). Common side effects are nausea, slight respiratory depression, sedation, and constipation. Hypotension may occur, and hallucinations and confusional states can develop, particularly with meperidine (its metabolite normeperidine is neurotoxic), and less frequently with morphine.

Pharmacological Adjuvants

Pharmacological adjuvants improve the efficacy of analgesics. Psychostimulants (amphetamines, methylphenidate), tricyclic antidepressants, anticonvulsants, benzodiazepines, antihistamines, neuroleptics, prostaglandin inhibitors, and nitrous oxide are effective adjuvants (Bouckoms 1988). Among antidepressants, amitriptyline or desipramine is recommended, whereas fluoxetine may be no more effective than placebo (Max et al. 1992). Trazodone is a frequently used adjuvant; in addition to effects on the pain syndrome itself, it significantly improves sleep and appetite.

■ TREATMENT AND MANAGEMENT OF CHRONIC PAIN

The treatment goal for the patient with chronic pain is to improve functional status, not eliminate the pain. Analgesics and surgical procedures are rarely curative in such patients. Treatment fads to alleviate pain come and go (Deyo 1991), and patients who have chronic pain are desperate for relief. Table 12–5 summarizes man-

---

TABLE 12–5. **Management principles for patients with chronic pain**

Evaluate the patient with a multidisciplinary team and treat the patient with active case management that prevents doctor shopping.

Ask how the pain and the condition causing the pain have affected the patient's life. The answer to that question frequently identifies potential psychosocial arenas for intervention.

Minimize medication use and eliminate narcotics (in most cases).

Do not rely on "rest" as the centerpiece of management.

Ask patients to set goals focused around improved physical and psychosocial functioning.

Use physical therapy and behavioral treatment methods (Table 12–6), which can markedly reduce or eliminate the need for analgesic medications.

Treat depression and anxiety disorders when present, and work to decrease psychosocial stressors that may sustain pain or increase suffering.

Mobilize the patient and work to improve function. The treatment plan should primarily aim to restore activity.

Reinforce increased activity (e.g., exercise), not maladaptive pain behaviors (e.g., groaning, medication-seeking).

Do no harm. Use surgical procedures only when clear evidence of reversible pathology exists.

TABLE 12–6.   **Behavioral treatment methods for pain**

Biofeedback	Computer-assisted measurement of physiological changes—previously thought to be involuntary—which brings them under voluntary control. Measurements can include surface electromyelography, temperature, galvanic skin response, respiration, pulse transit time, and distal plesmography.
Autogenic training	Mental exercises designed to produce relaxation imagery through suggestion that is sometimes coupled with relaxation and exercises.
Progressive muscle relaxation	A systematic approach to relaxation exercises involving the tensing and relaxing of muscle groups.
Hypnosis	A state of enhanced focus or awareness that can lead to increased levels of suggestibility. In some patients, this can reduce or block painful sensations.
Cognitive-behavioral therapy	Monitoring negative thoughts; recognizing the relationship among thoughts, affects, and behaviors; and altering or replacing dysfunctional thoughts with more reality-oriented ones.

Source.   Adapted from Smith G, Beers D: "Pain," in *Behavioral Medicine in Primary Care: A Practical Guide.* Edited by Feldman MD, Christensen JF. Stamford, CT, Appleton & Lange, 1997, p. 281. Copyright 1997, Appleton & Lange. Used with permission.

agement principles for patients with chronic pain syndromes. Table 12–6 defines behavioral and psychotherapeutic techniques that are effective treatments of chronic pain and help to decrease or obviate the need for medications.

■ REFERENCES

American Psychiatric Association: Diagnostic and Statistical Manual of Mental Disorders, 4th Edition. Washington, DC, American Psychiatric Association, 1994

Beecher HK: The powerful placebo. JAMA 159:1602–1606, 1955

Bouckoms A: Psychiatric aspects of severe pain and suffering in the critically ill, in Problems in Critical Care. Edited by Wise MG. Philadelphia, PA, JB Lippincott, 1988, pp 47–62

Bouckoms A, Hackett TP: The pain patient: evaluation and treatment, in Massachusetts General Hospital Handbook of General Hospital Psychiatry, 3rd Edition. Edited by Cassem NH. St. Louis, MO, Mosby-Year Book, 1991, pp 39–68

Butcher JN, Dahlstrom WG, Graham JR, et al: Manual for Administration and Scoring, Minnesota Multiphasic Personality Inventory—2: MMPI-2. Minneapolis, University of Minnesota, 1989

Deyo RA: Fads in the treatment of low back pain. N Engl J Med 325:1039–1040, 1991

Drasner K, Katz JA, Schapera A: Control of pain and anxiety, in Principles of Critical Care. Edited by Hall JB, Schmidt GA, Wood LDH. New York, McGraw-Hill, 1992, pp 958–973

Dworkin SF, Von Korff M, LeResche L: Multiple pains and psychiatric disturbance: an epidemiologic investigation. Arch Gen Psychiatry 47:239–244, 1990

Engle GL: "Psychogenic" pain and the pain-prone patient. Am J Med 26:899–918, 1959

Hyman SE, Cassem NH: Pain, in Scientific American Medicine (Current Topics in Medicine, Chapter II). Edited by Rubenstein E, Federman DD. New York, Scientific American, 1989, pp 1–17

Jaffe JH, Martin WR: Opioid analgesics and antagonists, in The Pharmacological Basis of Therapeutics, 8th Edition. Edited by Gilman AG, Rall TW, Nies AS, et al. New York, Pergamon, 1990, pp 485–521

Maciewicz R, Bouckoms A, Martin JB: Drug therapy of neuropathic pain. Clin J Pain 1:39–49, 1985

Mapou R, Spector J, Kay GG: Neuropsychological and psychological assessment, in The American Psychiatric Press Textbook of Consultation-Liaison Psychiatry. Edited by Rundell JR, Wise MG. Washington, DC, American Psychiatric Press, 1996, pp 86–115

Max MB, Lynch SA, Muir J, et al: Effects of desipramine, amitriptyline, and fluoxetine on pain in diabetic neuropathy. N Engl J Med 326:1250–1256, 1992

McCracken LM, Spertus IL, Janeck AS et al: Behavioral dimensions of adjustment in persons with chronic pain: pain-related anxiety and acceptance. Pain 80:283–289, 1999

Smith G, Beers D: Pain, in Behavioral Medicine in Primary Care: A Practical Guide. Edited by Feldman MD, Christensen JF. Stamford, CT, Appleton & Lange, 1997, pp 277–283

■ ADDITIONAL READINGS

American Pain Society: Principles of analgesic use in the treatment of acute pain or chronic cancer pain (special feature). Clinical Pharmacy 6:523–532, 1987

Brown DL, Flynn JF, Owens PD: Pain control, in Critical Care, 2nd Edition. Edited by Civetta JM, Taylor RW, Kirby RB. Philadelphia, PA, JB Lippincott, 1992, pp 219–229

Fields H, Liebeskind J (eds): Pharmacological Approaches to the Treatment of Chronic Pain: Concepts and Critical Issues. New York, IASP Press, 1994

Fishbain DA: Types of pain treatment facilities and referral selection criteria. Arch Fam Med 4:58–66, 1995

Houpt JL: Chronic pain management, in Principles of Medical Psychiatry. Edited by Stoudemire A, Fogel BS. Orlando, FL, Grune & Stratton, 1987, pp 389–401

13

PERSONALITY, RESPONSE TO ILLNESS, AND MEDICAL PSYCHOTHERAPY

Personality is a consistent and to some extent predictable set of behaviors that characterize a person's management of day-to-day living. These long-term traits are generally stable and usually ego-syntonic. However, stress can disturb the usual balance between needs, drives, external reality, and conscience. For example, medical illness and hospitalization present the patient with a strange, stressful, and demanding environment that may destabilize personality function. Most individuals are highly resilient and will cope well with an illness or injury. When personality issues complicate the treatment of an illness or hinder the patient's cooperation with the medical or nursing staff, the consultation-liaison (C-L) psychiatrist is often consulted.

■ PERSONALITY AND RESPONSE TO ILLNESS

Psychological Regression

A person with an acute serious illness who is admitted to a hospital may psychologically regress. This regression is catalyzed by a loss of control of basic body functions, such as eating, sleeping, and bladder and bowel control. The degree to which this is a problem depends on the severity of stress, the patient's baseline level of psychological functioning, and the quality of social supports. A patient's behavior during times of severe stress does not necessarily reflect long-term personality dysfunction or the presence of a personality disorder.

Levels of Ego Defenses

Understanding the patient's defense or coping mechanisms is one way to identify the patient's behavioral tendencies both during times of severe stress and, most important, during times of lower stress. If the C-L psychiatrist's interventions can reduce the patient's anxiety and discomfort, one might predict that the patient will return to more typical, hopefully mature, defenses. DSM-IV (American Psychiatric Association 1994) contains a method for the assessment of defense mechanisms and coping styles—the Defensive Functioning Scale. The Defensive Functioning Scale (Table 13–1) organizes these defense mechanisms from the highest (most adaptive) to the lowest (least adaptive) level.

■ PERSONALITY AND GENERAL MEDICAL CONDITIONS

Personality can interact with somatic illness in many ways. Maladaptive behaviors can directly increase the risk of diseases. For example, alcohol abuse can lead to liver disease, or failure to use a seat belt can lead to traumatic injury. Alternatively, chronic medical conditions, such as chronic pain or life-threatening chronic illness, can lead to maladaptive chronic behavior patterns (e.g., expectation of disappointment and rejection). Finally, neurological and medical conditions can produce profound personality change.

When an adult experiences a change in personality, the clinician should consider potential medical and toxic etiologies. Central nervous system (CNS) insults may either change personality traits or magnify preexisting ones. Various CNS lesions or conditions can cause secondary personality syndromes (see Table 13–2). The family of a patient with a secondary personality syndrome often reports that the patient is "not himself." Appropriate social be-

TABLE 13–1.	**Defenses: common responses to illness**

Individual defense mechanisms

High adaptive level (optimal adaptation in handling stress)

    Affiliation

    Altruism

    Anticipation

    Humor

    Self-assertion

    Self-observation

    Sublimation

    Suppression

Mental inhibitions level (keeps threats and fears out of awareness)

    Displacement

    Dissociation

    Intellectualization

    Isolation of affect

    Reaction formation

    Repression

    Undoing

Minor image-distorting level (distortions used to regulate self-esteem)

    Devaluation

    Idealization

    Omnipotence

Disavowal level (removal from awareness or misattribution)

    Denial

    Projection

    Rationalization

Major image-distorting level (gross distortion or misattribution)

    Autistic fantasy

    Projective identification

    Splitting of self-image or image of others

(continued)

TABLE 13–1.	Defenses: common responses to illness *(continued)*

Action level (deals with stressors by action or withdrawal)

  Acting out

  Apathetic withdrawal

  Complaining

  Help-rejecting

  Passive-aggression

Level of defensive dysregulation (pronounced break with reality)

  Delusional projection

  Psychotic denial

  Psychotic distortion

Source. Adapted from American Psychiatric Association: *Diagnostic and Statistical Manual of Mental Disorders,* 4th Edition. Washington, DC, American Psychiatric Association, 1994. Copyright 1994, American Psychiatric Association. Used with permission.

havior often disappears. Apathy, suspiciousness, affective instability, poor impulse control, and a change in demeanor can also occur.

Frontal lobe injuries, tumors, abscesses, and other lesions predispose patients to personality change or dysfunction. CNS frontal lobe lesions are common because of the vulnerability of the prefrontal and frontal cortex to injury; in many cases, cognitive abilities are relatively preserved. Table 13–3 lists the clinical features of patients with frontal lobe personality syndromes.

■ PERSONALITY DISORDER

Definition

Personality traits—characteristic behavioral response patterns—are the typical ways that an individual thinks, feels, and relates to others. When these patterns are fixed, inflexible, unresponsive to changes in the environment, and maladaptive, they can result in

TABLE 13–2.	**Medical causes of personality change**

Cortical dementia (may be late manifestation)

Central nervous system tumors

Frontal lobe disease (especially degenerative/ablative)

Head trauma

Poisons

Postconcussive syndrome

Psychosurgery

Stroke

Subarachnoid hemorrhage

Subcortical dementia (often a major manifestation)

Temporal lobe disease (especially irritative/seizure)

Source. Adapted from Popkin MK: "The Organic Brain Syndromes Presenting With Little or No Cognitive Impairment," in *The Medical Basis of Psychiatry.* Edited by Winokur G, Clayton PJ. Philadelphia, PA, WB Saunders, 1986, pp. 29–38. Used with permission.

psychological and social dysfunction. Such behavior patterns may constitute a personality disorder. DSM-IV includes 11 personality disorders: paranoid, schizoid, schizotypal, antisocial, borderline, histrionic, narcissistic, avoidant, dependent, obsessive-compulsive, and not otherwise specified; two proposed personality disorders, depressive and passive-aggressive, are listed in DSM-IV's Appendix B as "provided for further study."

Clinical Characteristics

Personality disorders are established by late adolescence or early adulthood. Behaviors associated with personality disorders are ego-syntonic. The behaviors feel "natural," and the individual may not understand why his or her actions upset others. The diagnosis of a personality disorder is based on long-term historical data, not on behavior at one point in time, especially a stressful time such as hospitalization with a life-threatening illness. Patients with personality

TABLE 13–3. **Clinical characteristics of frontal lobe syndromes**

Disinhibition

Talkativeness

Pranks and joking

Lack of concern for future

Sexual indiscretion

Unconcern for feelings of others

Concentration/attention impairment

Cognitive function largely intact

Lack of initiative

Slowed psychomotor activity

Hyperactive tendon reflexes may be present

Tactlessness

Childish excitement

Diminished social control

Lack of concern for consequences of actions

Mood elevation

Inability to carry out planned activities

Lack of spontaneity

Grasp reflex present

Babinski's sign may be present

disorders frequently lack empathy and usually believe that the environment must change when problems arise. CNS (especially frontal lobe) disease, head trauma, stressors, and situations that induce psychological regression can exacerbate personality dysfunction.

Patients with personality disorders also affect the physician's and staff's abilities to respond appropriately, leading to nontherapeutic behaviors, such as avoiding the patient, not responding to a change in symptoms, or assigning the patient's care to the least skilled member of the team. In this way, countertransference can influence the patient's clinical outcome.

Differential Diagnosis

Included in the differential diagnosis of a personality disorder are all Axis I psychiatric disorders, personality traits, stress-related psychological regression, and secondary personality syndromes. Other characterological disturbances exist besides the official list of Axis II conditions in DSM-IV (Ursano et al. 1999). Many of these conditions, such as alexithymia and type A behavior pattern, are of interest to C-L psychiatrists. As an example, alexithymia is an impaired ability to perceive or express emotions. In a severe form, it might qualify as a personality disorder because the individual's characteristic way of dealing with feelings is maladaptive and inflexible. However, the operational definition makes reliable measurement of alexithymia difficult. In various studies, alexithymia was highly prevalent in patients with psychosomatic conditions, chronic psychogenic pain, and psychological conditions affecting a physiological disorder (Taylor et al. 1990). Some conditions, such as dysthymic disorder, cyclothymic disorder, and dissociative identity disorder, are categorized by the DSM-IV classification committee as Axis I disorders even though they are more characteristic of a personality disorder.

■ TREATMENT AND MANAGEMENT

General Considerations

Patients with a personality disorder rarely seek treatment; patterns of behavior are ingrained, stable, and "comfortable." More commonly, someone else, such as a family member or hospital staff, wants the patient's behavior to change, especially when the behavior complicates medical management. The psychiatric consult that is requested is not desired by the patient, who will likely see himself or herself as a victim, not the problem.

After receiving a consult on a patient with personality or coping style problems, the psychiatrist must 1) identify and attempt to reverse any remediable organic factors (Table 13–2), 2) carefully consider whether other psychiatric disorders are present, 3) establish baseline and current levels of personality functioning and past responses to stressors, and 4) try to understand the meaning of the illness and hospitalization to the patient. Optimal management of maladaptive stress responses is not possible without an understanding of how the patient sees himself or herself with this illness at this time (Groves and Kucharski 1987). In other words, why this patient and why now? Armed with these data, the consultant can recommend the most appropriate psychopharmacological, psychotherapeutic, and ward management interventions.

Pharmacotherapy

Neuroleptics. Patients with borderline, schizotypal, or paranoid personality disorders sometimes experience micropsychotic episodes, especially when stressed and regressed. These episodes frequently respond to low doses of neuroleptic medication. Drug treatment also may improve impulse control, mood, and severe disabling anxiety.

Antidepressants. Antidepressant medications are indicated when clinical major depressive disorder occurs in a patient with a personality disorder. Antidepressants can also decrease affective instability in patients with borderline personality disorder. When such patients are taking antidepressants, the potential for overdose is often high, and a nonlethal medication should be used.

Lithium. Lithium helps to decrease affective symptoms and emotional lability in some patients with personality disorder. Patients with impulse control difficulty also may benefit from lithium.

Antianxiety agents and sedative-hypnotics. These medications should be prescribed with caution and avoided when possible because patients with personality disorders are at risk for substance abuse, disinhibition, and overdose. However, judicious use of low-dose benzodiazepines for acute anxiety is sometimes necessary.

Other medications.   Carbamazepine or propranolol may be effective in many patients with aggressive and assaultive behavior caused by secondary personality syndrome, explosive type (Patterson 1987). Patients with impulsive features (borderline, histrionic, antisocial, narcissistic, and dependent personality disorders) are at risk for suicidal gestures. Therefore, medications should be prescribed cautiously and in limited quantities at discharge. Antisocial patients often show drug-seeking behavior.

Group Psychotherapy

Group treatments are very useful for patients who tend to express affects through somatic representation. Such groups tend to facilitate communication with several people who may share similar diagnoses, characteristics, interests, anxieties, and misperceptions about illness (Lipsitt 1996). Patients learn from one another, depend less on the therapist, share stressful experiences, and sometimes model behavior after the therapist or other group members. Groups may be psychoeducational; supportive; expressive; homogeneous or heterogeneous (regarding illness); closed or open-ended; and inpatient, day hospital, or outpatient.

Clinic and Ward Management

Staff issues.   Patients with personality syndromes or regressive behaviors often engender anxiety, anger, rage, resentment, an urge to punish, or avoidance behavior in the staff. The consultant may defuse a tense situation by educating the staff about the patient's personality and why they feel or react as they do. This approach usually decreases the intensity of affect among hospital personnel and is hoped to translate into decreased affect in the patient. Giving the staff articles such as "Taking Care of the Hateful Patient" by Groves (1978) is helpful.

Patient issues.   When staff-patient conflict exists, the consultant should objectively consider whether the patient has legitimate complaints. If legitimate problems exist, the consultant should help correct them. For some patients, especially patients with obsessive-compulsive personality styles, consultants should work with the treatment team to resurrect the patient's intellectual defenses. Giving the patient as much control as possible over treatment and activity decisions may decrease anxiety and unreasonable demands.

More frequently, however, patients require appropriate boundaries, structure, and limit-setting. External control helps the primitively functioning or regressed patient retain internal control. Boundaries and limit-setting are not punitive; they provide structure for the patient. Borderline, histrionic, antisocial, dependent, and narcissistic personality disorder patients are most likely to require such structure.

Transference and countertransference. Illness, hospitalization, pain, and fear increase the frequency and intensity of transference reactions. The physician is seen as a reliable parent or as an authority figure from the past. Alternatively, the physician is viewed with fear and suspicion as a disappointing figure from the past (Ursano et al. 1991). Manifestations of the transference to the physician and the medical staff may prompt the request for a psychiatric consultation. During the assessment, the patient may also develop similar transference feelings toward the C-L psychiatrist. Usually, however, the patient's transference feelings toward the C-L psychiatrist are less intense because the consultant has had much less contact with the patient. To assess countertransference, the C-L psychiatrist uses his or her reactions to a patient as information to help understand what the treatment team experiences; this information can help the C-L psychiatrist make effective recommendations.

■ MEDICAL PSYCHOTHERAPY

Definition

Medical psychotherapy is defined as "that which is intentionally (as contrasted with coincidentally) exercised on patients with medical illness by physicians with psychiatric training" (Lipsitt 1996, p. 1054). The ultimate aim of medical psychotherapy is to systematically apply biopsychosocial interventions to encourage psychotherapeutic change. Attempts to remove psychological defenses are almost always counterproductive. The consulting psychiatrist must remember that patients under the stress of hospitalization and severe illness use less "mature" but nevertheless adaptive defenses. Even if they cause problems for the ward or clinic, these defenses are the patient's best available coping tools and, unless dangerous, should initially be supported. A frontal assault on defenses usually makes matters worse, causing intense fear, despair, anger, or psychosis.

Selection Process

Traditional selection criteria do not apply in the inpatient or even some outpatient C-L settings. The C-L psychiatrist goes to the patient; the patient does not select the C-L psychiatrist. Patients typically have not identified a particular emotional issue for which they need help; it is the attending physician, house officer, or nurse who requests consultation. In fact, in inpatient settings, the patient rarely knows about the psychiatric consultation until the psychiatrist presents at the bedside. Patients in the C-L setting therefore seldom have the motivation for or receptivity to psychotherapy in its usual sense (Lipsitt 1996).

Setting

Although C-L psychiatrists provide their services in a variety of outpatient facilities, the setting of the medical psychotherapist is often the bedside, a hospital or clinic conference room, an intensive care unit, or—in special circumstances—even a hallway; medical psychotherapy rarely occurs in a well-furnished, quiet office. Hospitalized patients wear hospital garb and have little privacy. The stereotypical 50-minute hour is nowhere more challenged than in medical settings, where encounters may last

---

TABLE 13–4. **Elements of medical psychotherapy formulation**

Character structure ("personality diagnosis")

Presenting problem (reason for request of consultation)

Patient's narrative (life "story"), including perceptions and attributions of current illness

Identified life event(s) or crisis that precipitated response

Defenses used by patient to negotiate stresses of medical illness, surgery, and hospitalization

Patterns from past are predictors of patient's response to caregivers and treatment interventions

---

Source. Adapted from Lipsitt DR: "Psychotherapy," in *The American Psychiatric Press Textbook of Consultation-Liaison Psychiatry.* Edited by Rundell JR, Wise MG. Washington, DC, American Psychiatric Press, 1996, p. 1067. Copyright 1996, American Psychiatric Press. Used with permission.

anywhere from a few minutes to more than 1 hour (Lipsitt 1996). Initial consultations or psychotherapy evaluations are often done in installments that are dictated by the patient's and staff's schedules.

Associative Anamnesis

One interview technique especially suited to C-L work is associative anamnesis (Deutsch and Murphy 1955), which was derived in part from the psychoanalytic free associative process. Deutsch and Murphy found that both physiological and psychological data could be obtained by allowing the patient considerable latitude in speaking about his or her symptoms. They noted that the patient "drifts into a communication in which he inattentively mixes emotional and symptom material" (p. 20). In this way, they said, "it is possible to observe the somatic and the psychic components more nearly simultaneously" (p. 19). Through repetition of key somatic or affective words (the interviewer is not passive) "the patient is stimulated to give the needed information" (p. 20).

Formulation

The C-L psychiatrist must use data from a variety of sources to derive a formulation. The formulation, as much as if not more than the DSM-IV diagnosis, is the C-L psychiatrist's road map to intervention (Lipsitt 1996). Table 13–4 summarizes essential elements of the medical psychotherapy formulation.

■ REFERENCES

American Psychiatric Association: Diagnostic and Statistical Manual of Mental Disorders, 4th Edition. Washington, DC, American Psychiatric Association, 1994

Deutsch F, Murphy W: The Clinical Interview. New York, International Universities Press, 1955

Groves JE: Taking care of the hateful patient. N Engl J Med 298:883–887, 1978

Groves JE, Kucharski A: Brief psychotherapy, in Massachusetts General Hospital Handbook of General Hospital Psychiatry. Edited by Cassem NH. St. Louis, MO, Mosby-Year Book, 1991, pp 321–341

Lipsitt DR: Psychotherapy, in The American Psychiatric Press Textbook of Consultation-Liaison Psychiatry. Edited by Rundell JR, Wise MG. Washington, DC, American Psychiatric Press, 1996, pp1052–1078

Patterson JF: Carbamazepine for assaultive patients with organic brain disease. Psychosomatics 28:579–581, 1987

Popkin MK: The organic brain syndromes presenting with little or no cognitive impairment, in The Medical Basis of Psychiatry. Edited by Winokur G, Clayton PJ. Philadelphia, PA, WB Saunders, 1986, pp 29–38

Taylor GJ, Bagby RM, Ryan DP, et al: Validation of the alexithymia construct: a measurement-based approach. Can J Psychiatry 35:290–297, 1990

Ursano RJ, Sonnenberg, S, Lazar S: Concise Guide to Psychodynamic Psychotherapy. Washington, DC, American Psychiatric Press, 1991

Ursano RJ, Epstein RS, Lazar SG: Behavioral responses to illness: personality and personality disorders, in The Essentials of Consultation-Liaison Psychiatry. Edited by Rundell JR, Wise MG. Washington, DC, American Psychiatric Press, 1999, pp 27–37

■ ADDITIONAL READINGS

Bloom BL: Focused single-session therapy: initial development and evaluation, in Forms of Brief Therapy. Edited by Budman S. New York, Guilford, 1981, pp 131–175

Groves JE: Management of the borderline patient on a medical or surgical ward: the psychiatric consultant's role. Int J Psychiatry Med 6:337–348, 1975

Gunderson JG: Personality disorders, in The New Harvard Guide to Psychiatry. Edited by Nicholi AM. Cambridge, MA, Belknap Press of Harvard University Press, 1988, pp 337–357

Horowitz MJ: Stress Response Syndromes. New York, Jason Aronson, 1976

Nardo JM: The personality in the medical setting: a psychodynamic understanding, in Consultation-Liaison Psychiatry and Behavioral Medicine. Edited by Houpt JL, Brodie HKH. Philadelphia, PA, JB Lippincott, 1986, pp 53–64

Rosenman RH: Type A behavior pattern: a personal overview. Journal of Social Behavior and Personality 5:1–24, 1990

Vaillant GE: Theoretical hierarchy of adaptive ego mechanisms. Arch Gen Psychiatry 24:107–118, 1971

14

MEDICOLEGAL ISSUES IN CONSULTATION

We begin this chapter on medicolegal issues with a disclaimer—we are not lawyers. The views expressed come from consultation-liaison psychiatrists who deal regularly with cases that raise forensic issues. Laws vary from state to state, and legal precedents change. Therefore, a consultation psychiatrist must be familiar with pertinent general legal concepts and state laws. As Groves and Vaccarino (1987) pointed out, it is better for the physician to practice good medicine than to attempt to function as a lawyer and practice bad medicine. There is no substitute for good faith, common sense, and a high standard of medical care (Shouton et al. 1991); however, consulting a lawyer who understands medical practice is occasionally necessary in difficult situations.

When a medicolegal issue arises, or could arise at some future time, detailed documentation in the patient's medical record is of paramount importance. Fear that the patient may read the record should not preclude documentation. The physician should write with the expectation that the patient will read the record. A person who claims malpractice by a physician must prove four things (Shouton et al. 1991): 1) that the physician, assuming he or she was treating the patient, did not perform up to the standards of care provided by an average physician in the local community; 2) that negligence occurred; 3) that the negligence was a direct cause of damage; and 4) that actual damage occurred.

■ CONFIDENTIALITY

Confidentiality is the right of a patient to have confidential communications withheld from outside parties unless authorization to release that information is given. Consultation-liaison work is unique in that the patient is not the customer. Once a consult is generated, an answer is due the consultee, not the patient. At the beginning of a consultation, psychiatrists should inform patients about the flow of information. Psychiatrists should not assume they have carte blanche authorization when speaking to hospital staff members about all matters revealed by the patient (Simon 1999). Information that will enable the staff to function effectively on behalf of the patient should be provided. Rarely is it necessary to disclose intimate details of the patient's life. This and other common statutory exceptions to confidentiality are summarized in Table 14–1.

In the strictest sense of the law, a psychiatrist performing a consultation should not speak to a patient's family or significant other without permission. When this is not possible, the psychiatrist should document the reasons in a clear note in the patient's medical record. Fortunately, the patient's refusal to allow the physician to

---

TABLE 14–1. **Common statutory exceptions to confidentiality between psychiatrist and patient**

Child abuse

Competency proceedings

Court-ordered examination

Danger to self or others

Patient as a litigant

Intent to commit a crime or harmful act

Civil commitment proceedings

Communication with other treatment providers

Source. Adapted from Simon RI: "Legal and Ethical Issues," in *The American Psychiatric Press Textbook of Consultation-Liaison Psychiatry.* Edited by Rundell JR, Wise MG. Washington, DC, American Psychiatric Press, 1996, pp. 178–200. Copyright 1996, American Psychiatric Press. Used with permission.

contact the family or significant other is uncommon. The reverse phenomenon can also occur; the family or significant other does not want the patient told about his or her diagnosis and prognosis. The most understandable reason for this request is to protect the patient from the emotional trauma of a terminal diagnosis. With reassurance and the realization that secrecy is impossible and is almost always destructive rather than helpful, full communications is usually restored. Sometimes the request for secrecy is symptomatic of long-standing maladaptive relationships within the family or companion relationship. A brief consultation is unlikely to correct this situation. In such cases, a useful focus is to help the staff deal with and provide care for a patient who has a difficult family or significant other.

■ COMPETENCY VERSUS CAPACITY

In general, *competency* refers to some minimal mental, cognitive, or behavioral ability, trait, or capability required to perform a particular legally recognized act or to assume some legal role (Simon 1999). The determination of incompetency is a judicial decision. In this regard, it is clinically useful to differentiate between the terms *incompetence* and *incapacity*. Incompetence refers to a court decision, whereas incapacity refers to a clinical determination (Mishkin 1989). Incapacity does not prevent treatment. It merely means the clinician must obtain substitute consent. Consultations to "evaluate competency" are actually evaluations for capacity; nevertheless, the term *competency* is in such wide use in clinical medicine that it is difficult to avoid using the term when discussing cases with consultees.

The consultation question "Is the patient competent?" requires immediate clarification by asking, "Competent for what?" The determination of "competency" is not an all-or-none phenomenon. For example, a patient may be judged incompetent by the court to manage his or her financial affairs but may still be competent to refuse a medical procedure.

"Competency" evaluations constitute about 4%–9% of the consults on a consultation service. These consults are often urgently requested; most patients are found "competent" (Farnsworth 1990, Mebane and Rauch 1990). Most are requested because a patient refuses treatment or disposition (usually transfer from the hospital to a nursing home) or threatens to leave against medical advice (Farnsworth 1990, Mebane and Rauch 1990). More rarely, physicians request competency evaluations to confirm a patient's capacity to give informed consent. Because the patient's mental status can change from one hour to the next, repetitive examinations are necessary.

Roth and colleagues (1977) proposed a standard of competency that is based on two variables: the treatment's risk-benefit ratio and the patient's decision regarding treatment (Figure 14–1). For example, a patient has a gangrenous leg, and amputation is proposed to save his life. The risk (potential consequences) of this procedure to the patient is low, and the benefits are high. Therefore, if the patient refuses amputation (cell B), a rigorous (high) test of competency is applied. Failure to pass this competency test, indicating that the patient is incompetent, would lead the psychiatrist to recommend that the physician and the patient's family or significant other pursue court action to appoint a surrogate decision maker. If the patient consents to amputation (cell A), a lenient (low) test of competency is used. On the other hand, in a clinical situation in which the surgical procedure is quite risky (e.g., heart transplant), a lenient (low) test of competency is applied to the patient who refuses the treatment (cell C). Consent to a heart transplant requires a more stringent (high) test of competency because of the high mortality and morbidity associated with the procedure (cell D).

The clinician should urge the patient and family, or significant other, to make early legal arrangements if the chance of future incompetency is high (e.g., Alzheimer's disease, cancer with brain metastasis). The patient, while still competent, can prepare a living will or a durable power of attorney (Howe 1988). The latter is a legal means of appointing a surrogate individual to make medical decisions when the patient is unable to.

Patient's decision	Treatment risk-benefit ratio	
Decision	Favorable	Unfavorable or questionable
Consent	Low test of competency (cell A)	High test of competency (cell D)
Refusal	High test of competency (cell B)	Low test of competency (cell C)

FIGURE 14–1.   **Factors in selection of competency tests.**

Source.   Reprinted from Roth LH, Meisel A, Lidz CW: "Tests of Competency to Consent to Treatment." *American Journal of Psychiatry* 124:279–284, 1977. Copyright 1977, American Psychiatric Association. Used with permission.

■ INFORMED CONSENT AND THE RIGHT TO REFUSE MEDICAL TREATMENT

Informed consent requires an informed patient (i.e., one who can understand the information provided and is capable of making a reasoned judgment about the treatment or procedure). According to Simon (1999), there are four basic exceptions to the requirement of obtaining informed consent:

1. *Emergencies:* When the physician administers appropriate treatment in a medically emergent situation in which the patient or other people are endangered, and it has proven impossible to obtain either the patient's consent or that of someone authorized to provide consent for the patient, the law typically "presumes" that consent is granted.
2. *Incompetency:* Only a competent person can provide informed consent. When the patient does not have the capacity to provide consent, it is obtained from a substitute decision maker.
3. *Therapeutic privilege:* This exception is the most difficult to apply. Informed consent is not required if a psychiatrist determines that a complete disclosure of possible risks and alternatives might have a deleterious effect on the patient's health and

welfare (Simon 1999). This determination and its rationale must be carefully documented; in such cases, it is very helpful to obtain a second opinion from a respected colleague.

4. *Waiver:* A patient may voluntarily waive his or her right for information (e.g., the patient does not want information on possible negative surgical outcomes).

Signing Out Against Medical Advice

Leaving a hospital or emergency department against medical advice (AMA) is the right of any competent patient, so long as he or she understands the nature and consequences of the act (Groves and Vaccarino 1987). The standard of competency will vary depending on the risk-benefit ratio in a particular situation (Figure 14–1). A threat or an attempt to sign out AMA often signifies a communication problem between the patient, who may have a personality disorder or is not coping well (or both), and the staff. Patients who leave AMA often return if a physician has not explicitly denied further care.

A patient is not required to sign the hospital's AMA form before departure. If he or she refused to sign the AMA form, the clinician should simply write on the form, "Patient refused to sign form" or "Patient departed without signing the AMA form," and then sign and date the document. A detailed account of the situation, along with the annotated AMA form, is placed in the medical record.

Do-Not-Resuscitate Orders

A competent patient has the right to reject or insist on resuscitative treatment (Miles et al. 1982). That right is rarely overruled (Simon 1999). One exception is when the rights of a spouse or child are considered more important than the patient's decision (Miles et al. 1982). When a competent patient either requests or declines resuscitation and later becomes incompetent, a court may be required to reverse the patient's original decision (Miles et al. 1982). In some states, the family or significant other, physician, and/or hospital ethics committee can intervene to resuscitate the patient if a chance of recovery exists. If a patient has a major mental disorder (e.g., severe depression) and rejects resuscitation because he or she desires death as an "appropriate deserved" outcome, the patient is considered incompetent (Simon 1999). The consultant in the latter case would recommend that the family or significant other seek guardianship. Do-not-resuscitate (DNR) orders should be written on the physician's order sheet, and the date, time, and reasons for the DNR order should be documented in the chart.

■ ADVANCE DIRECTIVES

The Patient Self-Determination Act was signed into law on November 5, 1990. This law establishes a patient's right, in advance, to accept or refuse medical or surgical treatment. An example of an advance directive is a living will. This law also states that a hospital must, if the hospital wishes to receive Medicare and Medicaid payments, 1) develop policies about advance directives, 2) ask all patients admitted to the hospital if they have advance directives and enter those into the chart, 3) give patients information about advance directives, and 4) educate the staff and community about advance directives (Greco et al. 1991).

■ GUARDIANSHIP

Guardianship is a method of substitute decision making for individuals who are judicially determined as unable to act for themselves (Brakel et al. 1985). In many jurisdictions, there are two separate types of guardianship. A *specific* guardian is authorized to make decisions about a particular subject area, such as major or emergency medical procedures. A *general* guardian, by contrast, has total control over the disabled individual's person, estate, or both (Sales et al. 1982).

■ INVOLUNTARY HOSPITALIZATION

The consultation-liaison psychiatrist may need to transfer medically ill patients involuntarily to a psychiatric unit. Three main substantive criteria serve as the foundation for all statutory commitment requirements (Simon 1999). These criteria require that the individual is 1) mentally ill, 2) dangerous to self or others, and/or 3) unable to provide for basic needs (i.e., gravely disabled). Clinicians do not legally commit patients; only a court can do that. The psychiatrist merely initiates a medical certification that brings the patient before the court, which usually occurs after a brief evaluation in the hospital (Simon 1999). Commitment laws vary greatly from state to state. A psychiatrist providing consultations to other physicians needs to become knowledgeable about local commitment laws and procedures, as well as local mental health treatment resources.

■ RESTRAINTS

Psychiatrists in most states can restrain a patient for the purpose of examination pending commitment. If the physician restrains a patient and determines that he or she is not committable, the physician is not liable if he or she acted in good faith. Also, in some instances, restraints (physical and/or chemical) are required for patients in an emergency department or general hospital. Clinical situations occur in which the patient is incapable of understanding the nature and consequences of his or her acts and/or has impaired judgment (Groves and Vaccarino 1987). A typical case is the patient with a hyperactive delirium. The consent of the next of kin is sought when possible; however, if the next of kin underestimates the danger of the situation, the medical decision should prevail.

Documenting the reasons for restraint and the type of restraint needed (e.g., 2-point, waist-belt, vest), the patient's bizarre or dangerous behavior, and the details of the psychiatric examination is essential. Recent rules issued by the Health Care Financing Administration state that a patient who is secluded or retrained, either chemically or mechanically, must be examined within 1 hour of the order for same. The order is valid for 4 hours in adults, 2 hours in patients age 7–17, and 1 hour in younger children. Unrestrained intensive care unit patients can pull out their endotracheal tubes, arterial lines, and intravenous lines. Moreover, confused, medically ill patients also climb over bed rails and fall onto the floor. Such falls frequently result in fractures and subdural hematomas. Generally, courts hold that restraints and seclusion are appropriate only when a patient presents a risk of harm to self or others and no less restrictive alternative is available.

■ REFERENCES

Brakel SJ, Parry J, Weiner BA: The Mentally Disabled and the Law, 3rd Edition. Chicago, IL, American Bar Foundation, 1985, p 370

Farnsworth MG: Competency evaluations in a general hospital. Psychosomatics 31:60–66, 1990

Greco PJ, Schulman KA, Lavizzo-Mourey R, et al: The patient self-determination act and the future of advance directives. Ann Intern Med 115:639–643, 1991

Groves JE, Vaccarino JM: Legal aspects of consultation, in Massachusetts General Hospital Handbook of General Hospital Psychiatry. Edited by Hackett IP, Cassem NH. Littleton, MA, PSG Publishing, 1987, pp 591–604

Howe EG: Forensic issues in critical care medicine, in Problems in Critical Care. Edited by Wise MG. Philadelphia, PA, JB Lippincott, 1988, pp 171–187

Mebane AH, Rauch HB: When do physicians request competency evaluations? Psychosomatics 31:40–46, 1990

Miles SH, Cranford R, Schultz AL: The do-not-resuscitate order in a teaching hospital. Ann Intern Med 96:660–664, 1982

Mishkin B: Determining the capacity for making health care decisions, in Issues in Geriatric Psychiatry (Advances in Psychosomatic Medicine Series, Vol 19). Edited by Billig N, Rabins PV. Basel, Switzerland, Karger, 1989, pp 151–166

Roth LH, Meisel A, Lidz CW: Tests of competency to consent to treatment. Am J Psychiatry 134:279–284, 1977

Sales BD, Powell DM, Van Duizend R: Disabled Persons and the Law: Law, Society, and Policy Services, Vol 1. New York, Plenum, 1982, p 461

Shouton R, Groves JE, Vaccarino JM: Legal aspects of consultation, in Massachusetts General Hospital Handbook of General Hospital Psychiatry, 3rd Edition. Edited by Cassem NH. St. Louis, MO, Mosby-Year Book, 1991, pp 619–638

Simon RI: Legal and ethical issues, in Essentials of Consultation-Liaison Psychiatry. Edited by Rundell JR, Wise MG. Washington, DC, American Psychiatric Press, 1999, pp 63–78

■ ADDITIONAL READINGS

American Psychiatric Association: Opinions of the Ethics Committee on the Principles of Medical Ethics With Annotations Especially Applicable to Psychiatry. Washington, DC, American Psychiatric Press, 1989

Appelbaum PS: General guidelines for psychiatrists who prescribe medication for patients treated by nonmedical therapists. Hosp Community Psychiatry 42:281–282, 1991

Guidelines for the Appropriate Use of Do-Not-Resuscitate Orders: Council on Ethical and Judicial Affairs, American Medical Association. JAMA 265:1868–1871, 1991

Simon RI: Clinical Psychiatry and the Law, 2nd Edition. Washington, DC, American Psychiatric Press, 1992a

Simon RI: Concise Guide to Psychiatry and Law for Clinicians. Washington, DC, American Psychiatric Press, 1992b

15

SUICIDALITY

For physicians, few events evoke more anguish than loss of a patient by suicide. Unlike many psychiatric symptoms or syndromes, suicidal statements or behaviors usually lead to prompt psychiatric referral. Unfortunately, considerable research has yet to identify specific indicators that would assist a population-based prevention program in making significant inroads into the baseline *population* suicide rate (Kessler et al. 1999). However, a clinically useful systematic approach to the assessment and management of suicidality among potentially suicidal *individuals* is possible.

■ EPIDEMIOLOGY

Completed Suicides

General population (Table 15–1). Suicide is the eighth or ninth leading cause of death in the United States. At a rate of 12 per 100,000 per year, it accounts for 1% of deaths from all causes (Roy 1989). The most successful suicide method is shooting. The elderly account for one-fourth of suicides, although they account for only 10% of the population. Suicides among whites occur at twice the rate as nonwhites, except for Native Americans. Clear warning signs precede 80% of suicides; 82% see a physician within 6 months and 53% within 1 month of a successful suicide.

The male-to-female ratio for suicide is 3:1. Over the course of the life cycle, men and women also have different patterns of suicide. For men, suicide rates gradually rise during adolescence, increase sharply in early adulthood, and parallel advancing age up to the 75- to 84-year age bracket, at which time they reach a rate of

TABLE 15–1.   **Suicide risk factors in the general population**

Psychiatric

Major depression—at least 40% of all suicides (particularly endogenous depression); risk is increased further if comorbid panic attacks are present

Alcohol dependence—25% of all suicides (rate 50–75 times the general population)

Drug addiction—10% die by suicide

Personality disorders—especially borderline and obsessive-compulsive

Schizophrenia—especially with hallucinations that command self-harm

Organic psychoses

Past history of suicide attempt(s)—especially if attempts were serious

Family history of suicide

Poor physical health—renal dialysis, cancer, HIV infection, cardiorespiratory disease, terminal illness, disfiguring illness

Psychological

History of recent loss (spouse, child, parent, job, financial)

History of parental loss during childhood

Important dates—anniversaries, holidays, etc.

Family instability

Social isolation—loss of social supports

Early life history of deprivation or abuse

Family exhausted with patient's illness

Giving away valued possessions

Social

Sex—males three times the rate of females

Race—whites twice the rate of nonwhites, except in urban areas where rate is the same; Native Americans have higher rates than other ethnic groups

Age—in men rates rise with age above 45; in women the peak risk is about age 55, then the rate declines

Religion—protestants and atheists have higher rates than Jews and Catholics

Geography—urban rates higher than rural

Marital status—divorced > single > widowed > married

Socioeconomic—high rates at both ends of spectrum; retired and unemployed at high risk

22.0 suicides per 100,000 (Schneidman 1989). Men tend to use more violent means, such as shooting, hanging, and jumping. For women, suicide rates peak in midlife, then decline. Marriage, especially if there are children, significantly lessens the risk of suicide. Marital separation, however, represents a higher risk than having never been married. Divorced men have seven times the suicide rate of married men, and divorced women have twice the rate of married women.

Medical-surgical patients (Table 15–2). Physical disease is an independent suicide risk factor, present in 25%–75% of people who commit suicide (Kontaxakis et al. 1988; Roy 1989). In nearly all suicides among medical-surgical patients, the patients had a history of recent loss of emotional support; anger was the predominant affect. Table 15–2 summarizes clinical observations associated with suicide among medical-surgical patients.

The reported suicide rate in most hospitals is lower than in the general population, varying between 3.2 and 15.0 per 100,000 per year (Sanders 1988). Access to means of suicide is more difficult in hospitals, and patients who give clear warning signs are usually promptly attended to. Jumping is the most successful suicide method in general hospital patients. Most general hospital patients who commit suicide have chronic, painful, or disfiguring illnesses (Sanders 1988). They also have a high frequency of psychiatric illness, particularly mood disorders and alcohol use disorders. Interpersonal problems with family members and ward staff are common.

Attempted Suicides

General population (Table 15–1). The ratio of suicide attempts to completions is about 10:1. In contrast to the 3:1 male-to-female ratio in completed suicides, a 3:1 female-to-male ratio exists for suicide attempts. Suicide attempts are a common reason for admissions to general hospitals. For example, 1%–2% of all admissions to emergency departments and 1%–5% of all admissions to medical intensive care units are drug overdoses (Bostwick

---

TABLE 15–2. **Factors associated with suicide in medical-surgical patients**

Chronic illness

Debilitating illness

Painful illness

Low pain tolerance

Renal dialysis

Cardiorespiratory disease

AIDS, AIDS-related complex, and HIV infection

Disrupted doctor-patient relationship

Interpersonal problems with family or staff

Medical staff may appear more important to the patient than family

Coexisting psychiatric illness, especially depression, substance use
  disorders, and personality disorder

Impulsivity

Alcohol, barbiturate, sedative-hypnotic, or narcotic withdrawal

Loss of emotional support

---

and Rundell 1996). The elderly attempt suicide less frequently than those younger than 65 but are successful more often. Drugs used in nonlethal suicide attempts are commonly available: benzodiazepines, alcohol, nonnarcotic analgesics, antidepressants, barbiturates, and antihistamines. Overdoses of acetaminophen, with its potential liver toxicity and over-the-counter availability, are particularly likely to result in a medical-surgical or psychiatric admission (Litman 1989).

Medical-surgical patients (Table 15–2). Although not well studied, the rate of attempted suicide in general hospital settings is estimated at 24 per 100,000 per year (Sanders 1988). The most frequent psychiatric diagnosis in attempters, in contrast to the depression and alcoholism in hospitalized suicide completers, is personality disorder. Again, a recent history of loss of emotional support is common. Wrist-slashing and drug overdose are the most common nonlethal suicide attempt methods in hospitals.

■ CLINICAL FEATURES AND RISK FACTORS

Whereas Table 15–1 summarizes psychiatric, psychological, and social risk factors for suicide, Table 15–3 describes a short useful mnemonic—SAD PERSONS—to help with rapid bedside evaluation of suicide risk (Patterson et al. 1983).

Psychiatric Disorders Associated With Increased Suicide Risk

Based on psychological autopsies, 95% of patients who completed suicides had psychiatric diagnoses, including 40% with mood disorders, 20%–25% with alcoholism, 10%–15% with schizophrenia, and 20%–25% with personality disorder (Litman 1989). More recent data suggests that the lifetime risk of suicide is lower: 6% for affective disorder, 7% for alcohol dependence, and 4% for schizophrenia (Inskip et al. 1998). Fifteen percent of patients with mood disorders will eventually commit suicide (Guze and Robins 1970), and 10% of patients with schizophrenia will eventually kill themselves (Miles 1977), with the risk for both highest early in the illness course. More recent data suggest that the lifetime risk of suicide is lower: 6% for affective disorders, 7% for alcohol dependence, and 4% for schizophrenia (Inskip et al. 1998).

History of a suicide attempt is an important predictor of future suicide risk. One of every 100 suicide attempter survivors will die by suicide within 1 year after the index attempt, a suicide risk approximately 100 times that of the general population (Hawton 1992). Suicide is often a response to a loss, real or metaphorical. Fantasies of revenge, punishment, reconciliation with a rejecting object, relief from the pain of loss, or reunion with a dead loved one may be evident (Furst and Ostow 1979). Holidays and anniversaries of important days in the life and death of the deceased also increase suicide risk.

TABLE 15–3.   **SAD PERSONS scale**

A positive factor counts one point

Scores:	0–2 = Little risk
	3–4 = Follow closely
	5–6 = Strongly consider psychiatric hospitalization
	7–10 = Very high risk, hospitalize or commit

Sex	Male—more men complete, more women attempt
Age	Elderly or adolescents
Depression	Especially with hopelessness
Previous attempt	Especially if potentially lethal
Ethanol abuse	Or other drugs
Rational thinking loss	Command hallucinations, OBS
Social support deficit	Or perception of poor supports
Organized plan	Will, available means
No spouse	Separated, divorced, widowed, single
Sickness	Especially chronic and debilitating illnesses

Source.   Adapted from Patterson WM, Dohn HH, Bird J, et al: "Evaluation of Suicidal Patients: The SAD PERSONS Scale." *Psychosomatics* 24:343–349, 1983. Used with permission.

Medical Disorders Associated With Increased Suicide Risk

Reviews of death certificates indicate that about 5% of suicide completers have a terminal illness (Murphy 1986); however, this rate may underrepresent the true prevalence. Many physicians misstate causes of death on death certificates to help patients' families avoid adverse financial and psychosocial consequences. Suicide rates higher than those in the general population are reported in cardiorespiratory patients, Alzheimer's disease patients, patients on renal dialysis, cancer patients, and patients infected with human immunodeficiency virus (HIV) (Bostwick and Rundell 1996). The fear of pain, disfigurement, and loss of function from cancer, HIV disease, and chronic renal failure can precipitate suicide, particularly early in the patient's course. The high relative risk just after diagnosis corresponds to a time of greatest fear.

■ APPROACH TO THE PATIENT

Epidemiological Risk Assessment

The proper assessment of suicidality requires a great deal of data. Much of the data can be collected, even from an uncooperative patient, by reviewing the medical record, interviewing the family, and talking to acquaintances and hospital staff. Simple demographic data such as age, sex, race, marital status, and religion provide other important epidemiological information.

Individual Risk Assessment

If suicide risk assessment is based on only epidemiological data, then many false-positive cases will result. Ultimately, the psychiatric examination of the individual patient leads to estimation of risk and a treatment plan. Asking a patient about suicidal ideation and plans does not increase suicide risk. Table 15–4 summarizes several important lines of inquiry. The psychiatrist should always inquire about recent real and perceived losses, including relationships, health, functional abilities, and physical integrity.

■ TREATMENT AND MANAGEMENT

Identifying the Risk Level

Initial management decisions are often difficult because patients are often ambivalent about suicide. There is a gradation of risk. Most patients examined are at "some risk." Information from a

TABLE 15–4.	Lines of questioning during examination of a potentially suicidal medical patient

Is there a wish to die?

Is there a plan?

What is the method planned?

Is there a history of recent substance abuse?

What medical illnesses are present?

What psychiatric diagnoses are present?

Is there a history of suicide attempts?

Is there a family history of suicide attempts?

Is there a history of impulsivity?

What is the level of psychological defensive functioning?

Has there been a will made recently?

Is there a history of recent losses, and how do they relate to past losses?

Is there talk of plans for the future?

What is the nature of the patient's social support system?

third party often helps the clinician gain other perspectives on the patient's situation. The clinician should always err on the side of safety. The response of both patient and third party to the treatment plan gives some indication of the patient's resilience and of the social resources available to aid in recovery from the suicidal crisis.

Protecting the Patient

The physician must be particularly vigilant in the emergency room, which is an easy place for a suicidal patient to obtain the means for self-harm (Anderson 1991). If the patient's suicide potential is questionable, he or she should be hospitalized, voluntarily or involuntarily. Once the patient is admitted to the hospital, his or her room should be secured (Bostwick and Rundell 1996). The staff must 1) remove anything that a patient could potentially use to injure himself or herself, such as sharp objects or material that could be fashioned into a noose; 2) search luggage and possessions; 3) monitor all objects coming into the room (e.g., the cutlery on the dinner tray) that are potential weapons; and 4) provide constant observation initially by using a sitter. The physician must carefully document the clinical diagnosis and treatment plan in the patient's chart; there is no room for communication error. Frequent updates and reassessments of suicide potential and the treatment plan are necessary.

Treating or Removing Risk Factors

Treatment of psychiatric disorders. Depressed patients should be given antidepressant medications. If the depressed suicidal patient is imminently suicidal, medically unable to tolerate antidepressants, or delusional, the psychiatrist should proceed directly to electroconvulsive therapy. He or she should observe the patient for a period of increased suicide risk as energy improves but hopelessness remains. Substance abuse issues should not be overlooked. Alcohol abuse is underdiagnosed in the general hospital. The psychiatrist should ask about command hallucinations and treat psychotic symptoms with neuroleptic medications. Any remediable causes of cognitive impairment must be removed.

Medical psychotherapy. Brief psychotherapy is quite helpful in some patients, especially when dealing with themes of loss. The psychiatrist should approach such patients with an accepting, supportive, empathic, and concerned manner and attempt to develop a therapeutic alliance. The patient's family should be involved, whenever possible. The clinician should make an effort to reestablish or strengthen the patient's connections to friends or community social service agencies.

Ward or outpatient management. Hospitals have suicide precaution guidelines, which should be placed in the chart and communicated to the ward staff. Suicide risk level must be continuously reassessed. Beware "hidden murderers" (i.e., individuals whose actions encourage a suicide attempt, such as a nurse who rejects/ignores the patient and "accidently" leaves a knife on the patient's meal tray); these may include family, hospital personnel, or even psychotherapists (Maltsberger and Buie 1974). The clinician should treat agitation and overt suicidal behavior promptly with physical restraints, chemical restraints, or both. Physical restraints are often required if a patient is unpredictable or impulsive. The consultant's chart notes should identify the level of risk, clearly state the plan, and report the interval at which the consultant will return to continue the assessment and recommend modifications to the plan (Bostwick and Rundell 1996). The consultant should also arrange follow-up care for the patient before discharge and detail it in the chart so that it is part of the inpatient's discharge plan.

In the emergency room or outpatient clinic setting, Davidson (1993) suggests that outpatient management is acceptable if the suicidal patient has 1) satisfactory impulse control, 2) no psychosis or intoxication, 3) no specific plan or easily accessible means, 4) accessible social supports to which he or she is willing to turn, and 5) a capacity for establishing rapport with the consultant.

■ REFERENCES

Anderson WH, Tesar G: The emergency room, in Massachusetts General Hospital Handbook of General Hospital Psychiatry, 3rd Edition. Edited by Cassem. St. Louis, MO, Mosby-Year Book, 1991, pp 445–464

Bostwick JM, Rundell JR: Suicidality, in The American Psychiatric Press Textbook of Consultation-Liaison Psychiatry. Edited by Rundell JR, Wise MG. Washington, DC, American Psychiatric Press, 1996, pp 138–161

Davidson L: Suicide and aggression in the medical setting, in Psychiatric Care of the Medical Patient. Edited by Stoudemire A, Fogel BS. New York, Oxford University Press, 1993, pp 71–86

Furst S, Ostow M: The psychodynamics of suicide, in Suicide: Theory and Clinical Aspects. Edited by Hankoff LD, Einsidler B. Littleton, MA, PSG Publishing, 1979, pp 165–178

Guze SB, Robins E: Suicide and primary affective disorders. Br J Psychiatry 117:437–438, 1970

Hawton K: Suicide and attempted suicide, in Handbook of Affective Disorders, 2nd Edition. Edited by Paykel ES. New York, Guilford, 1992, pp 635–650

Inskip HM, Harris EC, Barradough B: Lifetime risk of suicide for affective disorder, alcoholism and schizophrenia. Br J Psychiatry 172:35–37, 1998

Kessler RC, Borges H, Walters EE: Prevalence of and risk factors for lifetime suicide attempts in the National Comorbidity Survey. Arch Gen Psychiatry 56:617–626, 1999

Kontaxakis VP, Christodoulou GN, Mavreas VG, et al: Attempted suicide in psychiatric outpatients with concurrent physical illness. Psychother Psychosom 50:201–206, 1988

Litman RE: Suicides: what do they have in mind? in Suicide: Understanding and Responding. Edited by Jacobs D, Brown HN. Madison, CT, International Universities Press, 1989, pp 143–154

Maltsberger JT, Buie DH: Countertransference hate in the treatment of suicidal patients. Arch Gen Psychiatry 30:625–633, 1974

Miles CP: Conditions predisposing to suicide: a review. J Nerv Ment Dis 164:231–246, 1977

Murphy GE: Suicide and attempted suicide, in The Medical Basis of Psychiatry. Edited by Winokur G, Clayton PJ. Philadelphia, PA, WB Saunders, 1986, pp 562–579

Patterson WM, Dohn HH, Bird J, et al: Evaluation of suicidal patients: the SAD PERSONS scale. Psychosomatics 24:343–349, 1983

Roy A: Emergency psychiatry: suicide, in Comprehensive Textbook of Psychiatry/V. Edited by Kaplan HI, Sadock BJ. Baltimore, MD, Williams & Wilkins, 1989, pp 1414–1427

Sanders R: Suicidal behavior in critical care medicine: conceptual issues and management strategies, in Problems in Critical Care Medicine. Edited by Wise MG. Philadelphia, PA, JB Lippincott, 1988, pp 116–133

Schneidman ES: Overview: a multidimensional approach to suicide, in Suicide: Understanding and Responding. Edited by Jacobs D, Brown HN. Madison, CT, International Universities Press, 1989, pp 1–30

■ ADDITIONAL READINGS

Adams KS: Suicide and attempted suicide. Med Clin North Am 34:3200–3208, 1983

Kaplan A, Klein R: Women and suicide, in Suicide: Understanding and Responding. Edited by Jacobs D, Brown HN. Madison, CT, International Universities Press, 1989, pp 257–282

Morgan AC: Special issues of assessment and treatment of suicide risk in the elderly, in Suicide: Understanding and Responding. Edited by Jacobs D, Brown HN. Madison, CT, International Universities Press, 1989, pp 239–255

Tomb DA (ed): Suicidal and assaultive behaviors, in Psychiatry for the House Officer, 3rd Edition. Baltimore, MD, Williams & Wilkins, 1988

16

GERIATRIC PSYCHIATRY

■ EPIDEMIOLOGY

Elderly persons constitute the fastest-growing segment of the United States population (Department of Health and Human Services 1990). In 1900, people ages 65 years and older made up only 4% of the total population; people ages 65 years and older now make up 13% of the total population. The subgroup of elderly persons ages 85 years or older is growing at an even faster pace, constituting 10% of those ages 65 years and older in 1990 and a predicted 22% in 2050 (Small and Gunay 1996). The ages 85 years and older group has the greatest frequency of chronic physical illnesses, dependency, and long-term care needs. This means that the consultation-liaison psychiatrist, who already sees many medically ill geriatric patients, will increasingly function as a geriatric psychiatrist.

■ PSYCHIATRIC DISORDERS

Delirium

Because of neuronal loss with aging and the likelihood of other factors, geriatric patients are at high risk for delirium. Early signs include agitation, beclouded consciousness, sleep disturbance, irritability, hypoactivity or hyperactivity, disorientation, impaired short-term memory, perceptual disturbances, and fear or anxiety. As cognitive dysfunction progresses, disordered attention and concentration become prominent. (See Chapter 3 for a complete discussion of delirium.)

Dementia

Dementia is a major public health challenge. The most common dementia, dementia of the Alzheimer's type, occurs in 3% of individuals ages 65–74, 19% of individuals ages 75–84, and 47% of individuals older than 85 (Small and Gunay 1996). Patients with dementia remain as medical inpatients significantly longer and require more daily nursing care than their nondemented counterparts (Erkinjuntti et al. 1986). Elderly patients with dementia also may have psychosis and agitation (Wragg and Jeste 1989), and their clinical picture can mimic delirium if a longitudinal historical perspective is not taken. The clinician should use accessory sources of information in the assessment of cognitive function and the patient's ability to perform activities of daily living.

Depression

Geriatric depression often presents differently from depression in young adults (National Institutes of Health 1992; Small 1991) (Table 16–1). Elderly depressed patients are less likely to express guilt feelings or to seek help than are their younger counterparts (Small et al. 1986). They are more likely to minimize or deny depression, complain about memory problems, and become preoccupied with somatic symptoms. Symptoms such as loss of appetite, anhedonia, anergy, and insomnia are more prominent than depressed mood in elderly patients (Small and Gunay 1996). Elderly white men have very high suicide rates (Rabins 1992); men older than 65 commit suicide at a rate higher than any other age group.

Anxiety

About 5.5% of individuals age 65 years or older have an anxiety disorder, whereas 11% of elderly men and 25% of elderly woman take anxiolytic medications (Sadavoy et al. 1991). This disparity is partially explained by the fact that most patients are prescribed psychotropics, especially anxiolytics, by primary care physicians, whereas psychiatrists are more likely to prescribe antidepressants,

TABLE 16–1.	Clinical features of geriatric depression

Compared with young adult depressed patients, geriatric patients who are clinically depressed are

More likely to

Minimize or deny depressed mood

Become preoccupied with somatic symptoms

Complain about memory

Less likely to

Express guilt

Seek help from a psychiatrist

Accept a psychological explanation for their illness

Source. Reprinted from Small GW, Gunay I: "Geriatric Medicine," in *The American Psychiatric Press Textbook of Consultation-Liaison Psychiatry.* Edited by Rundell JR, Wise MG. Washington, DC, American Psychiatric Press, 1996, pp. 878–898. Copyright 1996, American Psychiatric Press. Used with permission.

particularly in cases of mixed anxiety and depression (Sadavoy et al. 1991). In addition, complaints of insomnia are extremely common; in a primary care setting, anxiety disorders were found in 35% of the individuals who complained of insomnia (Kroenke et al. 1994).

Psychosis

Approximately 13% of all schizophrenic individuals have onset of the disorder in their 50s, 7% in their 60s, and only 3% after age 70 (Sadavoy et al. 1991). Delusional disorder (lifetime risk 0.5%–0.1%) usually presents in middle to late adulthood, with an average age at onset in men of ages 40–49 and in women of ages 60–69 (Sadavoy et al. 1991). Psychosis associated with dementia is common; about 30% of patients with Alzheimer's dementia have delusions and visual hallucinations (Sadavoy et al. 1991). Zubenko and colleagues (1991) found associations between the presence of psychosis and the densities of senile plaques and neurofibrillary tangles in the brains of patients with Alzheimer's disease. Jeste and associates

(1992) reported that patients with Alzheimer's disease and psychosis show greater cognitive impairment than their counterparts without psychosis. Regardless of whether the psychiatric disorder is dementia with psychotic symptoms or primary psychosis, antipsychotics offer effective treatment (Lohr et al. 1992).

Substance-Related Disorders

Elderly persons often underreport their alcohol consumption (Atkinson 1990), and clinicians fail to recognize alcohol-related problems in elderly patients (Curtis et al. 1989). Decreased lean body mass and total body water cause the total volume of distribution for alcohol to decline with age (Small and Gunay 1996). Cognitive and cerebellar functions after a standard alcohol load worsen with age.

■ DIAGNOSTIC EVALUATION

Clinical History

The clinician must attend to the patient's physical symptoms and medical history, as well as to the patient's psychiatric history. Multiple medical conditions and multiple medications are the rule rather than the exception. Frequently, the signs and symptoms of medical and psychiatric disorders overlap. Because obtaining a history is sometimes difficult, a reliable collateral source saves time and contributes important clinical information.

Physical Examination

Sometimes, the consultation-liaison psychiatrist must perform a limited physical examination, particularly a neurological examination. Consultants occasionally discover a physical sign overlooked by the consultee. One situation in which this can occur is an agitated, disturbed patient (e.g., a frail elderly patient with psychosis) who makes the medical staff consultee anxious, clouding clinical assessment (Small and Gunay 1996).

Mental Status Examination

Depressed elderly patients who minimize dysphoria may divulge their depression nonverbally through facial expressions and sighs. A careful investigation of suicidal thinking and intent is essential because elderly people often choose lethal methods for suicide. Cognitive assessment of geriatric patients is also important. (The consultant should follow the cortical mapping guidelines for cognitive examination discussed in Chapter 2.)

Laboratory Findings

Abnormal sodium and chloride levels can indicate dehydration that may, if untreated, progress to delirium, lethargy, or convulsions. Serum creatinine levels may overestimate glomerular filtration rate in elderly patients, because decreased protein intake and decreased muscle mass cause a decline in creatinine production, which decreases serum creatinine levels. Therefore, normal serum levels for blood urea nitrogen (BUN) and creatinine may conceal decreased renal function, and small elevations may represent significant dysfunction. Liver function, as reflected by hepatic function tests, should remain adequate throughout life. To assess renal clearance accurately, a 24-hour creatinine clearance test is necessary (Greenblatt et al. 1982).

■ TREATMENT AND MANAGEMENT

Treatment of Medical Problems

Most psychiatric problems in elderly patients occur either because of or concurrently with medical illnesses. Even though the consultee is in charge of the medical treatment, the consultant, when appropriate, must recommend further diagnostic evaluations or alternative medical treatments.

Age-Related Pharmacological Issues

Pharmacokinetic Factors

Aging influences five main pharmacokinetic factors (Table 16–2): absorption, distribution, hepatic function, protein binding, and renal excretion. Although these factors usually change with age, considerable interindividual variability exists.

Absorption.   The aging process typically results in decreased gastric acidity, gastrointestinal motility, gastrointestinal blood flow, and gastrointestinal surface area (Sadavoy et al. 1991). These changes do not alter significantly the absorption of psychotropic drugs unless gastric pathology is present (Salzman 1992). In elderly patients, drug-drug interactions are more likely to influence absorption. For example, antacids may delay absorption of psychotropic drugs and therefore delay their onset of action. Anticholinergic drugs, such as amitriptyline, also slow absorption and gastric motility and ultimately delay onset of action of other drugs. In addition, medications such as cholestyramine can inhibit absorption and decrease effectiveness.

Distribution.   Lean muscle mass and total body water decrease with age, while total body fat tends to increase. For fat-soluble (lipophilic) drugs, this means an increased volume of distribution, more accumulation, and a prolonged elimination half-life (Jenike 1989). Because psychotropic drugs, except lithium, are highly lipophilic, they may remain in an elderly patient's system for days or even weeks after the medication is discontinued (Salzman 1992).

Hepatic function.   Lipophilic drugs are converted to water-soluble compounds, mainly by hepatic enzymes, before elimination by the kidney; therefore, the effects of age on the liver are particularly important to psychotropic drugs. Hepatic metabolism is dependent on hepatic blood flow and hepatic enzyme activity, two factors that tend to decrease with age. Hepatic blood flow may decrease as much as 40% by age 65 (Sadavoy et al. 1991). Demethylation and hydroxylation are the two metabolic mechanisms

TABLE 16–2. Pharmacokinetic changes associated with aging

Factor	Age effect	Consequence
Absorption	Decreased gastric acidity	In absence of gastric pathology or drug-drug interactions, absorption of psychotropic drugs not significantly altered
	Decreased motility	
	Decreased blood flow	
	Decreased gastrointestinal surface area	
Distribution	Increased volume of distribution of lipophilic drugs	Prolonged elimination half-life of psychotropic drugs (except lithium)
Hepatic function	Decreased hepatic blood flow	Increased circulating, unmetabolized, and partially metabolized psychotropic drug
	Decreased first-pass effect	
	Decreased hepatic enzyme activity	Prolonged time required for psychotropic drug elimination
	Decreased demethylation	Prolonged exposure to unmetabolized drug
	Decreased hydroxylation	
Protein binding	Decreased albumin	Increase in active drug (unclear effects)
	Increased (?) α_1 glycoprotein	Unclear effect on pharmacokinetics

(continued)

TABLE 16–2. Pharmacokinetic changes associated with aging *(continued)*

Factor	Age effect	Consequence
Renal excretion	Decreased renal blood flow	Decreased lithium clearance and increased risk of toxicity
	Decreased glomerular filtration rate	Decreased antidepressant hydroxy metabolite clearance
		Increased cardiotoxicity
	Decreased tubular excretory capacity	Decreased benzodiazepine clearance
		Prolonged elimination half-life

Source. Reprinted from Wise MG, Tierney J: "Psychopharmacology in the Elderly." *Journal of the Louisiana State Medical Society* 144:471–476, 1992. Used with permission.

that inactivate many psychotropics; both tend to slow with age, although hydroxylation typically slows first. The summary effect of these hepatic changes may prolong the duration of action and elimination half-life of many psychotropic drugs by as much as two- to threefold (Sadavoy et al. 1991).

Protein binding.   Except for lithium, most psychotropic drugs are highly protein-bound. This means that changes in protein concentrations may have significant effects on a psychotropic drug's pharmacological activity, metabolism, and elimination. Antidepressants mostly bind to sites available on α_1 glycoprotein, whereas benzodiazepines and neuroleptics bind mainly to albumin. Studies indicate that aging causes a decrease in serum albumin and a likely increase in α_1 glycoprotein, although the clinical significance of this is unclear (Greenblatt et al. 1982). Malnutrition, medical illness, and drug-drug interactions can profoundly alter the unbound (active) fraction of a drug.

Renal excretion.   Biotransformation to water-soluble metabolites is important in the renal clearance of psychotropic drugs. Elderly individuals may have decreased renal blood flow, decreased glomerular filtration rate, and decreased tubular excretion rate. Glomerular filtration rate may decrease 50% by age 70 (Rowe 1982). As a result, the renal clearance of lithium decreases 30%–50% between ages 25 and 75 (Jenike 1989). The clearance of long-acting benzodiazepines, such as diazepam, may increase from 20 hours in a 20-year-old to more than 90 hours in an 80-year-old (Jenike 1989). The clearance of tricyclic antidepressants' hydroxy metabolites also decreases, which is potentially toxic to the cardiac conduction system (Salzman 1992).

Pharmacodynamic Factors

Pharmacodynamics also change with age. Neurotransmitter synthesis and turnover, receptor binding, and synaptic neurotransmission change in many brain areas as people age. The precise clinical significance of such changes is unknown, but available evidence suggests that the elderly have greater receptor-site sensitivity for many drugs, particularly benzodiazepines (e.g., diazepam). By contrast, changes in β-adrenergic function result in lower sensitivity to β-adrenergic stimulation and blockade.

Polypharmacy

The use of multiple drugs affects all pharmacokinetic and pharmacodynamic processes. Because elderly persons are likely to use more than one medication, drug-drug interactions are a critical issue in management. Metabolism of psychotropic drugs is often complicated by chronic medical illnesses and medications that alter gastrointestinal, hepatic, or renal function. Because potential combinations of various drugs and diseases are too numerous to study systemically (Small and Gunay 1996), comprehensive data are unavailable.

■ ELECTROCONVULSIVE THERAPY

Electroconvulsive therapy (ECT) is generally the safest and most effective treatment for severely depressed, medically compromised elderly patients and is the treatment of choice for psychotic depression (Small and Gunay 1996). Patients with multiple medical problems and those older than 75 years are at increased risk for adverse effects, but modification of the treatment regimen helps to minimize risks. Short-term memory effects are common but short-lived in elderly patients. Overall, cognitive dysfunction should improve with ECT (Stoudemire et al. 1991).

■ PSYCHOTHERAPY

One of the problems constantly facing the older patient is loss—loss of physical function, loss of friends and loved ones through death or disability, and, possibly, loss of economic and social status. Bereavement and grief are common. Elderly people, especially the very old, do not seem to have much anxiety about death (Sadavoy et al. 1991). However, they often have fears of pain, abandonment, and disability. Appropriate, reality-based reassurance is often helpful. As with most medically ill patients seen by the consultation-liaison psychiatrist, the elderly ill patient has his or her psychological defenses stripped away by the medical insult and cumulative losses. As long as the elderly patient has reasonable cognitive function, there is no reason to expect that he or she cannot benefit from psychotherapeutic techniques used in other medically ill patients. Therefore, crisis intervention is no different with elderly people: help the patient adjust to the situation, correct the patient's distortions about the events at hand, and help the patient use intrapsychic strengths and mobilize external supports. Caregivers for elderly patients often need support and respites from caregiving duties, and they may need psychiatric treatment because clinical depression occurs so commonly.

■ ELDER ABUSE

An estimated 10% of Americans older than 65 years are abused (Council on Scientific Affairs 1987). The abuser is often a relative who lives with the victim; the abuse is generally recurring. According to Small and Gunay (1996, p. 886), "clinicians should consider the possibility of elder abuse when a caregiver 1) expresses frustration in providing care, 2) shows signs of psychological distress, 3) has a history of abuse or violence, or 4) has a history of alcohol or drug abuse."

■ CONCLUSION

Consultation-liaison psychiatrists will increasingly evaluate and treat geriatric patients, given the changing demographic patterns. Consultation on geriatric patients requires that consultation-liaison psychiatrists retain medical skills and knowledge of unique aspects of psychiatric syndromes in the elderly. Table 16–3 is a summary of suggested strategies for psychiatric consultation for geriatric patients.

TABLE 16–3.   **Suggested strategies for psychiatric consultation for geriatric patients**

Collect data from multiple sources

Recognize unique clinical presentations of geriatric syndromes

Search for medical and toxic causes of psychiatric syndromes

Reduce polypharmacy

Follow conservative and rational pharmacological guidelines

Identify adverse drug effects sooner rather than later

Emphasize nonpharmacological interventions

Source.   Reprinted from Small GW, Gunay I: "Geriatric Medicine," in *The American Psychiatric Press Textbook of Consultation-Liaison Psychiatry.* Edited by Rundell JR, Wise MG. Washington, DC, American Psychiatric Press, 1996, pp. 878–898. Copyright 1996, American Psychiatric Press. Used with permission.

■ REFERENCES

Atkinson RM: Aging and alcohol use disorders: diagnostic issues in the elderly. Int Psychogeriatr 2:55–70, 1990

Council on Scientific Affairs: Elder abuse and neglect. JAMA 257:966–971, 1987

Curtis JR, Geller G, Stokes EG, et al: Characteristics, diagnosis and treatment of alcoholism in elderly patients. J Am Geriatr Soc 37:310–316, 1989

Department of Health and Human Services, Public Health Service: Healthy People 2000: National Health Promotion and Disease Prevention Objectives. Washington, DC, Department of Health and Human Services, 1990

Erkinjuntti T, Wikstrom J, Palo J, et al: Dementia among medical inpatients: evaluation of 2000 consecutive admissions. Arch Intern Med 146:1923–1926, 1986

Greenblatt DJ, Sellers EM, Shader RI: Drug disposition in old age. N Engl J Med 306:1081–1088, 1982

Jenike MA: Geriatric Psychiatry and Psychopharmacology: A Clinical Approach. Chicago, IL, Year Book Medical, 1989

Jeste DV, Wragg RE, Salmon DP, et al: Cognitive deficits of Alzheimer's disease patients with and without delusions. Am J Psychiatry 149:184–189, 1992

Kroenke K, Spitzer RL, Williams JBW, et al: Physical symptoms in primary care: predictors of psychiatric disorders and functional impairment. Arch Fam Med 3:774–779, 1994

Lohr JB, Jeste DV, Harris MJ, et al: Treatment of disordered behavior, in Clinical Geriatric Psychopharmacology, 2nd Edition. Edited by Salzman C. Baltimore, MD, Williams & Wilkins, 1992, pp 79–113

National Institutes of Health Consensus Development Panel on Depression in Late Life: Diagnosis and treatment of depression in late life. JAMA 268:1018–1024, 1992

Rabins PV: Prevention of mental disorder in the elderly: current perspectives and future prospects. J Am Geriatr Soc 40:727–733, 1992

Rowe JW: Renal system, in Health and Disease in Old Age. Edited by Rowe JW, Besdine EW. Boston, MA, Little, Brown, 1982, pp 165–184

Sadavoy J, Lazarus LW, Jarvik LF (eds): Comprehensive Review of Geriatric Psychiatry. Washington, DC, American Psychiatric Press, 1991

Salzman C: Clinical Geriatric Psychopharmacology. Baltimore, MD, Williams & Wilkins, 1992

Small GW: Recognition and treatment of depression in the elderly. J Clin Psychiatry 52 (suppl):11–22, 1991

Small GW, Gunay I: Geriatric medicine, in The American Psychiatric Press Textbook of Consultation-Liaison Psychiatry. Edited by Rundell JR, Wise MG. Washington, DC, American Psychiatric Press, 1996, pp 878–898

Small GW, Komanduri R, Gitlin M, et al: The influence of age on guilt expression in major depression. Int J Geriatr Psychiatry 1:121–126, 1986

Stoudemire A, Hill CD, Morris R, et al: Cognitive outcome following tricyclic and electroconvulsive treatment of major depression in the elderly. Am J Psychiatry 148:1336–1340, 1991

Wragg R, Jeste DV: Overview of depression and psychosis in Alzheimer's disease. Am J Psychiatry 146:577–587, 1989

Zubenko GS, Moosy J, Martinez AJ, et al: Neuropathologic and neurochemical correlates of psychosis in primary dementia. Arch Neurol 48:619–624, 1991

■ ADDITIONAL READINGS

Busse EW, Blazer DG (eds): Geriatric Psychiatry. Washington, DC, American Psychiatric Press, 1989

Kalayam B, Shamoian LA: Geriatric psychiatry: an update. J Clin Psychiatry 51:177–183, 1990

Rodriguez MM, Grossberg GT: Estrogen as a psychotherapeutic agent. Clin Geriatr Med 14:177–189, 1998

17

SPECIAL
CONSULTATION-LIAISON
SETTINGS AND SITUATIONS

Consultation-liaison (C-L) psychiatrists practice in many different outpatient and inpatient settings. Some C-L psychiatrists conduct most or all of their work in subspecialty settings such as oncology units or human immunodeficiency virus/acquired immunodeficiency syndrome (HIV/AIDS) clinics. Although an exhaustive review of each of these settings is beyond the scope of this "pocket" guide, we want to highlight unique characteristics of subspecialty units and patient populations. Many "rules," pearls, and guidelines discussed in previous chapters are modified to fit special situations.

■ PREGNANCY AND THE POSTPARTUM PERIOD

Psychopharmacology During Pregnancy and Lactation

Medications may cause teratogenesis at all stages of pregnancy, although risk is greatest during the first trimester. In an ideal world, pregnant and breast-feeding women would never need to receive psychopharmacological agents. However, in the real world, clinicians must balance the risks of teratogenesis and effects on a breast-feeding child against the risks and effects of severe psychiatric illness on both the mother and the child. Each case is unique and must take into account stage of pregnancy, severity of psychiatric illness, degree of functional impairment when ill, quality of social supports, and compliance with medical follow-up and monitoring.

Teratogenic potential is neither proven nor disproven for neuroleptics, antidepressants, benzodiazepines, and sedative-hypnotics. It is accepted practice to avoid use of these medications during pregnancy, particularly during the first trimester. Clinicians substitute alternative therapies, including psychotherapy and electroconvulsive therapy (ECT), when possible.

Ample evidence indicates that antimania medications can cause birth defects, often cardiovascular (Baldessarini and Cole 1988). In pregnant women, lithium should be used only when life-saving benefits clearly outweigh this potential risk. Carbamazepine should be avoided as well, particularly if the patient is taking more than one anticonvulsant—combination therapy may increase the risk of teratogenesis. If a woman is taking lithium at the time of delivery, the obstetrical clinician should be informed that lithium clearance may shift drastically from unusually high during pregnancy to low with the physiological postdelivery diuresis (Baldessarini and Cole 1988).

Because of the potential for physiological dependency in the newborn, it is prudent to taper and stop medications a few weeks before delivery. Babies born to mothers who are physically dependent on opiates or sedative-hypnotics may experience withdrawal.

If a woman taking a psychiatric medication(s) is trying to become pregnant, she can continue taking the drug until she misses her first period. Stopping medication 2 weeks into the pregnancy is probably early enough to avoid malformations (Schatzberg and Cole 1991). Fortunately, ECT is a safe and effective option for psychotic and mood disorders that occur during pregnancy.

Nursing mothers who take psychotropic medications probably will excrete those medications in breast milk. Generally, concentrations in breast milk are much lower than levels in the blood, so that total amounts ingested by a nursing infant are small. However, most clinicians advise mothers who are breast-feeding their infants to avoid psychopharmacological medications and advise against breast-feeding if the psychiatric disorder is severe.

Postpartum Psychiatric Disorders

Postpartum depression.   After labor and delivery, 60%–80% of women develop mild transient dysphoria ("blues") (Stotland 1999). Postpartum depression usually occurs 1–2 weeks after delivery and may not occur until the second or third child. A woman who experiences postpartum depression is at increased risk for episodes with future births. Antidepressant medications should be administered, and the patient should be counseled to bottle-feed her infant. ECT is also an effective treatment for postpartum depression.

Postpartum psychosis.   Although psychotic symptoms following delivery in a woman with no past or family history of psychotic disorders may represent an initial episode of schizophrenia, the syndrome is more likely a secondary mental disorder. Postpartum psychoses are often associated with obstetrical events such as toxemia, malpresentations, hydramnios, and placental defects (Nadelson and Notman 1986). These medical events are not associated with other postpartum psychiatric disorders. One-third of patients who experience postpartum psychosis have similar difficulties in future pregnancies. Mothers taking neuroleptics should be advised not to breast-feed.

Fetal alcohol syndrome.   Alcohol abuse by pregnant women can cause fetal alcohol syndrome. Cardinal features include growth retardation before and after birth, small head circumference, flattened facial features, mental retardation, low birth weight, developmental delays, and behavioral abnormalities.

References

Baldessarini RJ, Cole JO: Chemotherapy, in The New Harvard Guide to Psychiatry. Edited by Nicholi AM. Cambridge, MA, Belknap Press of Harvard University Press, 1988, pp 481–533

Nadelson CC, Notman MT: The psychiatric aspects of obstetrics and gynecology, in Consultation-Liaison Psychiatry and Behavioral Medicine. Edited by Houpt JL, Brodie HKH. Philadelphia, PA, JB Lippincott, 1986, pp 367–378

Schatzberg AF, Cole JO: Manual of Clinical Psychopharmacology, 2nd Edition. Washington, DC, American Psychiatric Press, 1991

Stotland NL: Obstetrics and gynecology, in Essentials of Consultation-Liaison Psychiatry. Edited by Rundell JR, Wise MG. Washington, DC, American Psychiatric Press, 1999, pp 383–397

■ PEDIATRIC CONSULTATION-LIAISON

C-L psychiatrists may find themselves providing consultation for children and adolescents because of the scarcity of child and adolescent psychiatrists. The general psychiatrist involved in consultation work with children or adolescents cannot simply equate child and adolescent C-L psychiatry with the adult consultation process. Pediatric consultation has several important differences, including the developmental perspective, the family focus, the process of consulting to pediatricians, and differences in the children's medical system.

Developmental Perspective

To perform psychiatric consultation on children, the psychiatrist must understand and maintain a developmental perspective. A developmental perspective implies recognition that the rapid physical and psychological changes taking place in a child or an adolescent alter the manifestations of disease, the effect of illness on the patient's life, and coping capacities (Fritz and Brown 1996). The fact that developmental steps exist for each stage of childhood and adolescence presents a major organizing variable to the consultant who seeks to assess the meaning of a symptom or a behavior. The stress of an illness or hospitalization frequently leads to regression, in which a child appears much less mature (i.e., temporarily loses some of the cognitive, emotional, or behavioral advances previously achieved). Such regression is disconcerting for parents, difficult for caregivers, and often uncomfortable for the child. The assessment and management of regressive behavior is a common reason that pediatricians request psychiatric consultation (Fritz and Brown 1996).

Family Focus

In contrast to many adult consultations, with the possible exception of a geriatric patient with cognitive dysfunction, the medical history and past psychiatric history are virtually never obtained from only the pediatric patient; the examiner must interview a parent or an adult caregiver (Fritz and Brown 1996). A consultation that would take approximately an hour and a half with an adult may take three times that long with a child.

Consultation Process

The consultant should advise the referring pediatrician how to prepare both the patient and the parents for psychiatric consultation. Information is often provided by not only the parents but also people outside the family, including a child's schoolteacher, caseworker, or therapist. Although this information is often difficult to obtain quickly, the consultant should use the authority of the hospital or clinic and create the degree of urgency necessary to obtain facts rapidly from these outside sources (Fritz and Brown 1996).

The consultant should assess the child's understanding of the medical situation, as well as the child's associated fears and expectations. Regressive symptoms during hospitalization (e.g., immature behavior, clinging, enuresis) are extremely common in preschoolers, but the same behavior in a young adolescent is a cause for more concern. In addition to describing elements well known to every adult psychiatrist (e.g., affect, thought processes, and cognition), the consultant must observe and describe the quality of the child's relationship with parents and unit staff.

Administrative and Legal Issues

A child or an adolescent may request that the psychiatrist keep information from the parents or pediatrician. Adolescents, in particular, may request confidentiality as a condition for cooperation. In most cases, this request is appropriate to honor and must be explained to the parents. The age at which informed consent and the right to refuse treatment become the prerogative of the patient rather than the parent varies from state to state. In general, however, from mid-adolescence on, a consultant should err in the direction of assuming that the patient has the same legal rights and need for informed consent as an adult (Fritz and Brown 1996).

Psychopharmacology

Psychostimulants are used for attention-deficit/hyperactivity disorder (ADHD), which may occur in children following neurological events, such as head injury. Common side effects of psychostimulants include loss of appetite, irritability, abdominal pain, and insomnia. Antidepressants are used for major mood disorders, enuresis, anxiety disorders, and ADHD. Similar to the adverse effects seen in adults, the most common side effects of tricyclics in children are anticholinergic and quinidine-like cardiac conduction delays. An electrocardiogram and vital signs are used to establish a baseline; the clinician also should observe for congenitally prolonged Q-T interval and then repeat these tests frequently during treatment. Neuroleptics are used for psychotic disorders and severe agitation associated with brain disorders. Important adverse effects in children are similar to those seen in adults and include sedation, parkinsonism, dystonias, and neuroleptic malignant syndrome. Anxiolytics are used primarily for chronic anxiety disorders or anticipatory anxiety (e.g., prior to painful medical procedures). Sedation and blunting of cognition are especially common side effects in children. Behavioral disinhibition and dependence are serious but occur rarely. Analgesics are underused in pediatric settings.

Reference

Fritz GK, Brown LK: Pediatrics, in The American Psychiatric Press Textbook of Consultation-Liaison Psychiatry. Edited by Rundell JR, Wise MG. Washington, DC, American Psychiatric Press, 1996, pp 740–753

■ BURNS

Epidemiology

More than 2 million people experience burns serious enough to seek health care every year in the United States; 70,000 will require hospitalizations and 5,000 die (Warden and Heinbach 1999). Mortality risk depends on the severity of the burn and the age of the patient. Children and the elderly are at highest risk. Psychiatric disorders predispose people to severe burns: 14%–21% of hospitalized adult burn patients have substance-related disorders, 8%–12% have dementia, and 24%–39% have other psychiatric disorders (MacArthur and Moore 1975). Burn patients are at high risk for developing psychiatric syndromes in the hospital, including delirium, substance withdrawal syndromes, and mood disorders.

Delirium

During the first 24–72 hours after a severe burn, the patient typically has a brief period of initial lucidity, which offers an opportunity to assess the patient's history, personality dynamics, and coping patterns. After that, between 30% and 70% of hospitalized patients with severe burns develop delirium, presumably caused by stress and burn-induced metabolic disturbances (Andreasen et al. 1977). Correction of metabolic abnormalities and infections helps to reverse the psychiatric symptomatology. Neuroleptics are the best pharmacological treatment for the symptoms of delirium. Neuroleptics decrease fear, anxiety, agitation, pain, and insomnia.

Haloperidol is a good choice because of its low incidence of cardiovascular and anticholinergic side effects.

Mood Syndromes

Clinicians should strongly consider the possibility of a medically induced secondary mood syndrome in depressed burn patients (Pasnau et al. 1996). Burn patients are at risk for many of the causes of secondary depression, particularly metabolic/electrolyte abnormalities and infection. Burn patients lose water at a rate several times faster than normal; hypovolemic shock is common. Following the shock phase is a period of intense catabolism and negative nitrogen balance. In addition, associated anorexia, weight loss, exhaustion, and lassitude may lead unsuspecting clinicians to overdiagnose depression.

Psychoactive Substance Use Withdrawal Syndromes

As many as one-fifth of burn patients have substance-related disorders. Some of these patients will experience withdrawal syndromes while initially hospitalized with severe burns. Unfortunately, the time courses for most withdrawal syndromes coincide with the critical periods of burn patients' medical courses. The clinician should expect and observe closely for signs of alcohol, opiate, barbiturate, and sedative-hypnotic withdrawal; withdrawal can greatly complicate medical care if not managed early and aggressively. He or she should ask the family about the patient's substance use patterns; heavy or daily use indicates the need for pharmacological prophylaxis.

Pain Management

Although pain is a continuing and critical issue for the burn patient, it becomes especially important during dressing changes and debridement, which may produce acute excruciating pain. Narcotics are the drugs of choice for treatment of this pain. Methadone is a good choice because of its excellent absorption and slow clearance. Caution should be exercised with meperidine because its metabolite, normeperidine, is a central nervous system (CNS) irritant that causes mental status changes. Neuroleptics, antidepressants, and psychostimulants are effective narcotic adjuvants. Dressing changes often require additional preemptive analgesia. Short-acting narcotics such as fentanyl citrate are useful and are given about 45 minutes to 1 hour before dressing changes or debridement.

Many clinicians use hypnosis to help patients control pain. Hypnosis is not considered a substitute for adequate pharmacological control of pain; its use is complicated by the hypnotizability of the patient, the severity of the pain, the busy and noisy setting of the burn unit, and the high frequency of secondary mental disorders (e.g., delirium).

Psychosocial Issues in Burn Patients Likely to Die

Many patients with severe burns will die. They usually are told their prognosis early in the course of treatment, while they are still lucid. The C-L psychiatrist's role with these patients may include consultation on several issues: death, dying, sense of loss, pain control, do-not-resuscitate orders, unfinished business, religious requests, and last wishes.

Psychiatric Issues in Recovery

As patients recover from their burns, many issues arise: changes in body image, difficulties with finances, problems with postdischarge care, negative reactions by family, limitations in occupations, and low self-esteem. Facial burns usually cause more psychological difficulty than burns to other body areas. A patient should not be forced to view a deformity until ready; he or she may choose to wait several weeks before looking in a mirror. Brief psychotherapy, family discussions, and honest explanations help prepare the hospitalized burn patient for long-term consequences and the prolonged rehabilitation process. Giving the patient a decision-making role in the hospital helps reestablish a sense of control and reduces dependency. Potential areas for increased patient responsibility include eating schedules, visiting hours, dressing change times, physical therapy activities, sleep periods, and some medication decisions.

Longer-term psychotherapy is sometimes required to help severely burned patients adjust to permanent disfigurement and changes in body image and self-esteem. In one study, 35.3% of burn patients met criteria for posttraumatic stress disorder at 2 months, 40% met the criteria at 6 months, and 45.2% met the criteria at 12 months postinjury (Perry et al. 1992). Cognitive or group psychotherapy can help lead the patient toward acceptance and psychological growth.

References

Andreasen NJ, Hartford CE, Knott JR, et al: EEG changes associated with burn delirium. Diseases of the Nervous System 38: 27–31, 1977

MacArthur JD, Moore FD: Epidemiology of burns. JAMA 231: 259–263, 1975

Pasnau RO, Fawzy FI, Skotzko CE, et al: Surgery and surgical subspecialties, in The American Psychiatric Press Textbook of Consultation-Liaison Psychiatry. Edited by Rundell JR, Wise MG. Washington, DC, American Psychiatric Press, 1996, pp 608–639

Perry SW, Difede J, Musngi G, et al: Predictors of posttraumatic stress disorder after burn injury. Am J Psychiatry 149:931–935, 1992

Warden GD, Heinbach DM: Burns, in Principles of Surgery, 7th Edition. Edited by Schwartz SI, Shires GT, Spencer FC, et al. New York, McGraw-Hill, 1991, pp 223–262

■ CANCER

Primary Psychiatric Disorders

Primary psychiatric disorders occur in 20%–58% of cancer patients. The prevalence of current major depressive disorder in cancer centers is 5%–8% (Fawzy and Greenberg 1999), about the same as rates reported among patients with other medical illnesses. Antidepressant choice depends on target symptoms and the anticipated side effects in a given patient. In patients without cardiac conduction defects, tricyclic antidepressants are sometimes beneficial, especially if effects on sleep, appetite, and pain are sought. However, some of the newer, less toxic antidepressants also improve sleep and aid analgesia (e.g., nefazodone, mirtazapine) and stimulate appetite (mirtazapine).

A trial of a psychostimulant, such as dextroamphetamine (Fernandez et al. 1987), methylphenidate, or pemoline, is appropriate for a rapid effect in systemically ill patients who are depressed, apathetic, and not eating.

Trazodone is widely used among oncology patients, especially when sedation is desired. Unfortunately, potential adverse effects include nausea and orthostatic hypotension. Nevertheless, the lack of anticholinergic side effects makes trazodone an attractive agent to use alone or in combination with selective serotonin reuptake inhibitors (SSRIs). SSRIs lack anticholinergic (except paroxetine) and sedative side effects. However, they can add to anorexia, jitteriness, and agitation (Massie et al. 1991; Shuster et al. 1992). Most SSRIs inhibit metabolism by the P450 enzyme system. Fortunately, this is unlikely to affect chemotherapy regimens.

Secondary Psychiatric Disorders

Secondary psychiatric disorders due to CNS metastases occur with many cancers, especially lung, breast, gastrointestinal, renal, and prostate (Lishman 1987). The likelihood of these syndromes becomes greater as a cancer progresses and as the number and intensity of treatments increase. Structural lesions of the brain can cause

TABLE 17–1. Psychiatric manifestations of chemotherapeutic agents

Agent	Side effect
Hormones	
Tamoxifen	Hot flashes, sleep disorder, irritability
Aminoglutethimide	Initial syndrome of rash, malaise, fatigue
Fluoxymesterone	Irritability, increased libido, hirsutism
Corticosteroids	Dose-related manic and depressive features, psychosis, insomnia, hyperactivity
Chemotherapy	
Procarbazine	Somnolence, psychosis, delirium, disulfiram-like effect (do not mix with alcohol)
L-Asparaginase	Somnolence, lethargy, delirium; not dose related
Pyrimidine analogues (inhibit DNA synthesis)	
Cytosine arabinoside	Leukoencephalopathy may result from high dose: syndrome of personality change (drowsiness, dementia, psychomotor retardation, ataxia); cerebellar syndrome
5-Fluorouracil	Fatigue, rarely delirium or seizure
Folate antagonist	
Methotrexate	Neurological toxicity with high-dose or intrathecal regimens
Metaphase inhibitor	
Vincristine, vinblastine	Dysphoria, lethargy
Biologicals	
Interferon	Most get flulike syndrome, with fever, myalgias, malaise, which dissipates; diffuse encephalopathy noted at high doses; syndrome of fatigue, difficulty in concentration, psychomotor retardation, and general disinterest

(continued)

TABLE 17–1.	Psychiatric manifestations of chemotherapeutic agents *(continued)*
Agent	**Side effect**
Biologicals *(continued)*	
Interleukin-2 (IL-2)	Delirium (dose related); most get flulike syndrome, with malaise, chills, anorexia, fatigue, depression

Source. Adapted from Fawzy FI, Greenberg DB: "Oncology," in *The American Psychiatric Press Textbook of Consultation-Liaison Psychiatry.* Edited by Rundell JR, Wise MG. Washington, DC, American Psychiatric Press, 1996, pp. 672–694. Copyright 1996, American Psychiatric Press. Used with permission.

both focal and generalized neuropsychiatric signs. Psychiatric symptoms also occur secondary to chemotherapeutic agents (Table 17–1) or secondary to medications used for symptom control. Metoclopramide, for example, is used for gastroesophageal reflux and to prevent nausea. Because metoclopramide is a CNS dopamine antagonist, it can produce extrapyramidal symptoms that are misdiagnosed ("The patient has a conversion reaction").

Anticipatory Nausea and Vomiting

Patients who vomit with chemotherapy may develop a conditioned response, usually nausea and vomiting, to the hospital, nurse, or sight and smell of medical facilities. This clinical phenomenon can be prevented or managed in several ways, including use of optimal antiemetic treatment or hypnosis. If the patient develops a phobic response, the site of treatment should be changed and an antidepressant added to treatment (Fawzy and Greenberg 1999).

Pain Management

Occasionally, pain management is an issue during consultation. Fears of addiction have no place in the treatment of the cancer patient. Narcotics such as methadone are the treatment of choice. Neuroleptics, antidepressants, and psychostimulants help diminish psychiatric components of pain (suffering, fear, and insomnia) and are good narcotic adjuvants. When bone metastases are present, prostaglandin inhibitors such as aspirin and nonsteroidal anti-inflammatory drugs are very useful.

Delivering Bad News

Problems most frequently seen in cancer patients are anxiety, dysphoria, and anger about the illness and its implications for the future. Patients with cancer should be told the truth. In telling patients they have a malignant and possibly fatal cancer, Cassem (1987) suggests that physicians 1) rehearse the statement so it can be delivered calmly, 2) be brief—3 sentences or less, 3) encourage the patient to talk, and 4) reassure the patient that he or she will receive continued attention and care.

References

Cassem NH: The dying patient, in Massachusetts General Hospital Handbook of General Hospital Psychiatry, 3rd Edition. Edited by Cassem NH. St. Louis, MO, Mosby-Year Book, 1991, pp 343–371

Fawzy FI, Greenberg DB: Oncology, in Essentials of Consultation-Liaison Psychiatry. Edited by Rundell JR, Wise MG. Washington, DC, American Psychiatric Press, 1999, pp 351–364

Fernandez F, Adams F, Holmes VF, et al: Methylphenidate for depressive disorders in cancer patients. Psychosomatics 28: 455–461, 1987

Lishman WA: Organic Psychiatry, 2nd Edition. Oxford, England, Blackwell Scientific, 1987

Massie MJ, Heiligenstein E, Lederberg MS: Psychiatric complications in cancer patients, in American Cancer Society Textbook of Clinical Oncology. Edited by Holleb AI, Fink DJ, Murphy GP. Atlanta, GA, American Cancer Society, 1991, pp 576–586

Shuster JL, Stern TA, Greenberg DB: Pros and cons of fluoxetine for the depressed cancer patient. Oncology 6:45–56, 1992

■ DEATH AND DYING

People usually die as they have lived. Personality characteristics are often exaggerated with increased stress, and fewer mature defense mechanisms are used. The dying patient may not want to be alone and is generally comfortable talking about death. It is usually the family, and sometimes the ward staff, who are reluctant to engage in such conversations. The importance of religious faith and the belief in an afterlife in dying patients should not be underestimated. The clinician should discuss do-not-resuscitate orders, wills, and comfort measures early. If the patient wants, time at home or private times with family while in the hospital should be arranged.

Depression

In a medically ill dying patient, the attribution of neurovegetative symptoms is often difficult (i.e., Is the patient depressed?). Almost all seriously ill patients have problems with sleep, energy, and appetite and may have some difficulty with concentration. The following characteristics help identify a depressed medically ill patient: sustained depressed mood, decreased psychomotor movements, suicidal ideation, helplessness, worthlessness, and hopelessness. The depressed patient also has anhedonia. The depressed dying patient with less than 3 weeks to live may respond to a rapid-acting psychostimulant, such as methylphenidate. Patients who are within hours to days of death and in distress are likely to benefit most from the use of sedatives or narcotic analgesic infusions.

Anxiety

The threat of death can cause anxiety. If an individual does not mention fears of dying, the clinician should inquire either indirectly (e.g., "You look scared. How are you doing?") or directly (e.g., "Are you worried that you may die?"). If the patient believes he or she is dying, the clinician should respond according to the reality of the situation. If the fear is unrealistic, reassurance and an explanation about the current situation will usually decrease anxiety and fear. If death is imminent, the clinician should ask the patient, "What frightens you the most about dying?" Three common fears are abandonment, uncontrollable pain, and shortness of breath (Cassem 1991). Anxiety disorders are commonly associated with neurological insults (Wise and Rundell 1999).

Antianxiety medications are very effective if symptomatic or disabling anxiety persists after psychological support and the opportunity for abreaction are provided. Benzodiazepines, however, can also result in lethargy and/or confusion. When terror or extreme fear is present, low doses of major tranquilizers (neuroleptics) often are more efficacious than benzodiazepines. Haloperidol 0.5–2 mg twice daily, perphenazine 2 mg orally three times a day, thiothixene 1–2 mg three times a day, or trifluoperazine 2 mg three times a day can reduce panic or extreme anxiety markedly.

Pain

In patients with advanced cancer, 60%–90% have pain (Foley 1985). In addition, depression and anxiety increase the experience of pain. In the evaluation process, the first step is to assess quality of pain, time course, fluctuations, and factors that exacerbate or relieve it. Mental status examination and medical and neurological evaluations are performed. Pain is also assessed repeatedly to balance the analgesic dosage against the level of pain and alertness (Elliott and Foley 1990). Pain is frequently undertreated in medically ill and dying patients.

References

Cassem NH: The dying patient, in Massachusetts General Hospital Handbook of General Hospital Psychiatry, 3rd Edition. Edited by Cassem NH. St. Louis, MO, Mosby-Year Book, 1991, pp 343–371

Elliott K, Foley KM: Pain syndromes. Journal of Psychosocial Oncology 8:11–45, 1990

Foley KM: The treatment of cancer pain. N Engl J Med 313:84–95, 1985

Wise MG, Rundell JR: Anxiety and neurological disorders. Seminars in Clinical Neuropsychiatry 4:98–102, 1999

■ NEUROLOGY AND NEUROSURGERY

Head Injury

Because of the swirling movement of traumatic forces within the brain during acceleration/deceleration injuries, head trauma is likely to produce changes in the axial structure of the brain (Waziri 1986). Therefore, subcortical structures, such as the limbic system, are often affected. In addition, in closed head injuries, contrecoup lesions are more severe than lesions in portions of the brain closest to the source of trauma. The only exception to this is when the head is perfectly still at the time of impact (Lishman 1987), an uncommon event. Frequent neuropsychiatric findings in head trauma patients include emotional lability, irritability, personality change, fear, rage, impulsivity, memory loss, and apathy. Secondary depression and mania also can occur.

In most head injuries, consciousness is impaired, ranging from a momentary daze to prolonged coma. Retrograde (before the trauma) and anterograde (after the trauma) amnesia commonly occur with significant head trauma. The degree of anterograde and retrograde amnesia each correlates positively with trauma severity and negatively with prognosis for full recovery. Generally, the period of retrograde amnesia shrinks faster than the period of anterograde amnesia. The degree and speed of recovery after head injury depend on many factors: premorbid neuropsychiatric state, amount of brain damage, location of brain damage, emotional impact of the injury, quality of medical care, compensation/litigation, and motivation (Lishman 1987).

CNS Infection

Usually, CNS infections present with nonfocal findings such as obtundation, irritability, or restlessness. When focal findings occur, an abscess should be suspected. Fever and focal signs may or may not be present; however, their absence typically delays the diagnosis of an abscess. CNS abscesses also may present with headaches, confusion, personality change, and memory loss. Neurosyphilis may have a variety of neuropsychiatric presentations, most commonly progressive dementia, mania, depression, and psychosis. The physician should assess for the possibility of meningeal inflammation by flexing the neck and hip joints (Kernig's and Brudzinski's signs).

Primary and Metastatic CNS Tumors

Half of the patients with primary CNS tumors develop psychiatric symptoms. Focal findings are usually present, but nonspecific signs and symptoms, such as personality change and affective lability, also may occur. The nature of neuropsychiatric symptomatology depends on the location of the tumor, the degree to which intracranial pressure is raised, and the constitution of the individual. Neuropsychiatric findings are more likely when tumors are frontal, limbic, or temporal than when tumors are parietal or occipital.

Lung, breast, gastrointestinal, pancreatic, renal, and prostate cancers are the most likely to metastasize to the brain. CNS metastases eventually develop in 35%–45% of lung cancer patients (Lohr and Cadet 1987). CNS metastatic tumors are sometimes symptomatic before the primary tumor, especially when the primary tumor is in the lung. If discovered early, when a single CNS metastasis exists, neurosurgical intervention is often warranted.

Because psychiatric symptoms of brain tumors are nonfocal, the clinician must maintain a high index of suspicion in patients who have cancer. A brain tumor should be suspected in patients with psychiatric symptoms and 1) frequent or unremitting headaches, 2) vomiting, 3) seizures, 4) visual complaints, and 5) any focal neurological finding (Lohr and Cadet 1987).

Subcortical/Limbic System Disease

Parkinson's disease, Huntington's chorea, progressive supranuclear palsy, and some elements of HIV dementia are examples of conditions that principally involve subcortical and limbic areas of the brain. Neuropsychiatric symptoms, such as emotional lability, fear, rage, apathy, impulsiveness, hallucinations, and delusions, are therefore common, although they are diverse and nonspecific. The clinician must not mistake subcortical dementias for primary mood disorders.

Normal Pressure Hydrocephalus

Of patients with dementia, 7% have normal pressure hydrocephalus (NPH) (Martin and Black 1987). NPH is important to recognize because it is usually treatable. The classic NPH diagnostic triad is dementia, gait disturbance, and urinary incontinence.

Poststroke Depression

The major psychiatric sequela of stroke is depression, although anxiety disorders occur more commonly than appreciated (Wise and Rundell 1999). Robinson and colleagues (1983), as part of a 2-year longitudinal study, confirmed that depression (major depressive disorder and dysthymic disorder) occurs in half of acute poststroke patients. They reported that 26% of acute poststroke patients had a presentation consistent with major depressive disorder, whereas another 20% had dysthymic disorder or minor depression. Follow-up longitudinal natural history studies suggested that the average duration of poststroke major depression is approximately 1 year. Dysthymic disorder may last longer, often greater than 2 years (Robinson et al. 1983, 1987).

Lacunar strokes and infarcts also have psychiatric sequelae. Lacunar infarcts are small lesions, often the result of hypertension, that occur in the deeper subcortical parts of the cerebrum and in the brain stem (Fricchione et al. 1999). They result from occlusion of the small penetrating branches of the large cerebral arteries. A wide range of mood changes may occur following lacunar strokes, including emotional incontinence and depression.

References

Fricchione G, Weilburg JB, Murray GB: Neurology and neurosurgery, in Essentials of Consultation-Liaison Psychiatry. Edited by Rundell JR, Wise MG. Washington, DC, American Psychiatric Press, 1999, pp 365–382

Lishman WA: Organic Psychiatry, 3rd Edition. Oxford, England, Blackwell Scientific, 1998

Lohr JB, Cadet JL: Neuropsychiatric aspects of brain tumors, in The American Psychiatric Press Textbook of Neuropsychiatry. Edited by Hales RE, Yudofsky SC. Washington, DC, American Psychiatric Press, 1987, pp 351–364

Martin MJ, Black JL: Neuropsychiatric aspects of degenerative disease, in The American Psychiatric Press Textbook of Neuropsychiatry. Edited by Hales RE, Yudofsky SC. Washington, DC, American Psychiatric Press, 1987, pp 257–286

Robinson RG, Starr LB, Kubos KL, et al: A two-year longitudinal study of post-stroke mood disorders: findings during the initial evaluation. Stroke 14:736–741, 1983

Robinson RG, Bolduc PL, Price TR: Two-year longitudinal study of post-stroke mood disorders: diagnosis and outcome at one and two years. Stroke 18:837–843, 1987

Waziri R: The amnestic syndrome, in The Medical Basis of Psychiatry. Edited by Winokur G, Clayton PJ. Philadelphia, PA, WB Saunders, 1986, pp 20–28

Wise MG, Rundell JR: Anxiety and neurological disorders. Seminars in Clinical Neuropsychiatry 4:98–102, 1999

■ HIV DISEASE AND AIDS

AIDS is the leading cause of death in the United States among men and women aged 25–44 years (Centers for Disease Control and Prevention 1995). During the past 2 years, major gains have occurred in treating HIV disease. In fact, the availability of "triple therapy" with three different antiretroviral agents has caused many patients with HIV disease and HIV specialists to talk openly about HIV disease as a chronic medical condition rather than a relentlessly progressive infection.

The psychiatric treatment and management of HIV disease must take into consideration a wide range of ongoing etiological factors, including premorbid primary psychiatric disorders, disorders secondary to HIV-1 CNS infection, advanced systemic disease, and neuropsychiatric side effects of commonly used HIV/AIDS medications (Worth and Halman 1999). Advanced systemic disease and HIV-1 CNS infection can constrain the pharmacotherapeutic options available to the C-L psychiatrist. Psychotherapeutic interventions must take into account the perspectives of patients who come from communities that often have been marginalized, socially disenfranchised, and impoverished. Management plans frequently require liaison with community-based HIV/AIDS service organizations and highly diverse social and family support groups.

AIDS

More than 1 million Americans are infected with HIV. The end stage of this infection is AIDS. Neuropsychiatric complications in AIDS patients include memory deficits, concentration impairment, dementia, psychomotor slowing, motor deficits, apathy, withdrawal, depression, or psychosis. In the final stages of the disease, delirium, profound slowness, severe dementia, focal neurological signs, secondary neurological disorders (e.g., tumors, CNS toxoplasmosis), seizures, and agitation are common.

Neuropsychiatric findings in AIDS may be caused by primary effects of the virus itself, neurotoxic by-products of the immune responses to the virus, indirect consequences of systemic disease (e.g., hypoxia, malnutrition), or intracranial tumors or infections that occur as a result of the immunocompromised state. Unless the patient is near death from nonneurological causes, aggressive diagnostic workup is indicated when new neuropsychiatric symptoms emerge in AIDS patients. Treatment is possible for many AIDS-related CNS disorders, especially toxoplasmosis, herpes simplex infection, and cerebral lymphoma.

HIV Infection Without AIDS

Longitudinal studies of HIV-infected military personnel (Rundell et al. 1991) have shown that social and occupational difficulties are more likely during the first year following a seropositive diagnosis and when the patient has anxiety, depression, unusual anger, a helpless/hopeless attitude, overcontrol of emotions, and excessive stoicism. Secondary mental syndromes occur in HIV-infected patients without AIDS, although less commonly than in AIDS patients. Most early-stage patients have cerebrospinal abnormalities, including cerebrospinal pleocytosis, elevated protein, increased immunoglobulin, and oligoclonal bands. When neuropsychiatric findings occur in early HIV disease, they involve subcortical, integrative, and executive functions: visuospatial integration, visuospatial memory, reaction time, verbal fluency, nonverbal fluency, problem solving, conceptual skills, set shifting, concentration, speed of mental processing, and mental flexibility (Rundell et al. 1991). Language and related general intellectual skills are usually spared.

Psychopharmacological Issues

Rabkin et al. (1994) reported that fluoxetine is well tolerated and effective for HIV-related major depression, with an 83% response rate and no deleterious effects on immune status. Studies of antidepressant efficacy among HIV patients, however, are notable for substantial placebo response and attrition (Rabkin et al. 1999), suggesting that unknown factors are important in efficacious diagnosis and treatment of depression in HIV disease. For HIV/AIDS patients, the dosing principle of starting low and increasing slowly applies. Fluoxetine or paroxetine should be started at 10 mg/day, or 25 mg of sertraline should be given to patients with advanced disease (Worth and Halman 1999). The dosage of fluoxetine should be increased after 4–5 weeks, and sertraline or paroxetine should be increased after 1–2 weeks and titrated against response and side-effect profile.

At low doses, both dextroamphetamine and methylphenidate are effective for HIV-related major depression, as primary agents (Fernandez and Levy 1992) or as adjuvant agents, with response rates up to 80%. They are especially effective for anergia, apathy, and anorexia; some patients also report improved mood, attention, and concentration. Stimulants are preferred to conventional antidepressants in patients with a predominance of apathy compared with sadness and in patients who are unable to tolerate the side effects of conventional antidepressants.

Suicide Assessment

Patients with HIV/AIDS are at increased risk for suicide from multiple factors and markers, including demographics, psychopathology, psychoactive substance abuse and dependence, psychosocial stressors, and HIV disease–associated morbidity. There are reports of suicide attempts and suicide following HIV-1 serologic testing, but evidence suggests that suicide risk is strongly related to concurrent depression. In a longitudinal study of HIV-1 serologic testing with pre- and posttest counseling, Perry and Jacobsberg (1990) found that suicidal ideation decreased over time for both HIV-seropositive and HIV-seronegative patients.

References

Centers for Disease Control and Prevention: Update: AIDS—United States, 1994. MMWR 44:64–67, 1995

Fernandez F, Levy JK. Psychopharmacotherapy of psychiatric syndromes in asymptomatic and symptomatic HIV infection. Psychiatr Med 9:377–394, 1992

Perry S, Jacobsberg R: Suicidal ideation and HIV testing. JAMA 263:679–682, 1990

Rabkin JG, Rabkin R, Wagner G: Effect of fluoxetine on mood and immune status in depressed patients with HIV illness. J Clin Psychiatry 55:92–97, 1994

Rabkin JG, Wagner GJ, Rabkin R: Fluoxetine treatment for depression in patients with HIV and AIDS: a randomized, placebo-controlled trial. Am J Psychiatry 156:101–107, 1999

Rundell JR, Brown GR, McManis SE, et al: Neuropsychiatric morbidity in early HIV disease: implications for military occupational function. Presentation at the NATO AGARD Problems in Aerospace Medicine Conference, Rome, Italy, October 1991

Worth JL, Halman MH: HIV Disease/AIDS, in Essentials of Consultation-Liaison Psychiatry. Edited by Rundell JR, Wise MG. Washington, DC, American Psychiatric Press, 1999, pp 451–478

■ ORGAN TRANSPLANTATION

The C-L psychiatrist is often called on to fulfill many formal and informal functions as a member of the organ transplant team. The degree to which the psychiatrist is accepted as a member of the transplant team depends on his or her ability to communicate effectively and succinctly with other team members, the extent to which his or her clinical judgment is trusted, his or her ability to effectively diffuse adverse transplant team member reactions to patients, and the psychiatrist's ability to work collaboratively and effectively with other transplant team members (Strouse et al. 1999).

Transplant Donors

Heart and liver transplants involve brain-dead donors, whereas renal transplants frequently involve living family donors. The C-L psychiatrist should evaluate potential interpersonal, marital, or family problems encountered by donor families. For example, is the family "black sheep" donating out of a conscious or an unconscious desire to improve his or her standing in the family system?

Although mortality for donors is very low (calculated to be equivalent to the commuter who drives 16 miles to work each day), preoperative donor anxiety occurs (Surman 1987).

Transplant Recipients

In potential organ transplant recipients, the psychiatric consultant is sometimes asked to comment on whether psychiatric contraindications to transplantation exist. Psychiatric illness is only a minor factor in deciding whether a particular patient should receive a donor organ. Successful transplant outcomes have been reported in patients who have mental retardation, anxiety disorders, mood disorders, psychoactive substance use disorders, and personality disorders (Surman 1987). More important than psychiatric predisposition to successful postoperative psychosocial functioning are the success of the allograft and strength of social supports. Table 17–2 summarizes biopsychosocial criteria for psychiatric evaluation of potential transplant recipients.

Rating Scales

Two rating scales are available for the clinical assessment of psychosocial factors in transplant candidates: the Psychosocial Assessment of Candidates for Transplant (PACT), developed by Olbrisch and colleagues (1989), and the Transplantation Evaluation Rating Scale (TERS), developed by Twillman et al. (1993). Both scales include weighted ratings for psychiatric diagnoses, substance abuse, health behaviors, compliance, social support, prior coping, and disease-specific coping. The TERS also rates affective and mental states.

Perioperative Issues

Acute secondary mental disorders are common during the perioperative period. Common etiological factors for delirium in transplant recipients include the consequences to the brain of chronic organ failure, the residua of general anesthesia, lengthy transplant surgery, volume and electrolyte shifts associated with reperfusion of the new organ, cyclosporine loading, postoperative opiate treatment, early graft dysfunction, fever, coagulopathy, and infection (Plevak et al. 1989). Psychoactive substance withdrawal is also possible during the postoperative period.

The first signs of *cyclosporine neurotoxicity* are often seen in the intensive care unit (Strouse et al. 1999). After an early lucid period, patients are lethargic and confused and require reintubation despite previously adequate respiratory functioning (Craven 1991). Variable symptoms are seen, including seizures, cortical blindness,

---

TABLE 17–2. **Biopsychosocial screening criteria for solid organ transplantation**

Absolute contraindications

Active substance abuse

Psychosis significantly limiting informed consent or compliance

Refusal of transplant and/or active suicidal ideation

Factitious disorder with physical symptoms

Relative contraindications

Dementia or other persistent cerebral dysfunction, if unable to arrange adequate psychosocial resources to supervise compliance *or* if dysfunction known to correlate with high risk of adverse posttransplant neuropsychiatric outcome (e.g., alcohol dementia, frontal lobe syndromes)

Treatment-refractory psychiatric illness, such as intractable, life-threatening mood disorder, schizophrenia, eating disorder, character disorder

Noncompliance with the transplant system, unwillingness to participate in necessary psychoeducational/psychiatric treatment

---

Source. Adapted from Strouse TB, Wolcott DL, Skotzko CE: "Transplantation," in *The American Psychiatric Press Textbook of Consultation-Liaison Psychiatry.* Edited by Rundell JR, Wise MG. Washington, DC, American Psychiatric Press, 1996, pp. 640–670. Copyright 1996, American Psychiatric Press. Used with permission.

aphasia, paresthesia, neuropathy, delusions, and agitation. Obtundation, deeper coma, status epilepticus, and death rarely occur (Adams et al. 1987). Diffuse white matter changes are seen on magnetic resonance imaging, accompanied by symmetric electroencephalographic dysrhythmia. In some cases, cyclosporine holidays are associated with symptom remission and normalization of white matter changes (De Groen et al. 1987).

References

Adams DH, Ponsford S, Gunson B, et al: Neurological complications following liver transplantation. Lancet 1:949–951, 1987

Craven JL: Cyclosporine-associated organic mental disorders in liver transplant recipients. Psychosomatics 32:94–102, 1991

De Groen PC, Aksamit AJ, Rakela J, et al: Central nervous system toxicity after liver transplantation: the role of cyclosporine and cholesterol. N Engl J Med 317:861–866, 1987

Olbrisch ME, Levenson J, Hamer R: The PACT: a rating scale for the study of clinical decision-making in psychosocial screening criteria for organ transplant candidates. Clin Transpl 3:164–169, 1989

Plevak DJ, Southorn PA, Narr BJ, et al: Intensive care unit experience in the Mayo Liver Transplantation Program: the first 100 cases. Mayo Clin Proc 64:433–445, 1989

Strouse TB, Wolcott DL, Skotzko CE: Transplantation, in Essentials of Consultation-Liaison Psychiatry. Edited by Rundell JR, Wise MG. Washington, DC, American Psychiatric Press, 1999, pp 325–349

Surman OS: Hemodialysis and renal transplantation, in Massachusetts General Hospital Handbook of General Hospital Psychiatry, 3rd Edition. Edited by Cassem NH. St. Louis MO, Mosby-Year Book, 1991, pp 401–430

Twillman RK, Manetto C, Wolcott DL: The Transplant Evaluation Scale: a revision of the psychosocial levels system for evaluating organ transplant candidates. Psychosomatics 34:144–153, 1993

■ CRITICALLY ILL PATIENTS AND THE INTENSIVE CARE UNIT

Given the nature of their work, critical care physicians and nurses regularly encounter patients who have fear, anxiety, denial, anger, depression, dependency, or maladaptive personality features. A psychiatrist who is comfortable working in a critical care setting offers great assistance to both patients and medical colleagues. To perform optimally in a critical care setting, a psychiatrist must have sound medical skills. He or she must examine the patient with a mental status and a physical examination, including a basic neurological examination. The critically ill patient's mental status examination provides important information for decision making. If the patient has delirium or dementia, the focus of the differential diagnosis is to identify the etiological agent(s). The detection and correction of underlying cause(s) are often life-saving in the seriously ill patient (see Chapter 3).

Mental Status Examination

Examining patients in the intensive care unit (ICU) is a challenge. First, the patient's level of consciousness should be noted. Next, the psychiatrist must establish a method of communication. If the patient cannot communicate verbally, he or she can write answers on a tablet. The psychiatrist can administer the entire Mini-Mental State Exam to any patient who can write (see Chapter 2). Writing may show spatial disorientation, misspellings, inappropriate repetition of letters (perseveration), and linguistic errors.

For patients who are unable to speak or write, the psychiatrist may either use an eye blink method of communication (one blink = yes, two blinks = no) or have the patient squeeze the psychiatrist's finger with his or her hand (one squeeze = yes, two squeezes = no). Questions should be phrased to allow for a yes or no response (e.g., "Are you feeling frightened?"). To determine whether a patient is confused, the psychiatrist should also ask nonsense questions (e.g., "Do catfish fly?" "Do beagles yodel?"). If the patient looks surprised or amused and properly answers the question, a secondary mental syndrome is not as likely.

Changes in Medical-Surgical Management

Patients in ICUs have serious physical illnesses. A large proportion of the psychiatric symptoms and disorders seen in the ICU setting are secondary to these medical disorders and/or toxicity from their treatments. Consequently, the psychiatrist must consider whether changes in the medical management of a patient would alleviate the psychiatric symptoms. For example, it makes no sense (and would be ineffective) to treat delirium caused by hypoxia or hypoglycemia with neuroleptics alone. Whenever possible, delirium should be treated specifically (e.g., reversal of hypoxia with oxygen or hypoglycemia with glucose). A special note of temporal correlations between the onset of mental symptoms and changes in the medical-surgical management of the patient should be made. The ICU flowchart or laboratory summary sheet may reveal a metabolic or infectious problem that explains an altered mental status. The psychiatrist also should review the medication list, with special attention paid to medications added just prior to symptom onset or discontinued before symptom onset (i.e., a withdrawal reaction). These and other temporal correlations are often the primary (or only) clues available to help identify the cause of psychiatric symptoms in the ICU.

Psychopharmacological Treatment

Serious physical illness may increase the patient's sensitivity to drug side effects (Stoudemire et al. 1990). Symptomatic treatment alone may not solve the problem; it may even create new problems. A thorough knowledge of the pharmacological properties of psychotropic agents is crucial to their successful use in the ICU (Shuster and Stern 1996). Most psychotropics are metabolized in the liver and cleared through the liver or kidneys. Therefore, altered hepatic or renal function clearly influences the choice and dosing of psychotropic medications. Clinical experience shows that doses below the standard therapeutic range are often effective in patients with medical illness, especially when drug interactions or renal or hepatic impairment slows drug clearance. Some critically ill patients, however, require doses similar to those required in healthy adults. Higher doses are safely achieved by titrating beneficial effects to side effects.

Respirators

Anxiety is particularly common when a patient is weaned from the ventilator. According to Shuster and Stern (1996, p. 798),

> Several factors can play a role in the anxiety: patients may experience at least brief periods of relative hypoxia during weaning trials; prolonged ventilation usually leads to deconditioning of muscles of respiration, so patients become frightened by the unfamiliar difficulty they experience with breathing until these muscles are reconditioned; and patients often become psychologically dependent on the ventilator and fearful when the device is disconnected.

Intra-Aortic Balloon Pump

An intra-aortic balloon pump (IABP) renders a patient immobile. Because of the IABP, patients must remain on their backs. In addition, numerous intravenous and intra-arterial lines are typically present, restricting arm movement. These physical restrictions can cause severe anxiety. Lorazepam is usually a good choice to relieve anxiety. It can be given intravenously (1 or 2 mg) and has a low frequency of adverse effects in a critically ill patient population. When a patient's anxiety reaches panic proportions, administration of a neuroleptic at a low dose is often helpful (e.g., perphenazine 2 mg bid or tid).

References

Stoudemire A, Moran MG, Fogel BS: Psychotropic drug use in the medically ill: part I. Psychosomatics 31:377–391, 1990

Shuster JL, Stern TA: Intensive care units, in The American Psychiatric Press Textbook of Consultation-Liaison Psychiatry. Edited by Rundell JR, Wise MG. Washington, DC, American Psychiatric Press, 1996, pp 782–802

■ MALE ERECTILE DISORDER (IMPOTENCE)

Many medical diseases and pharmacological agents are associated with male erectile disorder. The ability to have an erection requires normal functioning in four areas: 1) adequate arterial flow to and through the penis; 2) normal neurological function, particularly the autonomic nervous system; 3) normal hormonal function; and 4) normal erotogenic input. Erotogenic function is impeded by depression, anxiety, interpersonal issues, and fatigue.

History

The pattern of erectile function and dysfunction helps the clinician decide whether a medical evaluation is necessary. If the patient has erections in the morning, during sleep, during masturbation, with a sexual partner other than the spouse, or spontaneously when intercourse is not planned, a psychological reason for impotence is very likely. If the patient has never had erectile function or has lost erectile function, a toxic or medical etiology is possible, and an evaluation is indicated.

Medications can cause impotence (Table 17–3). It is diagnostically helpful to correlate the onset of sexual dysfunction with initiation of or increases in prescribed or over-the-counter medications (Brown and Philbrick 1996).

TABLE 17–3.   **Medications that may cause male erectile disorder (impotence)**

Alcohol	Amitriptyline	Amoxapine
Amphetamines	Amyl nitrite	Atenolol
Atropine	Baclofen	Barbiturates
Benztropine	Bromocriptine	Bupropion
Captopril	Carbamazepine	Chlorambucil
Chlorothiazide	Chlorpromazine	Cimetidine
Clidinium	Clofibrate	Clomipramine
Clonidine	Cyclophosphamide	Cytosine arabinoside
Desipramine	Dichlorphenamide	Digoxin
Diphenhydramine	Disopyramide	Disulfiram
Fenfluramine	Glycopyrrolate	Guanethidine
Haloperidol	Hydralazine	Hydrochlorothiazide
Hydroxyzine	Imipramine	Indomethacin
Interferon alpha	Isocarboxazid	Ketoconazole
Lithium	Maprotiline	Melphalan
Methadone	Methaqualone	Methotrexate
Methscopolamine	Methyldopa	Metoclopramide
Metoprolol	Mexiletine	Morphine
Nadolol	Naproxen	Nortriptyline
Pargyline	Phenelzine	Phentolamine
Phenytoin	Pimozide	Pindolol
Prazosin	Procarbazine	Progestins
Propranolol	Protriptyline	Scopolamine
Selective serotonin reuptake inhibitors	Thiazide diuretics	Thioridazine
Thiothixene	Timolol	Tranylcypromine
Trihexyphenidyl	Trimipramine	Verapamil

Source.   Adapted from Brown GW, Philbrick K: "Sexual Disorders and Dysfunction," in *The American Psychiatric Press Textbook of Consultation-Liaison Psychiatry.* Edited by Rundell JR, Wise MG. Washington, DC, American Psychiatric Press, 1996, pp. 473–475. Copyright 1996, American Psychiatric Press. Used with permission.

Evaluation

The evaluation of erectile dysfunction includes a physical examination, with particular attention to neurological function. A full evaluation of impotence is expensive. It may include a sleep laboratory evaluation, which often is diagnostic. Strain gauges are connected to the penis and monitor whether nocturnal erections occur during rapid eye movement (REM) sleep. If full erections occur during REM sleep, a psychological etiology for impotence is probable. Other diagnostic studies may include Doppler blood flow studies, nerve conduction studies, tests of bladder function, and cavernosonograms. Laboratory studies may include glucose tolerance test, blood urea nitrogen and creatinine levels, liver function tests, and hormonal studies (e.g., thyroid, testosterone, prolactin, follicle stimulating hormone, and luteinizing hormone).

Treatment

Some causes of impotence are reversible (e.g., hyperthyroidism, alcohol, prescribed drugs) and others are usually irreversible (e.g., spinal cord injury, autonomic neuropathies such as those found in type 1 diabetes). In the latter case, a penile prosthesis may be considered. There are many reasons for psychological impotence. A thorough interview with the patient and sexual partner usually clarifies the underlying issues. If marital discord exists, marital therapy is recommended prior to referral for sexual therapy.

Reference

Brown GW, Philbrick K: Sexual disorders and dysfunction, in The American Psychiatric Press Textbook of Consultation-Liaison Psychiatry. Edited by Rundell JR, Wise MG. Washington, DC, American Psychiatric Press, 1996, pp 608–639

■ ADDITIONAL READINGS FOR THIS CHAPTER

Apfel RJ, Handel MH: Madness and Loss of Motherhood: Sexuality, Reproduction, and Long-Term Mental Illness. Washington, DC, American Psychiatric Press, 1993

Lyketsos CG, Hanson AL, Fishman M, et al: Manic Syndrome Early and Late in the Course of HIV. Am J Psychiatry 150: 326–327, 1993

Rabkin JG: Psychostimulant medication for depression and lethargy in HIV illness; a pilot study. Progress Notes 4:1, 1993

Shuster JL, Breitbart W, Chochinov HM: Psychiatric aspects of excellent end-of-life care. Psychosomatics 40:1–4, 1999

Wiener I, Breitbart W, Holland J: Psychiatric issues in the care of dying patients, in Essentials of Consultation-Liaison Psychiatry. Edited by Rundell JR, Wise MG. Washington, DC, American Psychiatric Press, 1999, pp 435–449

INDEX

Page numbers printed in **boldface** *type refer to tables or figures.*

Abstracting abilities, 14
  cortical mapping, **24–25**
Acetaminophen, suicide attempts
    and, 246
Acetazolamide, drug interactions,
    177
Acute anxiety, behavioral
    management, 106
Acute stress disorder, 95–99
  PTSD risk and, 99, 108
Acyclovir, delirium etiology and,
    36
Addison's disease, depression
    etiology and, **66**
Adjustment disorder, 137
  with anxiety, 93, 101
  with depressed mood, 63
  psychotherapy for, 137
Adolescents
  informed consent, 274
  patient confidentiality for, 274
  regressive behavior in, 273
  treatment refusal rights, 274
α-adrenergic blockade, for central
    or chronic pain relief, 212
Adrenocorticotropic hormone,
    delirium etiology and, **36**
Advance directives, 239
Affect, parameters, 12–13

Affective disorder, suicide risk
    and, 247
Aggression. *See also* Violence
  differential diagnosis, 196–197
  drugs associated with, 197
  etiologies, 198
  medications for, 56
Aggression (chronic)
  behavioral treatments, 197–199
  medications for, 197, **198–199**
Agoraphobia, without panic
    disorder, 95
AIDS, neuropsychiatric
    complications, 289–290
Akathisia, 101
Alcohol
  aggression and, 197
  as anxiety/panic cause, **97**
  cross-reactivity with
      benzodiazepines and
      sedative-hypnotics, 158
  dementia and, 45
  drug interactions, **176**, **177**, **178**
  effect changes with aging, 258
  intoxication, violence etiology
      and, 195
  male erectile disorder etiology
      and, **300**
  mania etiology and, **84**

Alcohol *(continued)*
  overdose, 151
    life-threatening signs, 151
    management, 151
  suicide attempts and, 246
  withdrawal
    as anxiety/panic cause, **97**
    violence etiology and, 195
  withdrawal delirium (delirium
    tremens), signs and
    symptoms, 155
Alcohol abuse. *See* Alcoholism
Alcohol dementia, 49–51
  epidemiology, 49–50
  Korsakoff's psychosis
    differentiation, 50
  neuropsychological
    abnormalities, 50–51
Alcohol dependence. *See*
  Alcoholism
Alcohol intoxication, 151, **152**
  management, 151, **152**
  medications for, **152**
Alcohol withdrawal, 153
  by burn patients, 276
  chlordiazepoxide for, 153,
    154
  diazepam for, 155
  folic acid for, **154**
  haloperidol for, **154**
  management, 153–155, **154**
  oxazepam for, **154**
  seizures, 155
    benzodiazepines for, 155
    phenytoin for, 155
  setting for, 153
  signs and symptoms, 153, **154**
  thiamine for, 153, **154**, 155
  tremors, 153

Alcohol withdrawal delirium
    (delirium tremens), 155–156
  benzodiazepines and, 156
  haloperidol for, 156
  management, 156
  neuroleptics for, 156
  thiamine for, 156
Alcohol-induced amnestic
    disorder, 156
  management, 156
Alcohol-induced psychotic
    disorder, 153
  management, 153
Alcoholics Anonymous, 150
Alcoholism, 149. *See also*
    Substance abuse
  depression etiology and, **67**
  diagnosis, 149–150
    CAGE screen, 149, **150**
    laboratory tests, 149
    physical signs, 150
  disulfiram for, 150
  fetal alcohol syndrome and,
    271
  management, 150
  medical complications, 150
  suicide risk and, 247
Alexithymia, 225
Alprazolam
  absorption rates, **103**
  cytochrome P450 enzymes and,
    181
  dosages, **103**
  drug interactions, **176**, **178**n
  half-life, **103**
  mania etiology and, **84**
  for panic disorder, 107
Alzheimer Family Support Group,
    57

Alzheimer's disease. *See also*
Dementia of the Alzheimer's
type (DAT)
psychosis and, 257–258
suicide risk, 248
vascular pathology and, 45
Amantadine
delirium etiology and, **36**
mania etiology and, **84**
Aminoglutethimide
delirium etiology and, **36**
side effects, **280**
Aminophylline, as anxiety/panic
cause, **97**
Amitriptyline
as analgesic adjuvant, 214
cytocochrome P450 enzymes
and, **182**
dosages, **70–71**
drug interactions, 260
male erectile disorder etiology
and, **300**
receptor affinities, **70–71**
Amnesia
in conversion disorder,
129
delirium and, 32
with head injury, 285
Amoxapine
dosages, **70–71**
male erectile disorder etiology
and, **300**
receptor affinities, **70–71**
Amphetamine abuse. *See also*
Substance abuse
anemia and, 163
diagnostic criteria, **148**
management, 163
polydrug abuse and, 163

Amphetamine delirium, 164
management, 164
Amphetamine delusional disorder,
164
haloperidol for, 164
management, 164
Amphetamine intoxication, **152**
benzodiazepines for, 163
haloperidol for, **152**, 163
lorazepam for, **152**, 163
management, 163–164
signs and symptoms, **152**, 163
Amphetamine withdrawal, 164
depression and, 165
desipramine for, **154**
diazepam for, 164
lorazepam for, **154**, 164
management, **154**, 164–165
neuroleptics for, 164
secondary depressive disorders'
etiologies and, **66**
signs and symptoms, **154**
Amphetamines, 162–163
aggression and, 197
as analgesic adjuvants, 214
as anxiety/panic cause, **97**
delirium etiology and, **36**
drug interactions, **176**, **178**
male erectile disorder etiology
and, **300**
mania etiology and, **84**
Amphotericin B
delirium etiology and, **36**
secondary depressive disorders'
etiologies and, **66**
Amyl nitrate, male erectile
disorder etiology and, **300**
Anafranil (clomipramine),
70–71

Analgesics. *See also names of
    specific drugs*
    for children, 274
    for continuous pain, 206
    delirium etiology and, **36**
    opiate dosage comparisons,
        213
    opiate potency comparisons, **213**
    patient-controlled analgesia
        (PCA) devices, 207
    pharmacological adjuvants,
        214–215
    suicide attempts and, 246
Anemia
    amphetamine abuse and, 163
    depression etiology and, **67**
Anhedonia, 283
Antacids
    drug absorption and, 172
    drug interactions, **176**, 260
Anti-inflammatory drugs. *See also
    Nonsteroidal
    anti-inflammatory drugs;
    names of specific drugs*
    delirium etiology and, **36**
Antianxiety medications. *See
    Anxiolytics; names of
    specific drugs*
Antiarrhythmic drugs, adverse
    effects, 68
Antiarrhythmics
    Class I, drug interactions, **178**
    cytochrome P450 enzymes and,
        181
    ECT risk reduced by, 76
    metabolization, 73
Antibiotics. *See also names of
    specific drugs*
    delirium etiology and, **36**

Anticholinergic coma, neuroleptic
    malignant syndrome and, 188
Anticholinergic delirium,
    neuroleptic malignant
    syndrome and, 188
Anticholinergics. *See also names
    of specific drugs*
    aggression and, 197
    as anxiety/panic cause, **97**
    delirium etiology and, **36**
    drug interactions, **176**, **178**
    for neuroleptic malignant
        syndrome, not
        recommended, 190
Anticonvulsants. *See also names
    of specific drugs*
    adverse effects, 89–90
    as analgesic adjuvants, 212, 214
    for chronic aggression, **198**
    for chronic or central pain
        relief, 212
    delirium etiology and, **36**
    dosages, **198**
    during pregnancy, 270
    for mania, 88–90
Antidepressants. *See also names
    of specific drugs*
    65.*See also* Tricyclic
        antidepressants
    adverse effects, 65, 73–74, 274
    as analgesic adjuvants, 212, 214
    for anxiety disorders, 105
    as anxiety/panic cause, **97**
    for cancer patients, 279, 281
    for chronic aggression, **198**
    for chronic or central pain
        relief, 212
    classes, **70–71**
    for depression treatment, 73–74

dosages, 65, **70–73**
efficacy in HIV patients, 290
HIV-related depression and,
290, 291
metabolization, 73
for pain management of burns,
278
for panic disorder, 106–107
for personality disorders, 226
for postpartum depression, 271
protein binding, 263
psychotherapy and, 76
for PTSD, 108
receptor affinities, 65, **70–73**
renal failure and, 175
suicide attempts and, 246
teratogenic potential, 270
Antihistamines
as analgesic adjuvants, 214
delirium etiology and, **36**
for insomnia, 112
suicide attempts and, 246
Antihypertensive drugs, secondary
depressive disorders'
etiologies and, **66**
Antihypertensives
as anxiety/panic cause, **97**
drug interactions, **176, 178**
Antimanic medications
birth defects from, 270
dosages, **87**
Antineoplastic drugs. *See also
names of specific drugs*
delirium etiology and, **36**
Antiparkinsonian drugs. *See also
names of specific drugs*
delirium etiology and, **36**
Antiprostaglandin drugs, for
continuous pain, 206

Antipsychotic drugs. *See also
names of specific drugs*
for delirium treatment, 39
Antipsychotics, drug interactions,
176, 177
Antiretroviral agents, mania
etiology and, **84**
Antispasmodic drugs, delirium
etiology and, **36**
Antituberculous agents, as
anxiety/panic cause, **97**
Anxiety
behavioral management of, 106
biology of, 94
fear of dying, 283–284
from respirator withdrawal,
105, 298
hospitalization and, 93, 101
mild, stress-related, 93, 101
in organ transplant donors,
293
pain and, 209
psychotherapy for, 106
severity, 93
substance-related disorders and,
101
Anxiety disorders. *See also* Panic
disorder; Posttraumatic stress
disorder
acute stress disorder, 95–99
PTSD and, 99
adjustment disorder with
anxiety, 101
characteristics, 94–95
cognitive-behavioral therapy
for, 106
diagnosis
differential psychiatric,
101–102

Anxiety disorders *(continued)*
  diagnosis *(continued)*
    medical vs psychiatric
      etiology, 101
    due to a general medical
      condition, 94
    treatment, 102
  epidemiology, 93–94, **96–99**
  generalized anxiety disorder,
    characteristics, 100
  in geriatric patients, 256–257
  obsessive-compulsive disorder,
    100
  phobias, characteristics, 100
  posttraumatic stress disorder,
    95, 99–100
    acute stress disorder and, 99
  psychotherapy for, 106
  somatoform disorders and, 138
  substance-induced, 95
    treatment, 102
  symptom confusion with
    medical disorders, 93
Anxiolytic amnesia disorder,
  management, 159
Anxiolytic amnestic disorder, 159
Anxiolytics. *See also names of
  specific drugs*
  adverse effects in children, 274
  aggression and, 197
  for chronic aggression, **198**
  gender differences in geriatric
    use, 256
  intoxication, 158
    management, **152**, 158
    signs and symptoms, **152**,
      159
  for personality disorders, 226
  withdrawal, 158

  management, **154**, 159
  signs and symptoms, **154**
Aphasia
  cortical mapping, **24–25**
  DAT and, 46
  in delirium, 33
  *Reitan-Indiana Aphasia
    Screening Test,* 17
Appearance (of patient),
  assessment, 12
Apraxia, *Draw a clock face test*
  for, 22
Asendin (amoxapine), **70–71**
Asparaginase, delirium etiology
  and, **36**
Aspartame, mania etiology and, **86**
Aspirin
  for cancer patients, 281
  for continuous pain, 206
  for vascular dementia, 55, **56**
Associative anamnesis, 230
Astemizole, cytochrome P450
  enzymes and, **181**
Atenolol, male erectile disorder
  etiology and, **300**
Atropine
  delirium etiology and, **36**
  male erectile disorder etiology
    and, **300**
Attention, 15
Attention-deficit/hyperactivity
  disorder (ADHD), 274
Autogenic training, for pain
  management, **216**

Baclofen
  male erectile disorder etiology
    and, **300**
  mania etiology and, **84**

Bad news, delivering, 282
Barbiturate withdrawal
  by burn patients, 276
  haloperidol for, 158
  lorazepam for, 158
  management, 158
Barbiturates
  abuse/dependence, diagnostic
    criteria, **148**, 157
  cytochrome P450 enzymes and,
    181
  delirium etiology and, **36**
  drug interactions, 176
  male erectile disorder etiology
    and, **300**
  secondary depressive disorders'
    etiologies and, **66**
  suicide attempts and, 246
  tolerance, 157
  tricyclic antidepressants and,
    68
Basal ganglia, idiopathic
  calcification, mania etiology
  and, **84**
BDD. *See* Body dysmorphic
  disorder
Behavior, assessment, 12
Behavior dysfunction, cortical
  mapping, **24–25**
Belladonna alkaloids, delirium
  etiology and, **36**
Benziodiazepines
  alcohol withdrawal delirium
    and, 156
  lithium use with, 83
  pain medications and, 209
Benzodiazepines
  2-keto-benzodiazepines, 102,
    103

3-hydroxy-benzodiazepines,
  103, 104
absorption rates, **103**
abuse/dependence
  diagnostic criteria, **148**, 157
  management, 157
adverse effects, 104, 112, 284
for alcohol withdrawal seizures,
  155
for amphetamine intoxication,
  163
for amphetamine withdrawal,
  164
as analgesic adjuvants, 214
classes, 102–104, **103**
cross-reactivity with alcohol
  and sedative-hypnotics,
  158
delirium etiology and, **36**
for delirium treatment, 39, 105
dependence, in pain disorder,
  131
discontinuing, 112
dosages, **103**
drug interactions, 90, **176**, **177**,
  178
for dying patients' anxiety, side
  effects and, 284
in geriatric patients, 264
half-lives, **103**, 104
haloperidol combined with, 105
for insomnia, 111–112
long-term use limitations, 102
metabolites, **103**
as neuroleptic adjuncts, 39–40
for neuroleptic malignant
  syndrome, not
  recommended, 190
oral compounds, **103**

Benzodiazepines (continued)
    overdose, flumazenil for, 158
    for panic disorder, 107
    for personality disorders, 226
    pharmacokinetics, **103**
    to prevent alcohol abstinence
        syndrome, 153
    protein binding, 263
    for PTSD, 108
    renal excretion, 263
    renal failure and, 175
    secondary depressive disorders'
        etiologies and, **66**
    suicide attempts and, 246
    teratogenic potential, 270
    tolerance, 157
    triazolo-benzodiazepines, 102,
        103
Benztropine
    delirium etiology and, **36**
    male erectile disorder etiology
        and, **300**
β-blockers. See also names of
        specific drugs
    adverse effects, 105
    for anxiety symptoms, 105
    for chronic aggression, 197,
        198
    cytochrome P450 enzymes and,
        181
    delirium etiology and, **36**
    drug interactions, **177**
    ECT risk reduced by, 76
    secondary depressive disorders'
        etiologies and, **66**
    withdrawal, as anxiety/panic
        cause, **97**
Biofeedback, for pain
        management, **216**

Bipolar disorder. See Depression;
        Mania
Birth defects, from antimania
        medications, 270
Body dysmorphic disorder (BDD)
    clinical features, 129–130
    defined, 129
    depression and, 130
    epidemiology, 129
    management, 130
    medications for, 130
    prognosis, 130
Borderline personality disorder,
        antidepressants for, 226
Brain, cortical anatomy, behavior
        dysfunction and, **24–25**
Brain damage, mania and, 81
Brain disease, delirium and, 29
Brain injury, violence etiology
        role, 196
Brain tumors, 286
Brain-behavior relationships, 23
Breast-feeding, psychiatric
        disorders and, 270, 271
Briquet's syndrome. See
        Somatization disorder
Bromide, mania etiology and,
        85
Bromocriptine, 109
    delirium etiology and, **36**
    dosages, 190
    male erectile disorder etiology
        and, **300**
    for neuroleptic malignant
        syndrome, 189
Bupropion, 73
    adverse effects, 73
    as anxiety/panic cause, **97**
    dosages, **70–71**

male erectile disorder etiology
and, **300**
for panic disorder, not
recommended, 106–107
receptor affinities, **70–71**
sedative-hypnotic medications
and, 112
Burns
delirium and, 275–276
epidemiology, 275
facial deformities from, 277
pain management, 276–277
preparing patients for death, 277
recovery issues, 277–278
substance-related disorders and,
276
Buspirone
action, 104
for acute anxiety, not
recommended, 104–105
adverse effects, 105
for chronic aggression, **198**
for chronic anxiety, 104
for dementia treatment, 56
dosages, 105, **198**
mania etiology and, **85**
for panic disorder, not
recommended, 105
therapeutic response onset,
104–105
Butorphanol, analgesics
compared, **213**

Cabbage, cytochrome P450
enzymes and, **183**
Caffeine
as anxiety/panic cause, **97**
cytochrome P450 enzymes and,
181, **183**

insomnia and, 110
Calcitonin, for phantom limb pain,
212
Calcium channel blockers, as
anxiety/panic cause, **97**
Cancer
anticipatory vomiting, 281
CNS metastases, 286
delivering bad news, 282
pain management, 281–282,
284
psychiatric symptoms, brain
tumors and, 286
Cancer patients
major depressive disorder
prevalence in, 279
medications for, 74
psychiatric disorders'
prevalence in, 279
suicide risk, 249
supportive group therapy for, 77
Cannabis, as anxiety/panic cause,
97
Capacity, competency vs, 235
Captopril
delirium etiology and, **36**
drug interactions, **177**
male erectile disorder etiology
and, **300**
mania etiology and, **85**
Carbamazepine
action, 88–89
adverse effects, 89
avoidance during pregnancy,
270
for chronic aggression, **198**
cytochrome P450 enzymes and,
89, **181**, **183**
diltiazem interaction with, 89

Carbamazepine *(continued)*
  dosages, **87**, 89–90, **198**
  drug interactions, 89, **176–177**
  male erectile disorder etiology
      and, **300**
  for mania, 83, 88
  mania etiology and, **85**
  for personality disorders, 227
  tricyclic antidepressants and,
      68
  verapamil interaction with, 89
Carbidopa, delirium etiology and,
      36
Carcinoid, mania etiology and, **86**
Cardiac catheterization, major
      depressive disorder and, 61
Cardiac drugs. *See also names of*
      specific drugs
  delirium etiology and, **36**
Cardiac patients, suicide risk, 248
Cardiovascular conditions, as
      anxiety/panic cause, **96**
Caregivers
  of dementia patients, 57
  elder abuse by, 265
  of elderly persons, support
      needed, 265
Catatonia, neuroleptic malignant
      syndrome and, 187
Catecholamine, 179
Causalgia, 204
Cephalosporins, delirium etiology
      and, **36**
Cerebrovascular disease,
      depression etiology and, **67**
Cerebrovascular lesions, mania
      etiology and, **84**
Charbroiled food, cytochrome
      P450 enzymes and, **183**

Chemotherapeutic agents,
      psychiatric manifestation,
      280–281
Chemotherapy agents, secondary
      depressive disorders'
      etiologies and, **66**
Children, patient confidentiality,
      274
Chloral hydrate
  avoidance with renal failure,
      175
  for insomnia, 173
  warfarin and, 173
Chlorambucil, male erectile
      disorder etiology and, **300**
Chlordiazepoxide
  absorption rates, **103**
  for alcohol withdrawal, 153,
      154
  dosages, **103**
  half-life, **103**
  renal failure and, 175
Chlorothiazide, male erectile
      disorder etiology and, **300**
Chlorpromazine
  avoidance in delirium
      treatment, 39
  avoidance in dementia
      treatment, 56
  drug interactions, **178**n
  epinephrine and, 173
  male erectile disorder etiology
      and, **300**
Cholestyramine
  drug absorption and, 172
  drug interactions, 260
Cholinesterase inhibitors
  for Alzheimer's type dementia,
      55

secondary depressive disorders'
etiologies and, **66**
Chronic illness, psychiatric
disorders and, 3
Chronic pain. *See* Pain (chronic)
Cigarettes, cytochrome P450
enzymes and, **183**
Cimetidine
cytochrome P450 enzymes and,
182
delirium etiology and, **36**
drug interactions, **176**
male erectile disorder etiology
and, **300**
mania etiology and, **85**
secondary depressive disorders'
etiologies and, **66**
Ciprofloxacin, cytochrome P450
enzymes and, **182**
Citalopram
CYP enzymes and, 180
drug interactions, 180
Clidinium, male erectile disorder
etiology and, **300**
Clofibrate, male erectile disorder
etiology and, **300**
Clomipramine
for BDD, 130
cytochrome P450 enzymes and,
181
dosages, **70–71**
drug interactions, **178**
male erectile disorder etiology
and, **300**
for obsessive-compulsive
disorder, 108
receptor affinities, **70–71**
Clonazepam
absorption rates, **103**

action duration, **110**
action onset, **110**
for chronic aggression, **198**
for chronic or central pain
relief, 212
for dementia symptoms, 56
dosages, **103**, **110**, **198**
drug interactions, **176**
excretion/metabolism, **110**
half-life, **103**, **110**
for insomnia, 112
lithium use with, 83
for panic disorder, 107
for sedative-hypnotics
withdrawal, **154**
Clonidine
adverse effects, 106
for anxiety, 105–106
for chronic or central pain
relief, 212
delirium etiology and, **36**
drug interactions, **178**
male erectile disorder etiology
and, **300**
for narcotic withdrawal
symptoms, 105
for panic disorder, 107
secondary depressive disorders'
etiologies and, **66**
withdrawal, mania etiology
and, **85**
Clorazepate
absorption rates, **103**
dosages, **103**, 104
half-life, **103**
Clozapine
CYP enzymes and, 180
cytochrome P450 enzymes and,
181

Clozapine *(continued)*
  neuroleptic malignant
      syndrome etiology and,
      180
CNS abscesses, 286
CNS infections, 285–286
CNS tumors
  metastatic, 286
  primary, 286
Cocaine, 165
  aggression and, 197
  as anxiety/panic cause, **97**
  delirium etiology and, **36**
  drug interactions, **178**
  mania etiology and, **85**
  withdrawal, secondary
      depressive disorders'
      etiologies and, **66**
Cocaine abuse. *See also* Substance
    abuse
  diagnostic criteria, **148**
  management, 165–166
Cocaine delirium, 166
  haloperidol for, 167
  lorazepam for, 167
  management, 166–167
Cocaine delusional disorder, 167
  haloperidol for, 167
Cocaine dependence
  diagnostic criteria, **148**
  management, 165–166
Cocaine intoxication, 166
  diazepam for, 166
  lorazepam for, **152**, 166
  management, **152**, 166
  signs and symptoms, **152**
Cocaine withdrawal
  depression and, 167
  desipramine for, **154**, 167
  dysphoria ("crash"), 166, 167
  lorazepam for, **154**
  management, **154**, 167
  signs and symptoms, **154**, 167
Cocaine-related disorders, 165–167
Codeine
  analgesics compared, **213**
  cytochrome P450 enzymes and,
      181
  metabolization, 73
Cognitive dysfunction
  in Alzheimer's type dementia,
      46
  dementia syndrome of
      depression and, 51
  in medical patients, 11
  medications and, 11
  multi-infarct dementia, 49
  not recognized by medical
      personnel, 11
Cognitive function tests, 17–22
  Draw a clock face test, 22, **38**
  Frank Jones Story test, 22
  Mini-Mental State Exam, 17,
      18–21, 53–54
  *Reitan-Indiana Aphasia
      Screening Test,* 17
  Set Test, 17
  Trail Part A and B, **38**
Cognitive therapy
  for adjustment disorder, 137
  for somatoform disorders, 141
Cognitive-behavioral therapy. *See
    also* Psychotherapy
  for anxiety with chronic pain,
      209
  for anxiety disorders, 106
  for burn patients, 278
  for depressive symptoms, 76

for medical-surgical patients, 76–77

for pain management, **216**

for panic disorder, 107

Coma

anticholinergic, neuroleptic malignant syndrome and, 188

hepatic, flumazenil for, 158

Competency

capacity vs, 235

do-not-resuscitate orders and, 239

evaluating, 235–237

guardianship, 239

informed consent and, 237

test selection factors, 236, **237**

Concentration, impaired, cortical mapping, **24–25**

Concussion, postconcussion, depression etiology and, **67**

Confidentiality

for adolescents, 274

for children, 274

families and, 235–236

psychiatric consultation and, 4, 234

statutory exceptions to, **234**

withholding prognosis from patient, 236

Consciousness level, 15

Consultation-liaison psychiatry. *See also* Pediatric consultation; Psychiatric consultation

combined residency training and, **2**

consultation vs. liaison work, 9–10

effectiveness, attributes needed for, **5**

history, 1

managed health care and, **2**

medication treatment principles, 171, **172**

medicolegal issues in, 233

multidisciplinary teams and, **2**

with outpatients, 7

settings for, **2**, 7, 269

trends in, **2**

Contraceptives. *See* Oral contraceptives

Conversion disorder

amnesia, 129

associated features, 128

chronic pain complaints and, 210

clinical features, 127–128

defined, 127

epidemiology, 127

management, 128–129

physical therapy for, 141

prognosis, 128

pseudoseizures, 129

psychotherapy for, 129

tremor, 129

Corticosteroids

delirium etiology and, **36**

mania etiology and, **85**

secondary depressive disorders' etiologies and, **66**

side effects, **280**

withdrawal, mania etiology and, **85**

Countertransference

illness and, 228

with somatoform disorders, 140

Critically ill patients. *See also* Patients
 delirium in, 297
 medical-surgical management changes for, 297
 mental status examination, 297
 psychopharmacological treatment, 297–298
Cushing's disease, depression etiology and, **66**
Cushing's syndrome, mania etiology and, **86**
Cyclobenzaprine, mania etiology and, **85**
Cyclophosphamide, male erectile disorder etiology and, **300**
Cyclosporine
 cytochrome P450 enzymes and, **181**, **182**
 drug interactions, **177**
 lithium interaction with, 83
 neurotoxicity in organ transplant recipients, 294–295
Cyproheptadine
 dosages, 190
 mania etiology and, **85**
 for serotonin syndrome, 190
Cytochrome P450 system, 179–180
 drug interactions, **176–177**, 180, **181–183**
 inducers of P450 enzymes, **183**
 inhibitors of P450 enzymes, **182**
 substrates of P450 enzymes, **181**
Cytosine arabinoside
 male erectile disorder etiology and, **300**
 side effects, **280**

Dantrolene
 dosages, 189
 for neuroleptic malignant syndrome, 189
DAT. *See* Dementia of the Alzheimer's type
Death, 283. *See also* Terminally ill patients
 depression as predictor of, 61
 fear of dying, 283–284
 preparing patients for, 277, 283
Debrisoquin, drug interactions, **178**
Defensive Functioning Scale, 220, **221–222**
Delirium, 29
 amphetamine delirium, 164
  management, 164
 anticholinergic, neuroleptic malignant syndrome and, 188
 assessment of patients with, **38**
 in burn patients, 275
 clinical characteristics, 30–34
 cocaine delirium, 166–167
 in critically ill patients, 297
 diagnosis
  diagnostic criteria, 30–31, **31**
  differential, 34, **35**, **37**
  mnemonics for, 34, **35**, **37**
 Draw a clock face test, 32
 epidemiology, 29, 30
 Frank Jones Story test response, 22
 in geriatric patients, 29, 30, 255
 hyperactivity in, 33
 hypoactivity in, 33
 intensive care unit psychosis and, 29

laboratory tests, **38**

language disturbances, 33

in medical patients, 11

medication management, 39–40, 275

medications associated with, 34, **36**

memory impairment, 32

mortality and, 29

neuropsychiatric impairments, 32–33

in organ transplant recipients, 293–294

perceptual disturbances, 33

prodrome, 32

psychomotor disturbances, 33

risk of, 30

sleep-wake cycle disturbances, 33–34

speech defects, 33

substance withdrawal and, 158

temporal course of symptoms, 32

thought processes, 33

treatment

    environmental interventions, 40–41

    medication management, 39–40, 105

    medications and, 36–37

    monitoring of patient, 36

    reduce psychiatric symptoms, 36

    reversible etiologies, 34–37

    symptomatic, 39–40

treatment goals, sleep normalization, 33–34

tremor with, 33

violence threats and, 195

Delirium tremens, 155–156. *See also* Alcohol withdrawal

    management, 156

    signs and symptoms, 155

Delusional disorder (somatic type), 139

    pimozide for, 139

Delusions, 13

Dementia. *See also* Dementia of the Alzheimer's type (DAT); Vascular dementia

    abstracting ability and, 14

    aggression and, 196

    caregiver support, 57

    causes, 45

    cortical, 46

        distinguishing features, **47**

    depression etiology and, **67**

    diagnosis

        clinical history, 52

        depression differentiation, 65, **68**

        laboratory tests, 53, **54**

        Mini-Mental State Exam (MMSE), 53–55

        neuroimaging, 53

        neuropsychological testing, 53–55

    differential diagnosis, 52–55

    Frank Jones Story test response, 22

    in geriatric patients, 30, 256

    hypothyroidism and, 55

    in medical patients, 11

    mental status examination for, 52–55

    mixed, 46

    multi-infarct, 49

Dementia *(continued)*
normal pressure hydrocephalus and, 287
pseudodementia differentiation, 51–52
psychiatric disorders and, 51–52
reversibility of, 45
Set Test, 17
subcortical, 46, 47–49, 287
distinguishing features, **47**
treatment, 55–57, **56**
of behavioral problems, 55–56
caregiver support, 57
of coexisting medical conditions, 55
cognitive function restoration, 55
environmental consistency, 57
medications, 56
reversible disorders, 55
Dementia of the Alzheimer's type (DAT). *See also* Alzheimer's disease; Dementia
cognitive dysfunction in, 46, **48**
diagnosis, 46, **48**
Huntington's disease differentiation, 49
language disturbance in, 46
medications for, 55
prevalence, 45, 256
treatment, 55–57, **56**
vascular dementia differentiation, 49
Dementia syndrome of depression, 51
Demerol (meperidine), analgesics compared, **213**

Depakote (valproate), dosages, **87**
Depression. *See also* Mood disorders
adjustment disorder with depressed mood, 63
amphetamine withdrawal and, 165
body dysmorphic disorder and, 130
chronic pain and, 208, **209**
cocaine withdrawal and, 167
as death predictor, 61
dementia syndrome of depression, 51
diagnosis, 208
criteria, 62, **62**
dementia differentiation, 65, **68**
differential, 64–65, **68**
in medical-surgical patients, 63
in dying patients, 283
dysthymic disorder and, 63
in elderly persons' caregivers, 265
epidemiology, 51, 61
etiologies, 63–64
geriatric, clinical features, 256, **257**
HIV-related, treatment, 290
medical conditions associated with, 64, **66–67**
in pain disorder, 131
postpartum, 271
poststroke, 287–288
prevalence in cancer patients, 279
remission relapse rates, 72
suicidality treatment, 251

toxic agents associated with,
64, **66–67**
treatment
antidepressants, 73–74
cognitive therapy, 76
MAOIs, 69
psychodynamic therapy,
76–77
psychostimulants, 74–75,
75
reversible etiologies, 65,
66–67
SSRIs, 72–73
tricyclic antidepressants,
65–68
Depression with, posttraumatic
stress syndrome (PTSD), 108
Desipramine
for amphetamine withdrawal,
154
as analgesic adjuvant, 214
for cocaine withdrawal, **154**,
167
dosages, **70–71**
male erectile disorder etiology
and, **300**
receptor affinities, **70–71**
Desyrel (trazodone), **70–71**
Dexamethasone, cytochrome P450
enzymes and, **183**
Dextroamphetamine
for cancer patients, 279
for depression, 74
dosages, 74
for HIV-related depression, 291
Diabetes mellitus, depression
etiology and, **66**
Diazepam
absorption rates, **103**

for alcohol withdrawal, 155
for amphetamine withdrawal,
164
for cocaine intoxication, 166
cytochrome P450 enzymes and,
181
dosages, **103**
in geriatric patients, 264
half-life, **103**, 104
for insomnia, 111
renal excretion, 263
renal failure and, 175
Dichlorphenamide, male erectile
disorder etiology and, **300**
Diet
cabbage, cytochrome P450
enzymes and, **183**
charbroiled food, cytochrome
P450 enzymes and, **183**
grapefruit juice, cytochrome
P450 enzymes and, **183**
monoamine oxidase inhibitors
and, 179
Digitalis
delirium etiology and, **36**
toxicity, as anxiety/panic cause,
97
Digoxin, male erectile disorder
etiology and, **300**
Dilaudid (hydromorphone),
analgesics compared, **213**
Diltiazem
carbamazepine interaction with,
89, **176**
cytochrome P450 enzymes and,
182
drug interactions, **176**, **177**
Diphenhydramine
action duration, **111**

Diphenhydramine *(continued)*
  action onset, **111**
  dosages, **111**
  excretion/metabolism, **111**
  half-life, **111**
  for insomnia, 112
  male erectile disorder etiology
    and, **300**
Disease, illness distinguished
    from, 119
Disopyramide
  drug interactions, **178**
  male erectile disorder etiology
    and, **300**
Disorientation
  in delirium, 32
  impaired, **24–25**
Disulfiram
  for alcoholic patients, 150
  delirium etiology and, **36**
  drug interactions, **176**
  male erectile disorder etiology
    and, **300**
  secondary depressive disorders'
    etiologies and, **66**
Diuretics
  secondary depressive disorders'
    etiologies and, **66**
  thiazide
    drug interactions, **177**
    lithium and, 88
    male erectile disorder
      etiology and, **300**
Do-not-resuscitate orders,
    238–239, 283
Dolophine (methadone),
    analgesics compared, **213**
Donepezil, for Alzheimer's type
    dementia, 55, **56**

Dopamine
  as anxiety/panic cause, **97**
  drug interactions, **178**
Dopaminergic medications. *See
    also names of specific drugs*
  for insomnia, 109
Doxepin
  for BDD, 130
  cytochrome P450 enzymes and,
    182
  dosages, **70–71**
  receptor affinities, **70–71**
Draw a clock face test, 22, 32
Droperidol, for delirium
    treatment, 39
Drugs. *See* Medications; *specific
    drugs by name or type*
Dysarthria, defined, 23
Dysbulia, defined, 23
Dyscalculia, defined, 23
Dysgnosia, defined, 23
Dysgraphia, defined, 23
Dyslexia, defined, 23
Dysphasia, defined, 23
Dyspraxia, defined, 23
Dysprosody, defined, 23
Dystaxia, defined, 23
Dysthymic disorder, diagnosis, 63

Edronax (riboxetine), **72–73**
Education, abstracting ability and,
    14
Effexor (venlafaxine), **70–71**
Elavil (amitriptyline), **70–71**
Elder abuse, signs of, 265
Electroconvulsive therapy (ECT)
  adverse effects, 75
  for depression, 75–76
  during pregnancy, 270

for geriatric patients, 264
for neuroleptic malignant
    syndrome, not
    recommended, 190
for postpartum depression, 271
risk conditions, 75–76
risk reduction, 76
for suicidal patients, 251
Electrolyte abnormalities,
    depression etiology and, **67**
Emergency treatment, informed
    consent and, 237
Enalapril, drug interactions, **177**
Encephalitis, depression etiology
    and, **66**
Encephalitis (Post-St. Louis type
    A), mania etiology and, **84**
Encephalopathy, posttraumatic,
    mania etiology and, **84**
Endocrine conditions
    as anxiety/panic cause, **96**
    posttraumatic, **96**
Endocrine disorders, depressive
    disorders' etiologies and,
    66
Ephedrine
    as anxiety/panic cause, **97**
    delirium etiology and, **36**
    drug interactions, **178**
Epilepsy
    aggression and, 196
    depression etiology and, **67**
Epinephrine
    as anxiety/panic cause, **97**
    chlorpromazine and, 173
    delirium etiology and, **36**
    drug interactions, **176**, **178**
Epstein-Barr virus, depression
    etiology and, **66**

Erythromycin
    cytochrome P450 enzymes and,
        181, **182**
    drug interactions, **177**
Estazolam
    action duration, **110**
    action onset, **110**
    dosages, **110**
    excretion/metabolism, **110**
    half-life, **110**
Estrogen
    for Alzheimer's type dementia,
        55, **56**
    as anxiety/panic cause, **97**
Ethchlorvynol, avoidance with
    renal failure, 175
Etiology, primary-secondary
    terminology for, 64
Extrapyramidal side effects, with
    fever, neuroleptic malignant
    syndrome and, 186–187

Factitious disorders
    by proxy, 133
    clinical features, 133
    defined, 132
    diseases simulated, **134**
    epidemiology, 132–133
    legal aspects, 133, **135**
    management, 133–134
    prognosis, 133
    signs and symptoms, **134**
Families
    consent to patient restraint, 240
    do-not-resuscitate orders and,
        238–239
    patient competency and, 236
    patient confidentiality and,
        234–235

Families *(continued)*
    patient refusal to allow contact,
        234–235
    withholding information from
        patients and, 235
Families (of patients), transplant
    donors, 292
Family therapy
    for chronic aggression, 197
    for manic patients, 90
Fenfluramine, male erectile
    disorder etiology and, **300**
Fentanyl citrate, for pain
    management of burns, 278
Fetal alcohol syndrome, 271
Flecainide, cytochrome P450
    enzymes and, **181**
Flumazenil
    for benzodiazepine overdose,
        158
    for hepatic coma, 158
5-Fluorouracil, side effects, **280**
Fluoxetine
    adverse effects, 73
    as analgesic adjuvant, 214
    as anxiety/panic cause, **97**
    for BDD, 130
    cytochrome P450 enzymes and,
        181, **182**
    dosages, **70–71**, 290, 291
    half-life, 72
    for HIV-related depression,
        290, 291
    for hypochondriasis, 127
    receptor affinities, **70–71**
    sedative-hypnotic medications
        and, 112
    tricyclic antidepressants and, 65
Fluoxymesterone, side effects, **280**

Flurazepam
    action duration, **110**
    action onset, **110**
    dosages, **110**
    excretion/metabolism, **110**
    half-life, **110**
    renal failure and, 175
Fluvoxamine
    CYP enzymes and, 180
    cytochrome P450 enzymes and,
        181, **182**
Folate, for alcohol intoxication,
    152
Folic acid, for alcohol withdrawal,
    154
Frank Jones Story test, 22
Frontal lobe dysfunction, *Set Test*
    used for, 17
Frontal lobe personality
    syndromes, clinical features,
    222, **224**
Functional symptoms. *See*
    Somatization; Somatoform
    disorders

Gabapentin
    dosages, **87**
    for mania, 83, 89
Ganciclovir, delirium etiology
    and, **36**
Gastrointestinal conditions
    as anxiety/panic cause, **99**
    anxiety/panic etiology and,
        98
Gentamicin, delirium etiology
    and, **36**
Geriatric patients. *See also* Patients
    aggressive behavior treatment,
        56

alcohol consumption by, 258
alcohol dementia in, 49–50
anxiety disorders in, 256–257
clinical history, 258
cognitive dysfunction, from
    medications, 2
crisis intervention with, 265
delirium in, 29, 30, 255
dementia in, 30, 256
depression in, clinical features,
    256, **257**
diagnostic evaluations with,
    258–259
elder abuse, 265
electroconvulsive therapy for,
    264
epidemiology, 255
insomnia in, 257
laboratory tests for, 259
mental status examination,
    259
multiple drug use by, 264
physical examination, 258
psychiatric consultation
    strategies, **266**
psychosis in, 257–258
psychotherapy with, 264–265
sedative-hypnotic drug
    withdrawal, 158
suicide attempts by, 246
suicide risk, 256
treatment of medical problems,
    259
Glutethimide, delirium etiology
    and, **36**
Glycopyrrolate, male erectile
    disorder etiology and, **300**
Grapefruit juice, cytochrome P450
    enzymes and, **182**

Group therapy. *See also*
    Psychotherapy
    for adjustment disorder, 137
    for medical patients, 76–77
    for personality disorders, 227
Guanethidine
    drug interactions, **178**
    male erectile disorder etiology
        and, **300**
    secondary depressive disorders'
        etiologies and, **66**
Guardianship, 239

Hachinski Ischemia Scale, 49,
    51
Halazepam
    absorption rates, **103**
    dosages, **103**
    half-life, **103**
Hallucinations, 13–14
    in alcohol-induced psychotic
        disorder, 153
Hallucinogens
    as anxiety/panic cause, **97**
    mania etiology and, **85**
Haloperidol
    for alcohol intoxication,
        152
    for alcohol withdrawal, **154**
    for alcohol withdrawal
        delirium, 156
    for amphetamine delusional
        disorder, 164
    for amphetamine intoxication,
        152, 163
    for anxiety upon respirator
        withdrawal, 105
    for barbiturate withdrawal,
        158

Haloperidol *(continued)*
  benzodiazepines combined
    with, 105
  benzodiazepines' use with,
    39–40, 105
  for burn patients, 276
  for cocaine delirium, 167
  for cocaine delusional disorder,
    167
  for cocaine intoxication, **152**
  cytochrome P450 enzymes and,
    181
  for delirium treatment, 39, 105
  for dementia treatment, 56
  dosages, 39, **40**, 105, **152**, 164,
    167, 193–194
  for dying patients' anxiety, 284
  lorazepam combined with, 40,
    105
  male erectile disorder etiology
    and, **300**
  for substance intoxication, **152**
  for violent behavior, 193–194
Head injury, 285
Heatstroke, neuroleptic malignant
    syndrome and, 187
Heavy metals
  as anxiety/panic cause, **98**
  depression etiology and, **67**
Hemispherectomy (right), mania
    etiology and, **84**
Hemodialysis
  mania etiology and, **86**
  for substance intoxication, 158
Hepatic coma, flumazenil for, 158
Hepatic function, psychotropic
    drugs and, 260, 297–298
Hepatitis, depression etiology and,
    66

Heroin
  analgesics compared, **213**
  receptor affinity for, 160
HIV dementia, 287
HIV disease, 288–289
  depression etiology and, **66**
  depression with
    dextroamphetamine for, 291
    fluoxetine for, 290, 291
    methylphenidate for, 291
    paroxetine for, 290, 291
  psychiatric management, 289
  psychostimulants for, **75**, 291
  psychotherapy with, 289
  suicide risk, 249, 291
  without AIDS, 290
HIV encephalopathy, mania
    etiology and, **84**
Hospitalization. *See also* Patients
  anxiety and, 93, 101
  decreases in, 3, 7
  depression precipitated by, 63
  factitious disorders and, 133
  intensive care units, restraint
    use in, 241
  involuntary, 240
  panic disorder and, 94
  regressive behavior, 219–220
    in adolescents, 273
    in children, 272, 273
  restraint use, 240–241
  signing out against medical
    advice, 236, 238
  staff-patient conflicts, 227–228
  for suicide attempts, 250, 251
  suicide precautions, 250–251,
    251–252
Human immunodeficiency virus.
    See HIV

Huntington's disease, 287
  Alzheimer's type dementia
      differentiation, 49
  characteristics, 49
  dementia and, 46
  depression etiology and, **67**
  mania etiology and, **84**
Hydralazine
  as anxiety/panic cause, **97**, **98**
  male erectile disorder etiology
      and, **300**
Hydrocephalus, dementia and, 45
Hydrochlorothiazide, male erectile
    disorder etiology and, **300**
Hydromorphine, receptor affinity
    for, 160
Hydromorphone (Dilaudid),
    analgesics compared, **213**
Hydroxycodone, metabolization, 73
Hydroxyzine
  action duration, **111**
  action onset, **111**
  dosages, **111**
  excretion/metabolism, **111**
  half-life, **111**
  male erectile disorder etiology
      and, **300**
Hyperbaric chamber use, mania
    etiology and, **86**
Hyperparathyroidism, depression
    etiology and, **66**
Hypertension
  depression etiology and, **67**
  nifedipine for, 179
Hyperthermia, malignant,
    neuroleptic malignant
    syndrome and, 187–188
Hyperthyroidism, mania etiology
    and, **86**

Hypnosis
  for burn pain management, 277
  for pain management, **216**
Hypnotherapy, for somatoform
    disorders, 141
Hypnotic amnestic disorder, 159
  management, 159
Hypnotics, aggression and, 197
Hypnotics. *See* Sedative-hypnotics
Hypochondriasis
  associated features, 126
  chronic pain complaints and,
      210
  clinical features, 125–126
  defined, 125
  diagnosis, 126
  epidemiology, 125
  fluoxetine for, 127
  management, 126–127
  monosymptomatic, 139
  prognosis, 126
  secondary, 138
Hypopituitarism, depression
    etiology and, **66**
Hypothyroidism
  dementia and, 55
  depression etiology and, **66**

Ibuprofen, for continuous pain,
    206
ICU psychosis, 29
Illness
  defense responses to, **221–222**
  disease distinguished from, 119
  false beliefs about, 76
  psychological regression and,
      219–220
Illness behavior, 120
  abnormal, 120

Illusions, 13
Imipramine
    for BDD, 130
    dosages, **70–71**
    male erectile disorder etiology
        and, **300**
    receptor affinities, **70–71**
Immunological/collagen vascular
        conditions, as anxiety/panic
        cause, **96–97**
Impotence. *See* Male erectile
        disorder
Incapacity, defined, 204
Incompetence, defined, 204
Indomethacin, male erectile
        disorder etiology and, **300**
Infections, depression etiologies
        and, **66**
Infectious mononucleosis, mania
        etiology and, **86**
Influenza, postinfluenza,
        depression etiology and, **66**
Informed consent, 237
    exceptions to obtaining, 237–238
    legal ages for, 274
Insight, ability assessment, 14
Insomnia, 108–109. *See also*
        Sleep disorders
    behavioral manipulations for,
        110
    caffeine and, 110
    chloral hydrate for, 173
    environmental manipulations
        for, 110
    in geriatric patients, 257
    medications for, **110–111**,
        111–112
    reversible etiologies, 109
    treatments, 109–112

Insulin, as anxiety/panic cause, **98**
Intensive care unit psychosis, 29
Intensive care units (ICUs)
    mental status examination in,
        296–297
    restraint use in, 241
Interferon
    delirium etiology and, 36
    secondary depressive disorders'
        etiologies and, **66**
    side effects, **280**
Interferon alpha, male erectile
        disorder etiology and, **300**
Interleukin-2 (IL-2), side effects,
        281
Intra-aortic balloon pump
    anxiety associated with, 298
        lorazepam for, 298
        perphenazine for, 298
Iproniazid, mania etiology and, **85**
Isocarboxazid, male erectile
        disorder etiology and, **300**
Isoniazid
    delirium etiology and, 36
    drug interactions, **176**, **177**

Judgment
    ability assessment, 14
    cortical mapping, **24–25**

Ketoconazole
    cytochrome P450 enzymes and,
        182
    male erectile disorder etiology
        and, **300**
Kidney function, psychotropic
        drugs and, 297–298
Kleine-Levin syndrome, mania
        etiology and, **84**

Klinefelter's syndrome, mania
    etiology and, **84**
Korsakoff's psychosis, alcohol
    dementia differentiation, 50
Korsakoff's syndrome, 156
    amnestic disorders' similarities,
    159
    thiamine for, 156

L-asparaginase, secondary
    depressive disorders'
    etiologies and, **66**
L-Asparaginase, side effects, **280**
L-dopa, delirium etiology and, **36**
L-Glutamine, mania etiology and,
    86
Laboratory tests, for delirium
    patients, **38**
Lactation, psychopharmacology
    during, 270
Lamictal (Lamotrigine), dosages,
    87
Lamotrigine
    dosages, **87**
    for mania, 83, 89
Language disturbances, 15
    in Alzheimer's type dementia,
    46
    cortical mapping, **24–25**
    in delirium, 33
    verbal fluency, *Set Test* for, 17
Levo-Dromoran (levorphanol),
    analgesics compared, **213**
Levodopa, 109
    as anxiety/panic cause, **98**
    drug interactions, **176**
    mania etiology and, **85**
    secondary depressive disorders'
    etiologies and, **66**

Levorphanol (Levo-Dromoran),
    analgesics compared, **213**
Lidocaine
    as anxiety/panic cause, **98**
    cytochrome P450 enzymes and,
    181
    delirium etiology and, **36**
    drug interactions, **178**
Liothyronine, drug interactions,
    178
Lithium
    adverse effects, 88
    avoidance during pregnancy, 270
    benziodiazepines' use with, 83
    for chronic aggression, **198**
    clonazepam use with, 83
    cyclosporine interaction with,
    83
    delirium etiology and, **36**
    distribution, 173
    dosages, 83, 86, **87**, 175, **198**
    drug interactions, **176**, **177**
    excretion, 174, 175
    half-life, 83
    male erectile disorder etiology
    and, **300**
    for mania, 83
    monitoring, importance of, 83
    neuroleptics' use with, 83
    for personality disorders, 226
    protein binding, 263
    renal failure and, 175
    renal function and, 83, 86, 175
    serum levels, monitoring
    importance, 83
    thiazide diuretics and, 88
    toxicity, 83, 86, 88
        dialysis treatment for, 86
        symptoms, 88

Lithobid (lithium), dosages, **87**
Liver disease, valproate
    contraindicated for, 90
Liver function, psychotropic drugs
    and, 260, 297–298
Loratadine, cytochrome P450
    enzymes and, **181**
Lorazepam
    absorption rates, **103**, 104
    action duration, **110**
    action onset, **110**
    for alcohol intoxication, **152**
    for amphetamine intoxication,
        152, 163
    for amphetamine withdrawal,
        154, 164
    for anxiety with intra-aortic
        balloon pump, 298
    for barbiturate withdrawal, 158
    for cocaine delirium, 167
    for cocaine intoxication, **152**,
        166
    for cocaine withdrawal, **154**
    for delirium treatment, 39
    dosages, **103**, **110**, **152**, 163,
        195, 298
    drug interactions, **178**n
    excretion/metabolism, **110**
    half-life, **103**, **110**
    haloperidol combined with, 40,
        105
    with liver impairment, 104
    for patients taking multiple
        medications, 104
    for substance intoxication,
        152
    for violent behavior, 194–195
Lupus erythematosus (systemic),
    depression etiology and, **67**

Male erectile disorder
    (impotence), 299
    evaluation, 299, 301
    history, 299
    laboratory tests, 301
    medications causing, **300**
    treatment, 301
Malingering
    assessment, MMPI for, 136
    clinical features, 135–136
    defined, 135
    epidemiology, 135
    legal aspects, 136
    management, 136
    pain and, 208, **209**
Malpractice, claims criteria, 233
Managed health care,
    consultation-liaison
    psychiatry and, **2**
Mania. *See also* Mood disorders
    brain injury and, 81
    brain lesions and, 81
    diagnosis
        diagnostic criteria, 81, **82**
        differential, 82–83
        mnemonic for, **82**
    prevalence, 81
    secondary, reversible etiologies,
        83, **84–86**
    treatment
        lithium, 83, 86–88
        pharmacological, 83–89, **87**
        psychotherapy, 90
    violence etiology and, 195
Maprotiline
    adverse effects, 68
    dosages, **70–71**
    male erectile disorder etiology
        and, **300**

receptor affinities, **70–71**
Marijuana (cannabis), as
    anxiety/panic cause, **97**
Medical conditions, psychological
    factors affecting, 132
Medical psychotherapy, 76–77.
    See also Psychotherapy
    associative anamnesis, 230
    defined, 228–229
    formulation, **230**, 231
    group therapy, 76–77
    selection process, 229
    settings, 229
Medical records, 233
Medications. *See also* names of
    specific drugs or types of
    drugs
    absorption, aging influence on,
        260, **261**
    absorption rates, 171–172
    age-related issues, 260–264,
        261–262
    aggression etiology and, 197
    as anxiety/panic cause, **97**
    for burn pain management,
        277–278
    cognitive dysfunction and, 11
    competitive inhibition, 173
    cytochrome P450 enzyme
        interactions, 179–180,
        181–183
    delirium etiology and, 34, **36**
    depressive disorders' etiologies
        and, **66–67**
    discontinuance during
        pregnancy, 270
    distribution, 173
        aging influence on, 260,
        261

excretion, 174–175
half-lives, 174–175
hepatic function, aging
    influence on, 260–263, **261**
interactions, 175–179,
    176–178, 180
male erectile disorder etiology
    and, 299, **300**
mania etiology and, **84–85**
metabolism, 174, 180
metabolism rates, 174
newborns' physiological
    dependency on, 270
oxidative metabolism, CYP
    enzymes and, 180
pharmacodynamic changes
    with aging, 263–264
pharmacokinetic changes with
    aging, 260–263, **261–262**
protein binding, 173
    aging influences on, **261**,
    263
receptor activity, 173–174
receptor alteration, 174
receptors, activation of multiple
    sites, 174
renal excretion, aging
    influences on, **262**, 263
secondary depressive disorders
    and, **66–67**
suicide attempts by overdosage,
    245–246
treatment principles in
    consultation-liaison
    settings, 171, **172**
Meditation, as therapy for
    somatoform disorders, 141
Melphalan, male erectile disorder
    etiology and, **300**

Memory impairment
    assessment, 16
    cortical mapping, **24–25**
    delirium and, 32
Meningoencephalitis, mania
    etiology and, **84**
Mental status examination
    anxiety disorder differentiation,
      101
    of somatizing patients, **121**
Mental status examinations, 11
    abstracting abilities, 14
    affect, 12–13
    attention, 15
    behavior, 12
    cognitive components, **12,**
      15–16
    cognitive function tests, 17–22
    consciousness level, 15
    for dementia, 52–55
    Draw a clock face test, 22
    Frank Jones Story test, 22
    for geriatric patients, 259
    insight, 14
    judgment, 14
    language, 15–16
    memory, 16
    Mini-Mental State Exam
      (MMSE), 17, **18–21,** 53–54
    mood, 12
    neurological examination, 22–23
    noncognitive components,
      12–14, **12**
    orientation, 16
    perceptions, 13–14
    physical appearance, 12
mental status examinations,
    Reitan-Indiana Aphasia
    Screening Test, 17

Mental status examinations,
    screening examinations,
    16–22
mental status examinations, *Set*
    Test, 17
Mental status examinations
    speech, 15–16
    thought content, 13
    thought processes, 13
Meperidine
    analgesics compared, **213**
    avoidance in pain management
      of burns, 278
    delirium etiology and, **36**
    drug interactions, **178**
    MAOI use with, 69
    receptor affinity for, 160
    withdrawal, management, 162
Mesoridazine, drug interactions,
    178n
Metabolic conditions, as
    anxiety/panic cause, **97**
Metabolic disturbances, dementia
    and, 45
Metaraminol, drug interactions,
    178
Methadone
    analgesics compared, **213**
    for cancer patients' pain
      management, 281
    dosages, 162
    male erectile disorder etiology
      and, **300**
    for opiate withdrawal, **154,** 162
    for pain management of burns,
      278
    receptor affinity for, 160
Methaqualone, male erectile
    disorder etiology and, **300**

Methotrexate
  delirium etiology and, **36**
  male erectile disorder etiology
    and, **300**
  side effects, **280**
Methscopolamine, male erectile
  disorder etiology and, **300**
Methyldopa
  delirium etiology and, **36**
  drug interactions, **177**
  male erectile disorder etiology
    and, **300**
  secondary depressive disorders'
    etiologies and, **66**
Methylphenidate
  as analgesic adjuvant, 214
  as anxiety/panic cause, **98**
  for cancer patients, 279
  cytochrome P450 enzymes and,
    182
  for depression, 74
  for depression in dying
    patients, 283
  dosages, 74
  for HIV-related depression, 291
  mania etiology and, **85**
Metoclopramide
  male erectile disorder etiology
    and, **300**
  mania etiology and, **85**
  neuroleptic malignant
    syndrome etiology and,
    180
  psychiatric manifestations of,
    281
  secondary depressive disorders'
    etiologies and, **66**
Metoprolol, male erectile disorder
  etiology and, **300**

Metrifonate, for Alzheimer's type
  dementia, 55, **56**
Metrizamide
  delirium etiology and, **36**
  mania etiology and, **85**
Mexiletine
  delirium etiology and, **36**
  male erectile disorder etiology
    and, **300**
Miconazole, cytochrome P450
  enzymes and, **182**
Midazolam
  cytochrome P450 enzymes and,
    181
  for delirium treatment, 39
Mini-Mental State Exam
    (MMSE), 17, **18–21**
  for dementia screening, 53–55
  in ICU setting, 296
Minnesota Multiphasic
    Personality Inventory
    (MMPI)
  interpretation for medical
    patients, 210
  for malingering assessment,
    136
  for pain complaint diagnosis,
    210
  for somatization evaluation,
    121
Mirtazapine, 73
  adverse effects, 74
  for cancer patients, 74, 279
  for depression, 74
  dosages, **72–73**
  receptor affinities, **72–73**
Mnemonics
  CAGE (screen for alcoholism
    diagnosis), 149, **150**

Mnemonics *(continued)*
FACT (*Set Test* categories), 17
GIDDINESS (mania diagnostic
criteria), **82**
I WATCH DEATH (delirium
differential diagnosis), **37**
SAD PERSONS scale (suicide
risk factors), **248**
SIG:E CAPS (diagnostic
criteria for major
depressive syndrome), 62
WHHHHIMP (delirium
differential diagnosis), 34,
35
Monoamine oxidase inhibitors
(MAOIs)
adverse effects, 69–72
for depression treatment, 69
diet and, 179
drug interactions, **176**, **177–178**
meperidine use with, 69
for panic disorder, 107
switching to another
antidepressant after, 69–72
sympathomimetics' use with, 69
Mononucleosis, mania etiology
and, **86**
Monosodium glutamate (MSG), as
anxiety/panic cause, **98**
Mood, defined, 12
Mood disorders. *See also*
Depression; Mania
in burn patients, 275, 276
epidemiology, 61
prevalence, 61
somatoform disorders and, 140
suicide risk and, 247
Mood stabilizers
adverse effects, 89–90

for mania, 88–90
Morphine
analgesics compared, **213**
for continuous pain, 206
cytochrome P450 enzymes and,
181
male erectile disorder etiology
and, **300**
Motor abnormalities
cortical mapping, **24–25**
in delirium, 33
MS-Contin
analgesic duration comparison,
213
for continuous pain, 206
Multidisciplinary medical teams,
consultation-liaison
psychiatry and, **2**
Multiple sclerosis
aggression and, 196
depression etiology and, **67**
Munchausen syndrome, 132,
133
Munchausen syndrome by proxy,
133

Nadolol
for chronic aggression, 197
male erectile disorder etiology
and, **300**
Nalbuphine, analgesics compared,
213
Naloxone
action, 160
dosages, **152**
for opiate intoxication, **152**,
173
Naproxen, male erectile disorder
etiology and, **300**

Narcotic abuse. *See also*
Substance abuse
signs of, 160, **161**
Narcotic-related disorders,
159–162
Narcotics, 159. *See also* Opiates
addiction risk, 206, 212–214
for cancer patients' pain
management, 281
for continuous pain, 206
dependence, in pain disorder,
131
for dying patients' anxiety, 206,
283
for pain management of burns,
277–278
for terminally ill patients, 206
underuse, 159
National Institute of Mental
Health (NIMH), 1
Nefazodone, 73
for cancer patients, 279
cytochrome P450 enzymes and,
182
dosages, **70–71**
for panic disorder, 107
receptor affinities, **70–71**
Neoplasms, dementia and, 45
Neuroleptic malignant syndrome
anticholinergic delirium or
coma and, 188
catatonia and, 188
characteristics, 180, 184, **185**
differential diagnosis, 186–189
epidemiology, 184
extrapyramidal side effects
with fever and, 186–187
heatstroke and, 188
laboratory abnormalities in, 184

malignant hyperthermia and,
188
risk factors, 184–185, **186**
serotonin syndrome and,
188–189
treatment, 189–190
Neuroleptics
adverse effects, 101, 105, 274
akathisia and, 101
for alcohol withdrawal
delirium, 156
for amphetamine withdrawal,
164
as analgesic adjuvants, 214
for anxiety, 105
for anxiety with chronic pain,
209
for anxiety disorders, 105
for anxiety from high-dose
steroids, 105
as anxiety/panic cause, **98**
avoidance if breast-feeding, 271
benzodiazepines' use with,
39–40
for burn patients, 275–276
for cancer patients' pain
management, 281
for chronic aggression, **199**
for cocaine delusional disorder,
167
for delirium, 105
for delirium treatment, 39, 275
for dementia treatment, 56
for dying patients' anxiety, 284
lithium use with, 83
metabolization, 73
neuroleptic malignant
syndrome etiology and,
180

Neuroleptics *(continued)*
    for pain management of burns, 278
    for panic disorder, 107
    Parkinson's disease sensitivity to, 49
    for personality disorders, 226
    protein binding, 263
    teratogenic potential, 270
    for violent behavior, 193–194
Neurologic conditions, as anxiety/panic cause, **98**, **99**
Neurological conditions, 285–288
    aggression and, 196
    mania etiology and, **84**
Neurological disorders, depression etiologies and, **67**
Neurological examination, 23
Neurological terminology, 23
Neuropeptides, for chronic or central pain relief, 212
Neuropsychiatric impairment in delirium, 32–33
    Draw a clock face test, 32
Neuropsychiatry, consultation psychiatry and, 23–24
Neurosyphilis, 286
    mania etiology and, **84**
Neurotonin (Gabapentin), dosages, **87**
Neurotransmitters, aggression etiology role, 196
Niacin deficiency, mania etiology and, **86**
Nicotine
    cigarettes, cytochrome P450 enzymes and, **183**
    drug interactions, **176**

Nicotinic acid, as anxiety/panic cause, **98**
Nifedipine
    cytochrome P450 enzymes and, **182**
    for hypertensive events, 179
Nitroprusside, for neuroleptic malignant syndrome, not recommended, 190
Nitrous oxide, as analgesic adjuvant, 214
Nomifensine, avoidance with renal failure, 175
Nonsteroidal anti-inflammatory drugs (NSAIDs). *See also* Anti-inflammatory drugs; *names of specific drugs*
    for Alzheimer's type dementia, 55, **56**
    as anxiety/panic cause, **98**
    for cancer patients' pain management, 281
    for continuous pain, 206
    cytochrome P450 enzymes and, **181**
    delirium etiology and, **36**
    secondary depressive disorders' etiologies and, **66**
Norepinephrine, drug interactions, **178**
Norfluoxetine
    cytochrome P450 enzymes and, **182**
    discontinuation, 72
    half-life, 72
Normal pressure hydrocephalus, diagnosis, 287
Normeperidine, 277
Norpramin (desipramine), **70–71**

Nortriptyline
   dosages, **70–71**
   male erectile disorder etiology
      and, **300**
   receptor affinities, **70–71**
NSAIDs. *See* Nonsteroidal
   anti-inflammatory drugs
Nubain (nalbuphine), analgesics
   compared, **213**

Obsessive-compulsive disorder,
   100
   clomipramine for, 108
   SSRIs for, 108
   treatment, 108
Obstetrical events, postpartum
   psychosis and, 271
Olanzapine, cytochrome P450
   enzymes and, **181**
Omeprazole, cytochrome P450
   enzymes and, **183**
Opiate abuse
   diagnosis, **148**, **152**, **154**, 160
   management, 160
   signs of, 160, **161**
Opiate dependence
   management, 160
   psychiatric disorders with, 160
   signs of, 160, **161**
Opiate intoxication
   management, **152**, 161–162
   naloxone for, **152**, 173
   signs and symptoms, **152**
Opiate withdrawal, 162
   by burn patients, 276
   management, **154**, 162
   methadone for, **154**, 162
   seizures, 162
   signs and symptoms, **154**, 162

Opiates, 212. *See also* Narcotics
   for acute pain relief, 211–212
   addiction risk, 206, 212–214
   adverse effects, 214
   analgesic dosage comparisons,
      213
   analgesic potency comparisons,
      213
   for central or chronic pain
      relief, 211–212
   delirium etiology and, **36**
   dosages, **213**
   overdose, 162
   for patients with abuse history,
      214
   receptors, 160
   respiratory depression
      tolerance, 160
   secondary depressive disorders'
      etiologies and, **66**
   tolerance, 160
Oral contraceptives
   drug interactions, **176**
   secondary depressive disorders'
      etiologies and, **66**
Organ transplantation, 292
   cyclosporine neurotoxicity,
      294–295
   donors, 292–293
   perioperative issues,
      293–294
   Psychosocial Assessment of
      Candidates for Transplant
      (PACT), 293
   recipients, biopsychosocial
      screening criteria, **294**
   Transplantation Evaluation
      Rating Scale (TERS), 293
Orientation, 16

Oxazepam
  absorption rates, **103**, 104
  for alcohol withdrawal, **154**
  dosages, **103**
  drug interactions, **178**n
  half-life, **103**
  with liver impairment, 104
  for patients taking multiple
     medications, 104
Oxycodone, metabolization, 73

Pain, 201–202. *See also* Pain
    (chronic)
  acute, 205
  anxiety and, 209, **209**
  behaviors with, 207–208
  in cancer patients, 281–282, 284
  causalgia, 204
  central, 204–205
    characteristics, **205**
  cognitive therapy for anxiety
    with, 209
  continuous, 205–206
    management, 206–207
  deafferentation. *See* Pain,
    central
  defined, 208
  diagnostic aids, 210–211
  drawing (graphic representation),
    203, 210–211
  malingering and, 208, **209**
  neuropathic. *See* Pain, central
  nioception, defined, 208
  nioceptive, 202, 211
  pain-prone patients, 208, **209**,
    211
  personality disorders and, 208
  phantom limb, 204
    treatment, 212

  posttherapeutic, 204
  reflex sympathetic dystrophy,
    204
  suffering, defined, 208
  terminology, 202–205, **203**,
    204, 208
  thalamic, 204
  treatment, analgesics, 211–212
Pain (chronic), 207. *See also* Pain
  cognitive therapy for, 138
  depression and, 208, **209**
  evaluation of, 202
  medical staff misinterpretation
    of, 207
  narcotic use, 159
  opiate use, 159
  psychiatric consultation for,
    201
  psychiatric syndromes
    associated with, 208, **209**
  somatoform disorders and,
    209–210
  treatment, 215–216
    behavioral methods, **215**
    management principles, **215**
Pain disorder
  benzodiazepine dependence in,
    131
  chronic pain complaints and,
    210
  clinical course, 131
  clinical features, 131
  cognitive therapy for, 141
  defined, 130–131
  depression and, 131
  epidemiology, 131
  forms of, 131
  management, 131–132
  narcotic dependence in, 131

Pain drawing, for pain complaint
     diagnosis, **203**, 210–211
Pain-prone patients, 208, **209**, 211
Palsy
     progressive supranuclear, 287
          depression etiology and, **67**
Pamelor (nortriptyline), **70–71**
Panic, 93
Panic disorder, 95. *See also*
          Anxiety disorders
     epidemiology, 94, 95
     hospitalization and, 94
     medications for, 106–107
     psychotherapy for, 107
     somatoform disorders and, 138
Paranoia
     cocaine use and, 167
     violence threats and, 195
Paresis, posttraumatic, mania
          etiology and, **84**
Pargyline, male erectile disorder
          etiology and, **300**
Parkinsonism,
          postencephalopathic, mania
          etiology and, **84**
Parkinson's disease, 287
     affect in, 13
     aggression and, 196
     antiparkinsonian drugs,
          delirium etiology and, **36**
     dementia in, 46, 47–49, **75**
     depression etiology and, **67**
     depression in, 47, **75**
     neuroleptic drug sensitivity in,
          49
Paroxetine
     adverse effects, 73
     cytochrome P450 enzymes and,
          181, **182**

dosages, **70–71**, 290, 291
half-life, 72
for HIV-related depression,
     290, 291
for panic disorder, 107
receptor affinities, **70–71**
side effects, 279
Patient confidentiality. *See*
          Confidentiality
Patient Self-Determination Act of
          1990, 239
Patients (medical-surgical)
     advance directives, 239
     alcohol abuse prevalence, 147
     burn patients, 275–278
     competency evaluation, 235–237
     delirium prevalence, 11, 29, 30
     dementia prevalence, 11
     depression in, 61
     depression prevalence, 51
     do-not-resuscitate orders,
          238–239
     ego defenses, 220
     false beliefs about illness, 76
     guardianship, 239
     hospitalization, 3
     informed consent by, 237–238
     mood disorders' prevalence, 61
     psychiatric illness in, 2–3,
          11–12
     record documentation, 233
     restraint use with, 240–241
Patients (medical-surgical). *See
          also* Critically ill patients;
          Geriatric patients;
          Hospitalization; Terminally
          ill patients
     signing out against medical
          advice, 236, 238

Patients (medical-surgical)
    (continued)
    staff-patient conflicts, 227–228
    substance-related disorders in,
        147
    suicide attempts by, 246–247
    suicide factors, **246**
    suicide rates, 245
    treatment refusal, 237–238
    viewing of new deformities by,
        277
Patients (surgical-medical),
    cognitive therapy for, 76–77
Paxil (paroxetine), **70–71**
Pediatric consultation, 272–275.
    See also Consultation-liaison
    psychiatry
    consultation process, 273
    developmental perspective
        needed, 272–273
    family focus, 273
    legal issues, 274
    patient confidentiality, 274
    psychopharmacology, 274
    regressive behavior, 272–273
Pemoline, for cancer patients, 279
Pentazocine, analgesics compared,
    213
Perceptions
    in delirium, 33
    disorders of, 13–14
Pergolide, 109
Perphenazine
    for anxiety with intra-aortic
        balloon pump, 298
    for anxiety upon respirator
        withdrawal, 105
    dosages, 105, 209, 298
    for dying patients' anxiety, 284

Personality
    change, medical conditions
        and, 220–223, **223**
    ego defenses, 220
    frontal lobe syndromes and,
        222, **224**
    illness and, 219
    staff reactions to unpleasant,
        227
Personality disorders
    antidepressants for, 226
    anxiolytics for, 226
    benzodiazepines for, 226
    carbamazepine for, 227
    characteristics, 223–224
    defined, 222–223
    differential diagnosis, 225
    group therapy for, 227
    lithium for, 226
    management, 225–226
    neuroleptics for, 226
    pain and, 208
    propranolol for, 227
    sedative-hypnotics for, 226
    somatization disorder and, 123
    suicide risk and, 247
Phantom limb sensation, 14
Phenacetin, cytochrome P450
    enzymes and, **181**
Phencyclidine, mania etiology
    and, **85**
Phenelzine
    adverse effects, 69
    dosages, 69
    male erectile disorder etiology
        and, **300**
Phenobarbital
    cytochrome P450 enzymes and,
        183

delirium etiology and, **36**
drug interactions, 177
Phenothiazines
antiparkinsonian drugs, **36**
cytochrome P450 enzymes and,
181, **182**
drug interactions, 178n, **178**
Phentolamine, male erectile
disorder etiology and, **300**
Phenylephrine
as anxiety/panic cause, **98**
delirium etiology and, **36**
drug interactions, **178**
Phenylpropanolamine
as anxiety/panic cause, **98**
drug interactions, **178**
Phenytoin
for alcohol withdrawal seizures,
155
cytochrome P450 enzymes and,
181, **183**
delirium etiology and, **36**
drug interactions, 177
male erectile disorder etiology
and, **300**
tricyclic antidepressants and, 68
Phobias, 100
social, medications for,
107–108
specific, graded exposure
treatment, 107
Pick's disease, mania etiology
and, **84**
Pimozide
for BDD, 130
cytochrome P450 enzymes and,
181
for delusional disorder, 139
dosages, 139

male erectile disorder etiology
and, **300**
Pindolol
for chronic aggression, 197
male erectile disorder etiology
and, **300**
Pneumonia, depression etiology
and, **66**
Polypharmacy
geriatric patients and, 264
with somatoform disorders, 140
Postoperative excitement, mania
etiology and, **86**
Postpartum depression, 271
Postpartum psychosis, 271
Posttraumatic stress disorder
(PTSD), 95, 99–100. *See also*
Anxiety disorders
95, comorbid psychiatric
disorders, 100
in burn patients, 278
depression with, 108
diagnosis, 99
medications for, 108
risk, acute stress disorder and, 99
Potassium iodide, drug
interactions, **177**
Pramipexole, 109
Prazepam
absorption rates, **103**
dosages, **103**
half-life, **103**
Prazosin, male erectile disorder
etiology and, **300**
Pregnancy
electroconvulsive therapy
(ECT) during, 270
medication discontinuance
during, 270

Pregnancy *(continued)*
  psychopharmacology during,
    269–270
Premenstrual psychosis, mania
    etiology and, **86**
Primary care clinics,
    consultation-liaison
    psychiatry in, 7
Primidone
  cytochrome P450 enzymes and,
    183
  drug interactions, **177**
Problem-solving ability
  cortical mapping, **24–25**
  Frank Jones Story test of, 22
Procainamide
  delirium etiology and, **36**
  drug interactions, **178**
  mania etiology and, **85**
Procaine, as anxiety/panic cause,
    98
Procarbazine
  as anxiety/panic cause, **98**
  male erectile disorder etiology
    and, **300**
  mania etiology and, **85**
  secondary depressive disorders'
    etiologies and, **66**
  side effects, **280**
Procyclidine, mania etiology and,
    85
Progestins, male erectile disorder
    etiology and, **300**
Progressive muscle relaxation, for
    pain management, **216**
Projective tests, for pain
    complaint diagnosis, 210
Promethazine, delirium etiology
    and, **36**

Propafenone
  cytochrome P450 enzymes and,
    181
  mania etiology and, **85**
Propoxyphene, drug interactions,
    177
Propranolol
  for aggressive behavior, 56
  for anxiety symptoms, 105
  for chronic aggression, 197, **198**
  cytochrome P450 enzymes and,
    181
  dosages, 190, **198**
  male erectile disorder etiology
    and, **300**
  for panic disorder, 107
  for personality disorders, 227
  for serotonin syndrome, 190
Prostaglandin inhibitors
  as analgesic adjuvants, 214
  for cancer patients' pain
    management, 281
Protease inhibitors, cytochrome
    P450 enzymes and, **182**
Protriptyline
  dosages, **70–71**
  male erectile disorder etiology
    and, **300**
  receptor affinities, **70–71**
Prozac (fluoxetine), **70–71**
Pseudodementia, dementia
    differentiation, 51–52
Pseudoephedrine, as anxiety/panic
    cause, **98**
Psychiatric consultation. *See also*
    Consultation-liaison
    psychiatry
  characteristics of effective, **5**
  consultation style, 4

cost-effectiveness, 3
follow-up, 5–6
for geriatric patients, 265
    strategies, **270**
medicolegal issues, 233
neuropsychiatry in, 23–24
patient confidentiality, 4
record documentation, detail
    importance in, 233
Psychiatric disorders
aggression and, 196–197
in burn patients, 275
in cancer patients, 279–281
chronic illness and, 3
in geriatric patients, 255–258
opiate addiction with, 160
in organ transplant recipients,
    293, **294**
postpartum, 271
prevalence in cancer patients,
    279
PTSD comorbidity, 100
suicide risk and, 247, 251
Psychogenic pain disorder. *See*
    Pain disorder
Psychological stress, exacerbation
    of medical conditions by, 132
Psychological tests
for delirium diagnosis, **38**
for mental status examinations,
    17–22
for pain complaint diagnosis,
    210–211
Psychomotor disturbances, in
    delirium, 33
Psychosis
Alzheimer's disease and,
    257–258
in geriatric patients, 257–258

monosymptomatic
    hypochondriacal, 139
pain and, 208
somatoform disorders and,
    138–139
violence etiology and, 195
Psychosocial Assessment of
    Candidates for Transplant
    (PACT), 293
Psychosomatic symptoms. *See*
    Somatization; Somatoform
    disorders
Psychostimulants
abuse potential, 75
adverse effects, 74–75, 274
as analgesic adjuvants, 214
for cancer patients, 279, 281
clinical situations for use, **75**
for depression treatment,
    74–75, **75**
for dying patients, 283
for pain management of burns,
    278
Psychotherapy. *See also*
    Cognitive-behavioral
    therapy; Group therapy;
    Medical psychotherapy
for adjustment disorder, 63, 137
antidepressants and, 76
for anxiety, 106
associative anamnesis, 230
burn patients' need for, 278
for chronic aggression,
    197–199
cognitive
    for adjustment disorder, 137
    for somatoform disorders,
        141
for conversion disorder, 129

Psychotherapy *(continued)*
  for depression, 76
  family therapy
    for chronic aggression, 197
    for manic patients, 90
  formulation, **230**, 231
  for geriatric patients, 264–265
  with HIV patients, 289
  for mania, 90
  in medical settings, 229–230
  for panic disorder, 107
  selection process, 229
  for somatoform disorders, 141
  for suicidal patients, 251
Puerperal psychosis, mania
    etiology and, **86**
Pyrimidine analogues, side
    effects, **280**

Quazepam
  action duration, **110**
  action onset, **110**
  dosages, **110**
  excretion/metabolism, **110**
  half-life, **110**
  for insomnia, 112
Quetiapine, cytochrome P450
    enzymes and, **181**
Quinacrine, delirium etiology and,
    36
Quinidine
  adverse effects, 68
  cytochrome P450 enzymes and,
    181, **182**
  delirium etiology and, **36**
  drug interactions, **178**

Ranitidine, delirium etiology and,
    36

*Reitan-Indiana Aphasia Screening
    Test,* 17
Relaxation therapies, for
    somatoform disorders, 141
Remeron (mirtazapine), **72–73**
Renal dialysis
  lithium and, 86
  suicide risk, 248
Renal function, psychotropic
    drugs and, 297–298
Reserpine
  as anxiety/panic cause, **97**
  secondary depressive disorders'
    etiologies and, **66**
Residency training,
    consultation-liaison
    psychiatry and, **2**
Respirators, withdrawal, anxiety
    from, 105, 298
Respiratory conditions, as
    anxiety/panic cause, **97–98**,
    98–99
Restless legs syndrome, 109
Restraint
  documentation requirements,
    240
  for examination, 240–241
  in intensive care units, 241
  legal aspects, 240–241
  of suicidal patients, 252
  of violent patients, procedure
    for, 193, **194**
Riboxetine
  dosages, **72–73**
  receptor affinities, **72–73**
Rifabutin, cytochrome P450
    enzymes and, **183**
Rifampin
  antiparkinsonian drugs, **36**

cytochrome P450 enzymes and,
183
drug interactions, **176**
Risperidone
cytochrome P450 enzymes and,
181
for delirium treatment, 39
Ritonavir, cytochrome P450
enzymes and, **182**
Rorschach Test, for pain
complaint diagnosis, 210
Roxanol-SR, for continuous pain,
206

Sadomasochistic index, for pain
complaint diagnosis, 211
Salicylates, as anxiety/panic
cause, **98**
Saquinavir, cytochrome P450
enzymes and, **182**
Schizophrenia
abstracting ability and, 14
ages of onset over 50, 256
suicide risk and, 247
Scopolamine
antiparkinsonian drugs, **36**
male erectile disorder etiology
and, **300**
Screening mental status
examinations, 16–22
Sedative amnestic disorder, 159
management, 159
Sedative-hypnotics, 111–112. *See
also names of specific drugs*
abuse/dependence,
management, 157
action durations, **110–111**
action onsets, **110–111**, 111–112
as anxiety/panic cause, **98**

cross-reactivity with alcohol
and benzodiazepines, 158
delirium etiology and, **36**
dosages, **110–111**
excretion/metabolism, **110–111**
half-lives, **110–111**
intoxication
management, **152**
signs and symptoms, **152**,
158
for personality disorders, 226
teratogenic potential, 270
tolerance, 157
withdrawal, 158
as anxiety/panic cause, **98**
by burn patients, 276
clonazepam for, **154**
in geriatric patients, 158
management, **154**, 159
signs and symptoms, **154**,
158
Seizures, in conversion disorder,
129
Selective serotonin reuptake
inhibitors (SSRIs), 72–73,
300
adverse effects, 73, 279
for anxiety disorders, 105
for chronic aggression, **198**
CYP enzymes and, 180
cytochrome P450 enzymes and,
279
for depression, 72–73
discontinuation, 72
dosages, **198**
drug interactions, **176**, **177**, **178**
enzyme inhibition by, 73
male erectile disorder etiology
and, **300**

Selective serotonin reuptake
inhibitors (SSRIs) *(continued)*
for obsessive-compulsive
disorder, 108
for panic disorder, 107
patient relapse rates and, 72
for phobias, 107–108
trazodone combined with, 74
Selegiline, for Alzheimer's type
dementia, 55, **56**
Serotonin syndrome
characteristics, **189**
cyproheptadine for, 190
neuroleptic malignant
syndrome and, 188–189
propranolol for, 190
treatment, 190
Serotonin/norepinephrine reuptake
inhibitors (SNRIs)
for anxiety disorders, 105
for social phobias, 107
Sertindole, cytochrome P450
enzymes and, **181**
Sertraline, 73
CYP enzymes and, 180
cytochrome P450 enzymes and,
181, **182**
dosages, **70–71**, 290
drug interactions, 180
half-life, 72
for HIV-related depression,
290–291
for panic disorder, 107
receptor affinities, **70–71**
Serzone (nefazodone), **70–71**
Set Test, 17
Significant others. *See* Families
Signing out against medical
advice, 236, 238

Sinequan (doxepin), **70–71**
Sleep apnea
depression etiology and, **67**
treatment, 109
Sleep disorders. *See also* Insomnia
myoclonic, 109
Sleep disruption, in dementia,
medications for, 56
Sleep-wake cycle, in delirium,
33–34
SNRIs. *See* Serotonin/
norepinephrine reuptake
inhibitors
Somatization, 119
abnormal illness behavior, 120
defined, 119
epidemiology, 120
evaluation, 120, **121**
MMPI for, **121**
illness behavior, 120
illness vs. disease, 119
psychological factors affecting
medical conditions, 132
symptom amplification, 117–118
Symptom Checklist-90 for, **121**
Somatization disorder
associated features, 122–123
chronic pain complaints,
209–210
clinical features, 122
diagnosis, 209–210
epidemiology, 122
management, 123, **124**
personality disorder and, 123
prognosis, 123
Somatoform disorder
(undifferentiated)
clinical features, 125
defined, 123

epidemiology, 123–124
management, **124**, 125
prognosis, 125
Somatoform disorders, 117–118.
    *See also names of specific
    disorders*
    adjustment disorder and, 137
    anxiety disorders and, 138, 140
    characteristics, 120–122
    chronic pain complaints,
        209–210
    cognitive therapy for, 141
    countertransference, 140
    depression and, 138
    differential diagnosis, 117–118,
        118, 136–139
    gain from, 127–128, 135, 141
    group therapy for, 141–142
    hypnotherapy for, 141
    management, 139–142
        approach to the patient, 140
        physical exercise, 140–141
        psychotherapy for, 141–142
        social dynamics, 140
    medical disorders and, 137
    mood disorders and, 140
    multiple medications with, 140
    not otherwise specified, 132
    panic disorder and, 138
    psychosis and, 138–139
    relaxation therapies for, 141
    secondary psychiatric disorders
        and, 137
    substance-related disorders and,
        138
Somatoform pain disorder. *See*
    Pain disorder
Spatial neglect, cortical mapping,
    24–25

Speech defects, 15
    in delirium, 33
Spouses. *See* Families
SSRIs. *See* Selective serotonin
    reuptake inhibitors
Stadol (butorphanol), analgesics
    compared, **213**
Steroids
    aggression and, 197
    anxiety from, treatment, 105
    as anxiety/panic cause, **98**
    cytochrome P450 enzymes and,
        181
    psychiatric disorders from,
        treatment, 105
Stroke
    aggression and, 196
    poststroke depression, 287–288
    poststroke depression and, 61,
        67, **75**
Subarachnoid hemorrhage,
    depression etiology and, **67**
Subcortical/limbic system disease,
    287
Substance abuse. *See also*
    Alcoholism; Amphetamine
    abuse; Cocaine abuse;
    Narcotic abuse; Opiate abuse
    diagnostic criteria, **148**
    violence etiology and, 195
Substance dependence, diagnostic
    criteria, **148**
Substance intoxication, signs and
    symptoms, **152**
Substance withdrawal, in burn
    patients, 276
Substance withdrawal syndromes,
    158
    management, **154**, 159

Substance withdrawal syndromes
(*continued*)
signs and symptoms, **154**
Substance-related disorders
as anxiety cause, 101
somatoform disorders and, 138
substance use disorders, 147–148
substance-induced disorders,
147–148
Succinylcholine, drug
interactions, **178**
Suffering, 208. *See also* Pain; Pain
(chronic)
Suicide, 243
attempts, 245–246
attempts as predictor of future
suicide, 247
by drug overdose, 245, 246
by medical-surgical patients,
245
clinical features, 247–249
emergency room vigilance
against, 250
epidemiology, 243–245
gender differences in, 243–245
geriatric patients and, 256, 259
"hidden murderers," 251–252
outpatient management
conditions, 252
potential, questions to ask, **250**
precautions, 250–251
psychiatric disorders associated
with, 247
psychotherapy for, 251
restraints against, 252
risk assessment, 249, **250**
risk factors, **244**
holidays, 247
medical disorders, 248–249

previous attempts, 247
psychiatric disorders, 247
SAD PERSONS scale, **248**
risk level determination,
249–250
treatment of attempted, 251
Surmontil (trimipramine), **70–71**
Sympathomimetic amines, mania
etiology and, **85**
Sympathomimetics. *See also*
names of specific drugs
as anxiety/panic cause, **98**
delirium etiology and, **36**
drug interactions, **178**
MAOI use with, 69
Symptom Checklist-90, **121**
Syphilis, tertiary, depression
etiology and, **66**

Tacrine
for Alzheimer's type dementia,
55, **56**
cytochrome P450 enzymes and,
182
Talwin (pentazocine), analgesics
compared, **213**
Tamoxifen
delirium etiology and, **36**
side effects, **280**
Tegretol (carbamazepine),
dosages, **87**
Temazepam
action duration, **111**
action onset, **111**
dosages, **111**
drug interactions, **178**n
excretion/metabolism, **111**
half-life, **111**
for insomnia, 112

Temporal lobe seizure, mania etiology and, **84**

Teratogenesis, antimania medications and, 270

Terfenadine, cytochrome P450 enzymes and, **181**

Terminally ill patients. *See also* Death; Patients
adjuvants to opiates for, 212
anxiety in, 283–284
delivering bad news, 282
depression in dying patients, 283
do-not-resuscitate orders, 238–239, 283
narcotics use, 206

Tetracycline
delirium etiology and, **36**
drug interactions, **177**

Thalamotomy, mania etiology and, **84**

Thematic Apperception Test, for pain complaint diagnosis, 210

Theophylline
as anxiety/panic cause, **98**
cytochrome P450 enzymes and, **181**
delirium etiology and, **36**

Therapeutic privilege, informed consent and, 237–238

Thiamine
for alcohol intoxication, **152**
for alcohol withdrawal, 153, **154**, 155
for alcohol withdrawal delirium, 156
for alcohol-induced amnestic disorder, 156

for Korsakoff's syndrome, 156

Thiazide diuretics
drug interactions, **177**
lithium and, 88
male erectile disorder etiology and, **300**

Thioridazine
avoidance in delirium treatment, 39
avoidance in dementia treatment, 56
drug interactions, **178**n
male erectile disorder etiology and, **300**

Thiothixene
for dying patients' anxiety, 284
male erectile disorder etiology and, **300**

The 36-Hour Day (Mace and Rabins), 57

Thought content, assessing, 13

Thought processes
assessing, 13
in delirium, 33

Thyroid preparations
as anxiety/panic cause, **98**
mania etiology and, **85**

Ticarcillin, delirium etiology and, **36**

Ticlopidine, for vascular dementia, 55

Timolol, male erectile disorder etiology and, **300**

Tobacco
cigarettes, cytochrome P450 enzymes and, **183**
drug interactions, **176**

Tocainide, delirium etiology and, **36**

Tofranil (imipramine), **70–71**
Tolbutamide, cytochrome P450
    enzymes and, **181**
Tolmetin, mania etiology and, **85**
Topamax (topiramate), dosages,
    87
Topiramate
    dosages, **87**
    for mania, 83, 89
Trail [test], **38**
Transference, illness and, 228
Transplantation Evaluation Rating
    Scale (TERS), 293
Tranylcypromine
    adverse effects, 69
    for BDD, 130
    dosages, 69
    male erectile disorder etiology
        and, **300**
Trazodone, 73
    adverse effects, 73–74, 112,
        279
    as analgesic adjuvant, 214–215
    for chronic aggression, **198**
trazodone, for dementia
    symptoms, 56
Trazodone
    dosages, **70–71**, 112, **198**
    for insomnia, 112
    for panic disorder, 107
    receptor affinities, **70–71**
    SSRIs combined with, 74
Treatment refusal, 237–238
    adolescents' right to, 274
    competency evaluation and,
        236
Tremor
    in conversion disorder, 129
    with delirium, 33

Triazolam
    action duration, **111**
    action onset, **111**
    adverse effects, 112
    cytochrome P450 enzymes and,
        181
    dosages, **111**
    excretion/metabolism, **111**
    half-life, **111**
    for insomnia, 111, 112
    mania etiology and, **85**
Tricyclic antidepressants. *See also*
    Antidepressants; *names of
    specific drugs*
    adverse effects, 68–69, 274
    as analgesic adjuvants, 214
    for cancer patients, 279
    conditions treated with, 65
    CYP enzymes and, 180
    cytochrome P450 enzymes and,
        181, **182**, **183**n
    delirium and, 36
    for depression treatment, 65–68
    dosages, 65
    drug interactions, **176**, **177**, **178**
    for panic disorder, 107
    renal excretion, 263
    treatment uses, 65
Trifluoperazine, for dying
    patients' anxiety, 284
Trihexyphenidyl
    delirium etiology and, **36**
    male erectile disorder etiology
        and, **300**
Trimipramine
    dosages, **70–71**
    male erectile disorder etiology
        and, **300**
    receptor affinities, **70–71**

Tuberculosis, depression etiology and, 66

Tumors
depression etiologies, **67**
mania etiology and, **84**

Tyramine
drug interactions, **178**
monoamine oxidase inhibitors and, 179

Understanding Alzheimer's Disease (Aronson), 57

Uremia, mania etiology and, **86**

Valproate
adverse effects, 90
contraindicated with liver disease, 90
cytochrome P450 enzymes and, 90
drug interactions, **177**
for mania, 83

Valproic acid
for chronic aggression, **198**
delirium etiology and, **36**
dosages, **87**, **198**
for mania, 88

Vascular dementia, 49. *See also* Dementia
Alzheimer's type dementia differentiation, 49
aspirin therapy for, 55, **56**
causes, 49
characteristics, 49
diagnostic criteria, 49, **50**
Hachinski Ischemia Scale, 49, **51**
ischemic vascular disease and, 49
mixed dementias and, 46

neuroimagery, 53
prevalence, 45
treatment, 55–57, **56**

Venlafaxine, 73
action, 72
cytochrome P450 enzymes and, **181**
dosages, **70–71**
receptor affinities, **70–71**

Verapamil
carbamazepine interaction with, 89, **176**
cytochrome P450 enzymes and, **181**
drug interactions, **176**, **177**
male erectile disorder etiology and, **300**

Vinblastine
delirium etiology and, **36**
secondary depressive disorders' etiologies and, **66**
side effects, **280**

Vincristine
delirium etiology and, **36**
secondary depressive disorders' etiologies and, **66**
side effects, **280**

Violence. *See also* Aggression
with cocaine delirium, 166–167
differential diagnosis, 196–197
emergency consultation, 193
etiologies, 195
physiological, 198
physical restraint, procedure for, 193, **194**
postviolent assessment, 196
threats of
family involvement, 195
how to deal with, 195

Visual analogue scale, for pain
    complaint diagnosis, 211
Vitamin B12 deficiency, mania
    etiology and, **86**
Vitamin E, for Alzheimer's type
    dementia, 55, **56**
Vivactil (protriptyline), **70–71**

Warfarin
    chloral hydrate and, 173
    cytochrome P450 enzymes and,
        181
    protein binding, 173
Wellbutrin (bupropion),
        70–71

Wernicke-Korsakoff syndrome, 156
    management, 156
    thiamine for, 156
Wernicke's encephalopathy, 156
Wilson's disease, mania etiology
    and, **84**

Yohimbine
    as anxiety/panic cause, **98**
    mania etiology and, **85**

Zidovudine, mania etiology and, **85**
Zoloft (sertraline), **70–71**
Zolpidem
    action duration, **111**